PRAISE FOR

# *Mothershift*

"*Mothershift* is medicine for every new mama's heart, and wisdom that this world so desperately needs as we relearn how to honor this profound transition into becoming 'Mother.' Even five years after first becoming a mother, Jessie's words orient me in a new way—and support me in the process of still becoming."

—DHYANA MASLA, author of *Ayurveda Mama*

"*Mothershift* is the real-deal companion every mother needs to support her through the complex emotional and spiritual landscapes that come up in new motherhood. It's so much more than a guide—Jessie Harrold provides the data, research, and grounded truths to validate a woman's complex experience of matrescence. I envision mothers gathering around kitchen tables discussing this book!"

—BECCA PIASTRELLI, author of *Root and Ritual*

"So many guidebooks for mothers focus on the baby, and yet Jessie Harrold knows that the root of family well-being begins with care for the mother. Rather than what we do as mothers, it is how we *feel* that truly matters in terms of an empowered and embodied mothering experience. The elemental framework in *Mothershift* for navigating the transformation of motherhood speaks to our mothering bodies, and the 'MotherPowers' that Harrold names are a road map for rebuilding a personal and collective mother-loving culture that will benefit us all."

—TAMI LYNN KENT, author of *Wild Feminine*, *Wild Creative*, and *Wild Mothering*

"*Mothershift* is a beacon and an essential read for the early years of motherhood. While reading it, all I could think about was how much less lonely I would have felt if I'd had this book when my babies were young. But even though my children are older now, Jessie Harrold's words reframed my memories, tenderly soothing remaining traces of not-enoughness or unattended grief. As Harrold says, when you become a mother, you become something new. Finally, we have a book to compassionately shepherd us through that process of becoming."

—MARA GLATZEL, author of *Needy*

"*Mothershift* is deep nourishment and potent medicine for modern mothers, and Jessie Harrold is the real deal, weaving hard-won wisdom, intersectionality, and heart throughout each page. At a time when most mothers don't have access to wise, initiated elders, *Mothershift* is especially essential as a source of mature guidance and support. I highly recommend this gem to new mothers and mother lovers alike."

—BETH BERRY, author of *Motherwhelmed*

# Mothershift

*Reclaiming
Motherhood as a
Rite of Passage*

## JESSIE HARROLD

SHAMBHALA

Shambhala Publications, Inc.
2129 13th Street
Boulder, Colorado 80302
www.shambhala.com

Cover art: Elvina Gafarova / Shutterstock
Cover design: Kate E. White
Interior design: Amanda Weiss

9 8 7 6 5 4 3 2 1

First Edition
Printed in the United States of America

Shambhala Publications makes every effort
to print on acid-free, recycled paper.
Shambhala Publications is distributed worldwide by
Penguin Random House, Inc., and its subsidiaries.

Library of Congress Cataloging-in-Publication Data
Names: Harrold, Jessie, author.
Title: Mothershift: reclaiming motherhood as a rite of passage / Jessie Harrold.
Description: Boulder, Colorado: Shambhala Publications, [2024] |
Includes bibliographical references.
Identifiers: LCCN 2023056024 | ISBN 9781645473060 (trade paperback)
Subjects: LCSH: Motherhood.
Classification: LCC HQ759 .H2957 2024 | DDC 306.874/3—dc23/eng/20240222
LC record available at https://lccn.loc.gov/2023056024

*For Ada and Max.*
*You made me, too.*

+

*For all the mamas who have honored me with the*
*opportunity to support them through pregnancy,*
*birth, and matrescence over the last fifteen years.*
*This book is for you.*

The moment a child is born, the mother
is also born. She never existed before.
The woman existed, but the mother, never.
A mother is something absolutely new.

—OSHO


We know more about the air we breathe,
the seas we travel, than about the nature
and meaning of motherhood.

—ADRIENNE RICH

# CONTENTS

# INTRODUCTION

Becoming a mother is so much more than just birthing or caring for a tiny human.

*(Which is, of course, a fairly superhuman feat in and of itself.)*

As you birth and nurture your baby, you are also birthing a new version of yourself. You, as Mother, will become a different person than you were before having a child.

It's a transformation that may start with conception, but we are mistaken to believe that the process is complete when our babies are born.

In fact, the rite of passage into motherhood is only just beginning.

Becoming a mother is one of those changes that changes *everything*. It's a seismic transformation that is biological, psychological, socio-cultural, economic, and spiritual in its scope. Perhaps more than anything, at its heart, the transition to motherhood represents a shift in the very tectonic plates of your identity. Despite the dominant "bounce back" cultural narrative of our times, motherhood is one of those transformations that makes your old self—your old jeans, your old dreams, and that way you used to drink hot coffee in the mornings—simply N/A. Not applicable. At least for now. And maybe forever.

In times long ago and places far away, mothers were ushered through this transformative time with the support of their communities and with ritual and ceremony to celebrate their shifting lives. But in our Western culture today, this incredibly important life transition is not protected and revered. Everything from social media to social policy denies the value of motherhood and denies mothers the opportunity to fully own, embody, and find power in their mothering identity. Instead, we are encouraged to buy the right stuff, to "do it right" via the instruction of Google and myriad other how-to books on parenting, and to rush to "get back to normal," while secretly struggling with loneliness, sadness, and feeling lost.

As a result, modern mothers are in crisis. As many as one in five mothers experience postpartum mood disorders,[1] which have become so common that the term *postpartum* is now shorthand for *depression* and not for the period of time following birth.

More and more people *are* talking about what happens to a woman when she transitions into motherhood, and terms like *the fourth trimester* have risen in the public consciousness. But even though women have been becoming mothers since the *actual* dawn of humanity, we in modern Western society *still* lack a deep and nuanced understanding of the normal, yet often challenging, process of this transformation.[2] Instead, we've normalized the Hallmark version of motherhood, full of milk-drunk smiles and moms who "have it all," leaving women who feel like they've lost themselves or who experience grief or disorientation to believe they are broken.

But they are not broken: they're *becoming*.

It's not something that takes six weeks, or three months, or even a year. No.

The transition to motherhood takes two to three years.

Before you close this book in horror, I *know*: that seems like an awfully long time to feel the way you might be feeling right now, to be stumbling along this journey without a map for the road ahead.

But now, you *do* have a map.

You're holding it.

And if this book is the map for your transition into motherhood, then I hope you'll trust me as your guide. Let me first share with you a little bit about my own *becoming* and why I came to write this book.

When I became a mother for the first time, I was taken aback by the changes that motherhood called me to make to my life—

despite the fact that, by that time, I had had a side hustle as a doula, supporting other women as they birthed their babies and became mothers, for four years.

I realized, swiftly and unequivocally, that motherhood wasn't just about diaper changing and breastfeeding and not sleeping very much anymore but about shifting many of my values, beliefs, and ways of being in the world. Suddenly I was no longer able to do the things that made me *me*. Gone were the hot cups of coffee and most of my business-casual wardrobe, yes, but as I lost myself in the endless hours of breastfeeding and rocking, my sense of self-worth and value in the world as a "productive" member of society who could *get things done* felt lost to me as well. My marriage, bonded through shared adventure and a love of late-night Scrabble games, needed redefining if it was going to survive this massive shift to our lives. The thought of returning to the job I had come to loathe became suddenly *unfathomable*, as was remaining in the home where we lived—all granite countertops and precariously placed pieces of art—thousands of miles away from our family support networks.

And so, for the first two or three years of being a mother, I felt utterly unmoored in so many ways. Some days, I railed against the fact of my own motherhood, longing for the time when I had more physical and emotional autonomy, yearning to feel sure of myself once again.

The steep learning curves and bleary-eyed nights eventually passed, and I quit my day job as a public health researcher and dove into my birth work full-time. I spent my days doing on-call breastfeeding support and teaching prenatal classes to increasingly jam-packed rooms of expectant parents, and I spent my nights rubbing the backs and holding the hands of birthing mothers.

Although it was in my job description to do things like show women how to achieve a great latch when breastfeeding and help them navigate the challenges of infant sleep, I started to realize that these conversations had a deeper context that went well below the everyday problems of early motherhood.

And so I started asking more questions. *Different* questions.

Suddenly, in so many cases, the problem of a baby not napping well was actually not so much about infant sleep but about a mother's ability to feel like herself again for a couple hours. The challenges of breastfeeding were often not so much about supply and demand but about autonomy and the shifting dynamics of formerly equal intimate partnerships.

I came to understand that *these* were the things that women were referring to when they said, "No one ever told me . . . " *These* were the conversations that would happen *after* prenatal class or infant massage class or playdates. *These* were the words that were whispered over the phone, staccato'ed with sobs and sighs and the shame of not being "normal" or "good enough."

I began to piece together, from my own experience and that of the women I was supporting, that what we were all traversing was a deeper, more profound, and more interior shift—not necessarily the series of definable problems with actionable solutions that I, the women I supported, and the culture we were steeped in had assumed.

I made it my mission to start unearthing this hidden inner experience women were having of the transition to motherhood—to start putting language to it in my blog posts and when I taught prenatal classes. More and more mothers started reaching out to me, saying things like "It's like you are reading my mind" and "I feel so much less alone now."

At the same time, I started noticing something else: I realized that as the women I was working with felt more supported through their transitions to motherhood, their *whole lives* flourished. Motherhood became a crucible that burned away all the parts of them that were inauthentic or unhappy or misaligned and allowed them to become laser-clear about who they were and what mattered most to them. They became even more deeply compassionate and more resilient. They learned to listen for and trust their intuition; they saw their bodies as powerful sources of pleasure and wisdom and sought fiercely honest and supportive communities of like-minded mothers. These women quit their jobs and followed their passions, picked up their pens and paintbrushes again, and renegotiated the terms of their intimate partnerships.

And so I started to ask, *What if?*

What if we reclaimed motherhood as a radical transformation to a woman's *whole* life—as the rite of passage that it truly is?

And what if we decided that losing yourself in motherhood is not the problem but *the point*?

What if we saw motherhood as an opportunity for a woman to access a deeper sense of her own power and authenticity?

What would that mean not just for mothers but for a world in desperate need of people who feel more empowered, more embodied, more interconnected and who find worthiness in rest and play and creativity, whose wisdom comes from their hearts just as much as their heads, and who are leaders and elders in the wider community?

What if?

*That* is the world I'm here for.

*That* is why I wrote this book.

Will you join me?

## WELCOME TO *MOTHERSHIFT*

My intention for writing this book is that these pages are where you will turn when your postpartum doula has packed up her magic Mary Poppins bag and your neighbors have stopped delivering casseroles.

This book is where you can receive support in making sense of who *you* are, as a woman, now that you're a mother. It's a place to seek refuge, to receive guidance through your transition to motherhood, and to feel as if you are being *mothered as you mother*. It's a place where you can understand, in your bones, that your experience of this radical transformation in your life is real, meaningful, and *okay*.

The journey that you will travel as you turn these pages begins, in chapter 1, with more of my own story and how I came to write this book. It also dives into how women's experience of the transition

to motherhood *beyond the fourth trimester* is still uncharted territory that we know very little about. You see, after years of research
and supporting women through this time in their lives, I noticed
that even the best books on the transition to motherhood focused
on the fact *that* the transition happens—and that it takes a long
time, that it is normal to have mixed feelings about motherhood,
and that mindfulness or gratefulness or self-care help. But none of
these excellent resources touch on *how* the transition to motherhood
happens. Because of that, mothers feel deeply disoriented as they
navigate this transformative time. The final section of chapter 1 outlines how I developed what I like to call *a map for your becoming*: a
research-based, four-phase model that describes how the transition
to motherhood unfolds and helps you to navigate every step along
the way.

Part 1 is a deep dive into that model, which I have used to guide
the thousands of women I've supported through the shift into motherhood. This section will help you to identify the cascade of changes
you can expect to your life as you enter motherhood, normalize the
feelings of grief and loss of self you may feel along the way, navigate
the discomfort of not knowing who you are anymore now that you're
a mother, and then gently guide you to explore who you're becoming.

Part 2 of the book is all about reclaiming the power and potential of the transition to motherhood. Let's face it: for reasons I've
already shared and many more that I will reference throughout this
book, motherhood in today's culture can be profoundly disempow-
ering. But there is another, adjacent reality in our experiences of
modern mothering: despite the challenges we face—*or perhaps,
sometimes, because of them*—the transition to motherhood is a
time in a woman's life that has tremendous potential. It invites us
to unearth parts of ourselves we may have hidden away to fit into
cultural norms and expectations. It allows us to develop new skills
and capacities that not only support us as individuals but are also
exactly what our *world* needs right now. I call these skills and capacities your MotherPowers. There are seven of them: self-tending,
creativity, embodiment, ritual, community, inner knowing, and earth

connection. My intention with this section of the book is to help you claim a greater sense of power and authenticity in your motherhood, to explore the idea of motherhood-as-revolution, and to support you to join the cadre of mothers who are change agents in a world that desperately needs mothering.

Woven throughout the entire book are stories of my own transition to motherhood as well as those of the women I've supported, and sections at the end of each chapter called "Your Turn" contain journal prompts and practical guidance for you to use to traverse this radical transformation in your life with grace and support.

## WHO THIS BOOK IS FOR

This book is for you if you carry Mother as a role or an identity in your life.

But what is a Mother? Who can be a Mother?

Sociologists have been grappling with this question for decades and have come to differentiate *Mother* as an identity, *Mothering* as a practice, and *Motherhood* as a set of social norms. Complicated, eh? Let's unpack this a little further. You might call yourself a *Mother*, and that might feel like an identity you hold or wish to hold. That identity might mean you're a biological mother—or not. It might mean you're a woman—or not. *Mothering*, on the other hand, is a verb. As Alexis Pauline Gumbs, China Martens, and Mai'a Williams write in their anthology *Revolutionary Mothering*, "Mothering [is the act of] creating, nurturing, affirming and supporting life."[3] From this perspective, mothering can be done by people who birth babies *and* others who care for those babies, including fathers, queer and gender nonconforming parents, aunts, uncles, grandmothers, grandfathers, and other carers (see note for more).[4] Finally, *Motherhood* is the term used by sociologists to refer to the social norms surrounding mothers and mothering—the "institution of motherhood," as the feminist scholar and poet Adrienne Rich called it in her groundbreaking book *Of Woman Born*.[5] The institution of motherhood is a quagmire of ideals

regarding *who* a mother "should be" (usually most societally accepted if she is white, cisgender, heterosexual, educated, able-
bodied, and economically privileged, to name a few) and *how* a
mother "should be" (always-present, nurturing, self-sacrificing, do-
mestically inclined, and quite satisfied with it all, for example—see
note for more).[6] Some of these social norms of motherhood are ones
that you may be able to recognize and scrutinize, but some may be
invisible to you—especially if you fit into them.

Though, dear reader, we are leaning into the idea that the identity
of Mother and the work of Mothering could be gender-neutral terms,
you'll note that I've already made a number of references to female
mothers and women in this introduction. My choice to focus on
female mothers in this book is in no small part because I am a female
mother and most of the mothers I have supported have been women.
It is the context that I know most deeply and feel I can speak to most
confidently. In addition, many of the topics I write about in this book
are tangled inextricably in the gendered social norms surrounding
motherhood. Finally, becoming a parent as a trans or nonbinary person is a unique experience that requires its own book(s!), written by
and for gender nonconforming parents. Some defining elements of
this complex experience may include gender dysphoria, the constant
need to disclose and explain their gender, and facing discrimination
and even threats to their safety.[7] These are topics I cannot speak to
with authority, and I defer to those who can give a first-voice account
of what it is to become a parent outside the gender binary.

I have endeavored to conscientiously research and write this book
in a way that includes the diverse experiences of mothers from many
walks of life—and also, this book is written from my own, inherently
biased lens as a white, cisgender, female, heterosexual, biological
mother of two children. There are many references to biological
mothering throughout the book, because the process of gestating
a tiny human is an important part of becoming a mother for the
majority of women and because, in my role as a doula, this is the
journey to motherhood with which I'm most intimate. However,
women who have not gestated their children will still find so much

value in the words here. There are also references to intimate partnerships in this book. I endeavor to refer to these in a way that could include partners of any gender, and women who are not partnered will resonate deeply with many of the other parts of this book. It is my hope that fourth-time mamas will find value in these words just as much as first-time mamas. I dearly wish that mothers who have had long fertility journeys will find meaning and support here just as much as those who didn't choose pregnancy and motherhood at all.

My hope is that you will find your own experience reflected here in many, if not all, of these pages, and that reading these words will be of service to you, helping you to feel a little less alone, a little more *a part of* a community of women birthing and raising the next generation while also birthing *ourselves*.

# MOTHERSHIFT

# 1

# Beyond Pelvic Floors and Emotional Roller Coasters

*The Uncharted Territory of Motherhood*
*after the Fourth Trimester*

It is as though when each cell of my children's bodies
was formed within my womb, a corresponding
cell of my own body was also transformed.
In building a baby, I also built a mother.
—Lucy Pearce, *Moods of Motherhood*

The seeds of this book were planted during my own transition to motherhood, which, for me, began about four months before I was to conceive my first child. My husband and I had been talking about having kids, and I was deeply ambivalent about the idea.

It was, perhaps, an especially strange perspective because I had been in practice as a doula for several years by this time. I had recently supported two clients who went through particularly challenging *postpartums*—one in which the mother dealt with a deep postpartum depression and the other in which the mother chose, unexpectedly, not to raise her baby, surrendering the child for adoption one week after being born. Though my years of supporting birth made me aware of the particulars of the birthing process—the part that many women have the most concern about when they are pregnant—these two experiences had me wondering: What will happen *afterward*? What is it like *becoming a mother*?

Perhaps most importantly: What will happen to *me*?

This knowledge wasn't covered in my doula training. Usually, I and most of the other birth doulas I knew parted ways with the newborn mothers we served by their sixth postpartum week. I knew how to support women with the pragmatics of this early postpartum time, and so I felt like I would probably be able to handle diaper changes and even the learning curve of breastfeeding with relative ease. But I didn't have a firsthand understanding of what would happen *next*.

Like, would motherhood *change me*?

Being a researcher at heart, I sought out answers. I asked the handful of my friends who had already become mothers themselves: What's it *like*? Is it really that hard? Is it really that joyful?

No one could give me a straight answer.

I understand now that no one could give me a straight answer because there isn't one. Even the most skillfully applied words and nuanced descriptions couldn't hold a candle to the complexity of what it is to become a mother—though poets and novelists and midwives and maybe every woman with a pen and paper and a propensity to pour her heart onto the page have been trying to find those words forever.

Now, when I describe motherhood to friends and clients, the only word I can think of to encompass it is *exhilarating*—meaning, by my way of thinking, simultaneously terrifying, delightful, uncomfortable, joyous, awful, and wonderful. See also: polar bear dips, roller coasters, whitewater rafting, and most experiences I've had of traveling in India.

But I digress.

In the winter of 2010, my process of "maybe baby" soul-searching had come to a head. My husband had decided he wanted, and was ready, to start a family. It was important to me to make my own choice in my own way, to call on some wild wisdom that lived somewhere between my head and my heart to make the single most life-changing decision I would ever make.

Katharina, the woman who would become my doula (spoiler alert: I got pregnant), still remembers the night I pulled into her driveway, the first of many times we would come to spend together. I had slipped on the ice outside my home the week before and dislocated my knee, the remnants of an old tackle football injury that reared up every so often. The snowbanks were piled high, and I clambered out of my car and shuffled up to her doorstep while leaning gingerly on crutches so as not to slip on the icy pavement.

I had seen Katharina give a talk a few months previous, and there, she was the first person I had ever heard say—like I said to you a few pages ago—"the transition to motherhood takes two to three years."

At the time, given the trepidation I was feeling about motherhood, I could have taken this as a warning. That seemed like a *very* long time to get used to this gig.

But instead, hearing that made me breathe an enormous sigh of relief. To me, this meant I had two to three years to start feeling at home in my role as a mother. I had two to three years to screw it all up sometimes, not really enjoy it sometimes, maybe even regret it sometimes, and we could all come out the other side a-okay.

I knew, in the moment I heard these words—that the transition to motherhood would take two to three years—that I had to speak with Katharina. I felt that her statement had the potential to validate all the curiosities, questions, and fears I had about *who I would become* when I became a mother.

Although I don't remember the substance of our conversation that wintry night, I do distinctly remember what it felt like to finally be deeply heard and held in my fear of the unknowns that lay ahead. After so many people had rolled their eyes and said throwaway lines like "You'll never be the same again," or had become awash with sentimentality and told me "You'll never know a love like this," I was *so very ready* to talk about my confusing mixture of desire and ambivalence, fear and yearning, and be told: Yes, this is normal. And yes, *everything* will change. And yes, it will take some time. Two to three years, even. And yes, you will be okay.

I don't think I realized back then how lucky I was to receive Katharina's wisdom about the transition to motherhood, how fortunate I was to hear it before my motherhood journey began. Even just ten years ago, we in Western society weren't really talking about the postpartum time in terms of anything other than what it meant to learn how to care for a baby. Though we were *beginning* to be cognizant of the presence and prevalence of postpartum mood disorders, our collective cultural understanding of what happens to a woman when she becomes a mother—beyond her role as a baby care machine or beyond what might happen when that transformational time was fraught with diagnosable mental health challenges—was bereft.

## TO THE FOURTH TRIMESTER AND BEYOND

Thankfully, in recent years there have been a great many pioneers talking about *the fourth trimester*, which usually refers to the time of particularly intense physical and emotional healing that occurs in the first three months postpartum. Many of these thought leaders have been contributing to this increasing understanding by unearthing the postpartum wisdom of times past and cultures far away and bringing it to the service of today's mamas. Heng Ou, founder of MotherBees, a postpartum meal delivery service in the western United States, cowrote the book *The First Forty Days* in 2016, which continues to rock many a new mama's world, mine included.[1] Ou combines Ayurvedic and Traditional Chinese Medicine philosophy in a book that is not just a compendium of nourishing recipes but a vision for what might be possible for mothers—and an entire culture of mothers—who receive holistic postpartum support. Others, like Kimberly Ann Johnson, author of *The Fourth Trimester*, offer specific tools and resources to help mothers successfully navigate this emotionally and physically vulnerable time with more ease.[2]

Though the importance of this tremendous work cannot be overstated, what I hear more often than anything from the women I work with, especially as they traverse the uncharted territory of motherhood beyond the fourth trimester, aren't necessarily lamentations about their pelvic floors and the roller coaster of their emotions, but "I don't know *who I am* anymore."

That is, what I see more often—and what I experienced myself—is a shift that feels *existential,* not merely physical and emotional. And what I also see is a lot of *confusion, isolation, and distress* about this part of the transition to motherhood.

And so it is that the fourth trimester is just the tip of the iceberg when it comes to our collective cognizance of what it means for a woman to become a mother. I know: it is amazing (and kind of sad) to think that we in our modern, Western culture could still only be *just beginning* to understand the experience of what is actually, by definition, the oldest human endeavor on earth. But there is a slowly increasing recognition among researchers, psychologists, and popular media of the experience of motherhood that goes beyond the physical and emotional realities of the fourth trimester, exploring the two- to three-year transformation that Katharina helped me to prepare for all those years ago. That is the focus of this book.

## FINALLY, THERE'S A WORD FOR IT

*Matrescence.*

This word was first coined by social anthropologist Dana Raphael, PhD, who is also credited with the modern use of the word *doula.* Raphael wrote, way back in 1975, that "childbirth brings about a series of very dramatic changes in the new mother's physical being, in her emotional life, in her status within the group, even in her own female identity." She goes on to claim "the critical transition period which has been missed is *matrescence*: the time of mother-becoming. Giving birth does not automatically make a mother out of a woman. The amount of time it takes to become a mother needs study."[3]

But then, Raphael's groundbreaking ideas on the transition to motherhood disappeared from the academic consciousness, and the study required to understand the period of *mother-becoming* was all but abandoned—at least until reproductive psychologist Aurélie Athan, PhD, came along and began to dive more deeply into evolving our collective understanding of matrescence.

In a conversation I had with Athan, she shared with me that the word *matrescence* sounds like *adolescence* for a reason.[4] Adolescence is a life transition that we have come to assume takes many years, involves big emotions, and is the result of massive hormonal shifts, brain changes, and equally massive physical shifts, as well as changes in relationships, social standing, and even economic standing. It is a time of general awkwardness at best and absolute agony at worst, and, *perhaps most importantly*, is not something we ever expect people to "bounce back from." We know, intuitively, that teenagers will never become children again: we expect young adults to have changed forever through the process of adolescence, *and we see that as a good thing*, full of potential and possibility and power.

Once again, I feel like I have to say it: somehow, we are *only just beginning* to understand the transition to motherhood with the same level of complexity and compassion we've offered awkward teenagers for decades.

Having a *word* in our lexicon to describe the radical transformation of motherhood has allowed so many women to find meaning and camaraderie in the experience: to feel a little less alone and a lot more normal. Matrescence activist and coach Amy Taylor-Kabbaz, in her book *Mama Rising*, writes: "If I'd known what matrescence was, I would have softened into the whole experience in a completely different way. If I'd known this was an awakening, a whole self-transformation, an invitation to evolve and rise, then I would have been so much kinder on myself. I would have seen my own grace; I would have forgiven myself for all the times I felt lost; I would have trusted it all."[5]

I've talked about the power and potential of the transition to motherhood—the possibility of *awakening* and *whole self-transformation*—a few times in this book already, but if you are reading this through the fog of depression or with the vigilance of anxiety, or if motherhood has dragged you by the hair into oppressive social norms, perhaps you're rolling your eyes right now. Perhaps this idea of power and potential feels like yet another one of the impossible expectations of pastel perfection and bliss with which motherhood gets painted. Though we'll dive much deeper into the nuance of these seemingly disparate experiences of motherhood, it is first necessary to acknowledge that, indeed, mothers today are experiencing postpartum mood disorders on a level that some have called "epidemic." And there's good reason for it. In fact, I firmly believe that, in many ways, the transition to motherhood is more challenging for women today than it ever was for our foremothers.

## SICK MOTHERS, A SICK CULTURE, AND THE POSTPARTUM DEPRESSION PARADOX

Though even just a decade ago our awareness of postpartum mood disorders was quite limited, now postpartum depression has become so prevalent in our cultural lexicon that we've dropped the *depression* and just started calling it *postpartum*, as though it were a given that having a baby would result in a psychiatric diagnosis.

There's a reason why we assume postpartum comes with a mental health diagnosis: for so many mothers, it does. Worldwide postpartum depression rates vary between 10 and 20 percent of new mothers. An additional 17 percent of mothers report experiencing postpartum anxiety, and 3 to 5 percent of mothers experience postpartum obsessive-compulsive disorder.[6] For Black and Indigenous mothers, these numbers are nearly double.[7] These already unacceptably high numbers rose to levels nearly three times higher during the COVID-19 pandemic.[8] But despite their prevalence, we still know little about the nuanced inner workings of postpartum mood disorders. In fact, postpartum depression is referred to by many mental health practitioners as a "garbage bag term"—a diagnostic category into which many misunderstood mental health symptoms get placed.[9] Indeed, in her book *Ordinary Insanity* about the prevalence and impact of postpartum anxiety in America, Sarah Menkedick critiques the inaccuracy of postpartum depression diagnostic testing, reports research that indicates that postpartum anxiety may be far more prevalent than postpartum depression, and hypothesizes that actually *both* experiences are grossly underreported.[10]

In so many ways, these data are unsurprising. The world mothers are being birthed into today stacks the deck against them. In the paragraphs to follow, I will share some of the conditions that most dramatically shape modern mothers' postpartum challenges, even from the very moment of their babies' births.

The vast majority of women start their motherhood journeys having experienced a highly medicalized birth in a hospital where cesarean section rates are two to three times higher than World Health Organization recommendations.[11] Birth interventions have a known effect on postpartum mental health. For example, research by Dr. Sarah Buckley on the hormonal physiology of childbearing indicates that the widespread use of medical interventions such as epidurals and synthetic oxytocin (known by its trade names Pitocin or Syntocinon and used to induce or augment uterine contractions) has a direct impact on women's postpartum hormone balance, and thus their postpartum mental health.[12] In addition, rates of birth trauma and birth-related PTSD are skyrocketing, with nearly 45 percent of mothers reporting experiencing a traumatic birth and up to 18 percent of those reporting symptoms of PTSD.[13] I often say that I see birth as a microcosm of the macrocosm of motherhood, meant to be a crash course in everything you *really* need to know when you become a mother. But so many women are being robbed of this potentially empowering experience, or going in misinformed (or disinformed) about the long-term impact of common medical interventions and then wondering what's wrong with *them* when their postpartum well-being is affected (see endnote for more).[14]

These birth and early postpartum challenges are dramatically augmented for BIPOC mothers. Research shows that Black mothers are more than twice as likely to die in childbirth and to experience postpartum mood disorders as white mothers.[15] Mothers who experience systemic racism and discrimination are also more likely to experience higher overall levels of chronic stress as well as being less likely to have access to safe, affordable health care.[16]

The widespread lack of social policy that supports mothers is also to blame for the postpartum challenges they face. Many companies—and entire countries—lack comprehensive maternity leave benefits. This puts mothers in a position of returning to work sometimes while they are *literally still bleeding from birth* lest they face lost wages or even be forced out of full-time employment in order to take time off to heal and care for their babies. Meanwhile, the cost of childcare is so prohibitive that, for some mothers, it either doesn't make economic sense to work outside the home or they are left with the labor of piecing together alternative care options for their children.

Another way in which what you're experiencing *ain't your mama's transition to motherhood* is that many of us have lost "the village" that supported our foremothers and ancestors through the physical and emotional challenges of postpartum. Anthropologist Sarah Blaffer Hrdy, PhD, has studied the evolution of "the village" in primates and humans. She describes humans as "reproductively hyperburdened," meaning that we have helpless babies fairly close together and, as a result, the needs of a mother's offspring often exceed her capacity to provide for them.[17] Hrdy posits that humans literally *evolved* to become more socially sensitive and altruistic creatures so that we could distribute the burden of care for our resource-intensive offspring to what she calls "alloparents"—the grandmothers, fathers, aunties, sisters, and brothers that we call kin.[18] But many modern mothers find themselves mothering in solitude. The COVID-19 pandemic thrust us even more deeply into this isolation, preventing new mothers from accessing even modern-day approximations of the village such as mom and baby groups and other social lifelines.

Though we may be mothering in relative social isolation, we are far from being isolated from the social norms about motherhood that run rampant through Western culture. These norms, which maternal theory scholar Andrea O'Reilly, PhD, groups into an ideology of "normative motherhood," include the ideas that childrearing is the purview of women and that this role is to be held by one self-sacrificing person—the biological mother—within the confines of a nuclear family.[19] All of this is thought to come naturally to mothers, of course, but also not without constant reference to "experts" that ensure this sacred work is being done "properly." Mothers who do not fit the insidious cultural norm that holds that "good" mothers are white, cisgender, heterosexual, and able-bodied are judged even more harshly if they fail to live up to the impossible ideals of normative motherhood. Helena Andrews-Dyer in her book *The Mamas* writes about her experience in a racially disparate social group of mothers: "As the only Black woman in the group, I had to be twice as good at something we all suck at."[20]

The dictates of normative motherhood have their roots in the end of feudalism and the early days of capitalism, but they mutated and intensified at several historical junctures, including when post-WWII mothers were pushed out of the workforce and back into the home, when parenting "experts" like Spock, Bowlby, and Sears came on the scene in the 1950s and '60s, and again when mothers headed to work in larger numbers in the late twentieth century.[21] With this latter shift came what sociologist Sharon Hays, PhD, calls "intensive mothering"—a motherhood ideal characterized as "child-centred, expert-guided, emotionally absorbing, labor intensive and financially expensive."[22] Shari Thurer, PhD, author of *The Myths of Motherhood*, states: "The current standards for *good mothering* are so formidable, self-denying, elusive, changeable, and contradictory that they are unattainable. Our contemporary myth heaps upon the mother so many duties and expectations that to take it seriously would be hazardous to her mental health."[23]

To make matters *even worse*, in our modern context this ideal of the "perfect mother" plays out writ large on the stage of social media. Though social media sometimes offers new mothers a sense of camaraderie and community, portrayals of perfect motherhood online can also shape unrealistic expectations of the actual work of mothering—a demonstrated predictor of anxiety, depression, stress, and low self-esteem in new mothers.[24] These portrayals often find mothers striving toward impossible ideals of perfectionism in motherhood, comparing their insides to other people's outsides and, inevitably, coming up short. The result isn't just feelings of inadequacy. When a mother cannot see herself in other people's experiences or does not see her experience of motherhood reflected positively in the outer world, the result, perhaps more devastating than her perfectionistic striving, is a loss of her sense of belonging to a community of other mothers.

There are so many more influences on and challenges to today's mothers: these are just a few, and I could write an *entire book* about how our modern context shapes women's experience of matrescence. Maybe someday I will, but for now, all of this is to say that *it's no wonder mothers today are suffering*. It's also to point out that many of the challenges modern-day mothers are experiencing are the result of *societal and systemic* problems. That is, you're not suffering because you're not *doing motherhood right*. You're not broken. It's our culture that's broken.

As Krishnamurti said: "It is no measure of health to be well adjusted to a profoundly sick society."

All of this is true, and *all* of these realities of modern motherhood need our attention, activism, and change, but there's more to the story of matrescence than this.[25]

As we slowly grow a more nuanced understanding of the complex landscape of postpartum mental health, reproductive psychologists and psychiatrists are positing that while modern mothers are experiencing tremendous and unprecedented challenges in the postpartum period, we are also, paradoxically, pathologizing and prescribing for a great many of the very normal, but difficult, experiences of the transition to motherhood.[26]

Let's unpack this paradox of postpartum depression a little, shall we?

We, as a culture, have a storied history of pathologizing women's normal processes, including menstruation, birth, and menopause.

We also tend to pathologize other life processes that make us uncomfortable or get in the way of our societal drive to strive, such as normal healthy grief, normal healthy seasonal fluctuations in our bodies and moods, and normal healthy stress responses. We are quicker, generally, to assume abnormality—and prescribe for it—rather than to ask the questions: *Could this be normal? Could my experience fit on the very broad spectrum of what is, in fact, normal and healthy?*

Dr. Alexandra Sacks, perinatal psychiatrist and author of the book *What No One Tells You: A Guide to Your Emotions from Pregnancy to Motherhood*, wrote in *Psychology Today*: "Matrescence is not a disease, but it's being confused with a serious condition (that deserves its own expanded outreach, research and advocacy) called Postpartum Depression."[27]

Because, as I've wholeheartedly established, we are *only just* beginning to understand the experience of becoming a mother in modern Western culture, it makes a lot of sense that we might see a woman who is feeling grief about losing her connection to who she used to be before having a baby, for example, and call her depressed.[28] In our modern culture—at least until the concept of matrescence makes its way into mainstream lexicon—we literally have *no other way* to conceptualize it, and precious little language to describe it.

Athan and other matrescence scholars are calling for us to broaden our perspective on the wildly complex and nuanced experience of becoming a mother, viewing it through a developmental lens in addition to the lenses of pathology or oppression that we often default to. She writes: "If contextualized within a lifespan . . . 'becoming a mother' can instead be affirmed as a normative phenomenon, a turning point in the trajectory of some women's lives with its natural 'disequilibrium and reorganization.' Anchored within the framework of a developmental model, a mother undergoes a maturational 'crisis' with its requisite upheaval, demanding adaptation, much like any other critical turning point in a human life."[29] Matrescence scholar and counselor Allison Davis, PhD, further clarifies: "Contextualizing distress within a developmental model does not erase clinically significant experiences of distress in the form of perinatal mood and anxiety disorders. The question isn't 'matrescence or postpartum depression?' It could be both."[30] In a 2023 paper, Davis notes that as many as 40 percent of mothers make up a "silent majority" who do not show clinical levels of distress, but who are nevertheless challenged and experience stress during the transition to motherhood.[31]

It is easy to see the potential for matrescence—especially with the unique challenges that modern-day society presents during that transition—to be fertile ground for depression. But I wonder all the time: What if women were received into motherhood *knowing* that it would shift the tectonic plates of their lives and that it's *supposed to*? That it's *normal* to feel lost, unsure of who you are anymore, ambivalent sometimes, angry or sad sometimes, and that all of these feelings are okay, can be supported with resources and guidance, and will end (but not quickly)?

One of the most compassionate, reassuring things *any* of us can ever hear is *you are normal.*

Before you scoff and say, "Well, what is normal anyway?" notice how much power being "normal" can hold in our lives. Feeling normal, or *okay*, is another way to say, "You belong." You belong with the rest of us because your experience is a lot like ours. Postpartum depression and anxiety, as Sacks states, are indeed real and serious clinical conditions. But there is also a generously broad spectrum of what is actually normal and healthy that has been labeled as pathology because our collective "postpartum depression radar" has become almost too sensitive, resulting in both the misdiagnosing of women who are *actually* experiencing postpartum anxiety or obsessive-compulsive disorder *and* the overdiagnosing of women who are *actually* experiencing the tumultuous but normal identity shift into motherhood.[32]

All of this has led us very, very astray from *what is possible* for women as they transition into motherhood. In advocating for a fuller perspective on what matrescence means for mothers, Athan and colleagues have likened the adaptations and subsequent self-awareness that are *also* common among new mothers to the experience of post-traumatic growth.[33] In a study of over a hundred mothers' experience of growth during matrescence, a group of researchers found that when they were well supported, "women may gain self-esteem, new meaning in life, and a sense of competence," citing, importantly, that "some degree of enduring psychological distress is necessary not only to set the process in motion, but also for the enhancement and maintenance of growth."[34] Research by Athan explored the spiritual growth that is common among many new mothers as they traverse matrescence, finding that women experienced increased mindfulness, heightened sensory experiences, increased pleasure and satisfaction in "the simple things," an elevated sense of the "magic in the ordinary," uncanny intuitive engagement, and a "striking comfort with ambiguity."[35]

Indeed, those experiences of whole self-transformation and awakening I described earlier and the experiences of disorientation and grief that also tend to come with motherhood are *all* part of what women traverse in matrescence. In fact, I could argue, *you can't have one without the other*. Let me be clear: this is not to say that we shouldn't work to change the challenging societal conditions into which today's mothers are born, any more than we should stop researching treatments and cures for diseases because those afflicted might "grow" as a result. But, as we tend to do in our binary, all-or-nothing way of thinking in our culture, we've failed to fully appreciate the complexity and nuance of matrescence, and in so doing, we may be limiting mothers' ability to experience this transformative time in its fullness.

There is another fascinating layer to the postpartum depression paradox: preliminary research shows that when women hold beliefs about motherhood as a time of inner and even spiritual evolution they *report lower depressive symptoms throughout their entire first postpartum year*.[36] In addition, seeing difficult periods of our lives as times of spiritual development has been demonstrated to support people to adapt more readily to future times of challenge, catalyze them toward meaningful life goals, ease anxiety and depression, and reduce addictions and compulsions.[37] Finally, research from other fields has shown that making meaning of challenging life circumstances encourages us to question and change the conditions under which we're living and step into more authentic lives.[38] And so it is that having an understanding of matrescence as a developmental, challenging but ultimately normal process that is also full of potential may in fact be *protective* against postpartum depression.

But, as Athan posits in her research, because we lack a schema for matrescence as a powerful, positive, transformational experience, mothers may be the last to know about the immense potential of their transition to motherhood. She writes: "Without any rites of passage or alternative interpretive frameworks to illuminate the presence of their spiritual work, mothers are finding themselves traversing a path to enlightenment in isolation. Where are women being informed that to embark on the transition to motherhood is to undergo a spiritual transformation?"[39]

And that brings us here, now, ready to explore the uncharted territory of matrescence—the rite of passage into motherhood—with all its challenges *and* its possibilities.

## WHAT *IS* A RITE OF PASSAGE, ANYWAY?

In the introduction, I shared that though the field of matrescence is growing day by day, our understanding of it is still only *that* it happens, rather than *how* it happens. With that current wisdom at our fingertips, we mothers can locate ourselves and find camaraderie and normalcy in the *fact* of our experience, but we still often feel like we're fumbling through the dark on a nebulous, all-consuming journey without a map for the road.

As my own curiosity about the transition to motherhood began to grow over the last decade—having experienced the total existential shift myself and then witnessing it in the clients I was supporting—my questions were all about the *how*. *How* do we transform when we become mothers? What happens to *who we are*, not just to our waist circumference and how we spend our Friday nights?

Most of our current discourse around the postpartum time focuses on the transition to motherhood as being a *behavioral* one—about *information* rather than deep *transformation*. In short, this perspective holds that once you've learned how to change diapers and make really strong coffee, you've essentially nailed it. It's a change to the things you *do*.

But becoming a mother is not just a series of new skills or behaviors, it's a complete reorientation of a woman's identity, her values, and how she makes her way through the world.

And so, alongside wanting to know *how* the transition to motherhood happened, I also wanted to explore the possibilities for motherhood when viewed from the *developmental model* posited by Athan—as in psychology-speak for how motherhood can be a process of intense transformation that, although challenging and confronting, also gifts mothers with an opportunity to grow and develop as *human beings*.

I began to realize that, at the heart of it all, I wanted to explore motherhood as a *rite of passage*: as nothing less than a total, irreversible, and powerful transformation of body, psyche, soul, and identity.

If the term *rite of passage* sounds a little bit foreign to you or like something that's relegated to teenage boys going on wilderness expeditions and coming back as men, let me share my working definition of what a rite of passage is:

A rite of passage is the kind of life change that changes everything. It is a transformation that runs deeper than changes we might experience to the things we do, think, or feel, and right into the very marrow of how we identify ourselves in the world. A rite of passage has the potential to bring us closer to our own sense of who we are and what matters most to us. Far from being solitary endeavors of self-actualization, rites of passage grow us up into mature adults that know and use their gifts to contribute to their community, as leaders and elders.

Nothing fits this description better than motherhood.

As you've likely already surmised, I'm a total geek. In more ways than not, I'm still the ten-year-old who used to spend my summer vacations in the library doing research projects for fun. And so, as I started formulating these questions about *how* the rite of passage into motherhood happens, I got my nose in some books.

A lot of books.

I explored research on adult development psychology; I read mythology; I studied neuroscience and attachment theory; I dove into feminist literature; I mined texts on rites of passage theory. I analyzed Arnold van Gennep's *The Rites of Passage*, Joseph Campbell's *The Hero's Journey*, and psychoanalyst Maureen Murdock's feminist take on the latter, *The Heroine's Journey*.[40]

(In other words, even though motherhood is often considered to be the consummate human rite of passage, I had to look way outside the wisdom of the pregnancy and parenting literature to find what I was searching for. Though I'm far from the first person to describe motherhood as a rite of passage, our concept of this transformation tends to focus on birth as the moment of metamorphosis. But, in my experience, birth is just the beginning of the journey. A clue: I was indeed navigating uncharted territory in our understanding of matrescence.)

As I did my research, what I was really searching for was a framework of some kind: a set of steps or a process that would describe the patterns in the journey that the mothers I was working with were navigating. In wanting to understand the *how* of matrescence, I was looking for a map for this uncharted territory so that I could help guide mamas along the way. But as I pored through the books, I found that a lot of the research and thinking on rites of passage and life transition had been generated by, about, and for—*how best to say this?*—old white guys. For example, the text that originated most of modern-day thought around rites of passage—*The Rites of Passage*—was based on van Gennep's once-contentious "armchair anthropology"[41] wherein he, a white man, read the accounts of various cultures' rites of passage witnessed by other mostly white, male field anthropologists and surmised a unifying structure by which he imagined *all* transformative processes in the human lifespan occurred (see note for more).[42] Other models of life transition tended to describe change as though it were a linear process happening in a vacuum, not within the nuanced ecosystem of roles, responsibilities, and realities that the women I worked with tended to have, which, in turn, dramatically affected the how, why, and when of the changes they traversed as they became mothers.[43] These models of life transition also didn't acknowledge the complex modern-day cultural contexts within which we operate that, of course, as I shared earlier in this chapter, deeply impact women's matrescence.

As you can imagine, my search for a map to help guide women through the transition to motherhood ended in the realization that I was going to have to chart it myself. And so the Four Elements of Radical Transformation were born.

## THE FOUR ELEMENTS OF RADICAL TRANSFORMATION: A MAP FOR YOUR *BECOMING*

The Four Elements model is composed of the elements Earth, Water, Air, and Fire as metaphors that describe the phases of identity shift and life transition. It is informed by the experiences of the women I've worked with and pulls in the wisdom from all those books I pored over—but with a feminist, nonlinear, relational, and complexity-oriented foundation. And the *radical* part? It doesn't just *sound* like the wild journey of whole self-transformation; it also draws upon the Latin word for *root*: *radicle*—as in, a transformation that brings you back to your roots, to who you are and what matters most to you. The model itself is a nod to the mythic underpinnings of rites of passage but also draws from the research on adult development psychology and adds a splash of complexity theory, attachment theory, and a few others for good measure . . . and modern-day relevance.

In other words? It's legit.

The Four Elements model is a map for not only the rite of passage into motherhood, but other transformations you'll likely find yourself making during your lifetime, too. In this way, this process and even aspects of this book can serve as a touchstone and a resource for your life well beyond the early years of matrescence.

Are you ready to dive in?

I'll give you an overview of the model here, and then the coming chapters in this section of the book will take you on a journey deeper into the Four Elements.

Here's how it works: Any major transformation in our lives begins with a *catalyst*. If you're reading this book, that catalyst is likely to be motherhood, but might also be other life circumstances that are shaping your experience at this time.

Once the catalyst (or catalysts) has occurred, we enter the Four Elements process of transformation. The first phase of transformation, or element, is Earth. I liken it to putting your feet on the earth of your life and getting grounded with *what is*—like an orientation to your lived reality. When I teach and mentor women in the postpartum period, I do this by inviting mothers to take an inventory of all the shifts that have happened since they've begun the transition to motherhood. It's a way of taking stock so you can begin to make meaning of the transformation that's happening in your life.

The next phase of the Four Elements model is Water, which describes the sense of grief and loss that so many mothers feel but often cannot articulate. In any life transition, we must let go of what is no longer—sometimes for a little while, and sometimes forever. It's watery work indeed, often marked by lots of tears and the washing away of what you are letting go. This is a challenging but healthy part of traversing any major life transformation, including motherhood.

We then enter the element of Air, which is the space of *liminality* or the in-between. So many women experiencing this phase of transformation throw their hands up and say, "I don't know what's next, or what I'm doing, or who I am. *Everything is up in the air*." This is when you might be feeling like you're not *not* a mother anymore, but maybe you're *not quite yet* fully embodied in your motherhood. It is a time to learn meaningful self-care so that you have the resilience and fortification to do the often-difficult work of learning to sit in the unknown of who you are becoming.

The final element is Fire. This is where the spark of the new life that's awaiting you begins to ignite and gather strength. It's a time of exploration, of discovering who you are now that you are a mother, and who you are as a *woman* who *happens to be a mother*. This is when you get to experiment with what feels good and true for you now. It's the "fun" part of the process, the part that we often try to take a shortcut to, bypassing all the gnarly experiences of grief and the unknown. I most often see this bypassing when women struggle to "get back to normal" (aka the old jeans, the old sex life, and the hot coffee) after they have babies, only to realize that that normal—*and the woman who lived in that version of normal*—doesn't actually exist anymore. The element of Fire is also where you begin to explore your MotherPowers—those counterculture skills and capacities that will not only support you in your motherhood but are also what our world needs more of right now.

Finally, as we emerge from the Fire, we begin the process of *integration*: we make sense of how we have changed in relation to the environments we find ourselves in and reshape the circumstances of our lives so they match and support our "new selves." Sometimes this means we make shifts in our relationships, friendships, or communities. Sometimes motherhood catalyzes a transformation in other areas of our lives like our careers or our homes or external environments. Even though this might seem like the (phew!) end of the process, this phase can sometimes be the most challenging, as we explore how our changed selves fit or don't fit into contexts that may or may not have changed along with us. It takes courage—and time.

The next chapters of this book will use the Four Elements model as a guide to help you navigate your transition to motherhood and will offer you specific tools and resources to help you along the way. But before we begin, there are some important nuances about the Four Elements model to take note of:

- The Four Elements model is not a linear process. Becoming a mother wouldn't be the rite of passage it is if it were easy, or linear, or if there were an instruction manual to follow. It wouldn't be the rite of passage it is if we didn't also have to step into the unknown along the way, or if we didn't also experience some hardship as we traverse this path. I see the Four Elements process not as one that has a beginning, middle, and end, but as a spiral, revolving from one Element to the next in an ongoing, iterative process of change and discovery. Very often, for example, women spend a lot of time moving back and forth between Water and Earth, consciously or subconsciously asking: *Okay, if I'm not that anymore, who am I now? If that's no longer part of my identity, then what is?* It can take a while before we then move into Air, or the liminal space, and often it takes some deliberate effort and extra support to be able to move into the fiery work of then beginning to create and define your own motherhood experience.

- And so it is that you will move through the Four Elements in your own sweet time. This process is slow and unfurling and, it bears mentioning, cannot be hacked with the tools of determination, striving, or cleverness. Indeed, the spiral of your motherhood journey will continue for the rest of your life, drawing you inward into deep contemplation and reflection and then pulling you back out into "the world," asking you to live into and enact your more deeply refined values and identities. You'll likely engage in this work again at other major transformational milestones in your mothering journey, like when your kids go to school or enter adolescence (which, someone recently pointed out to me, often coincides with women's experience of peri-menopause—a veritable adventure in hormones!) or leave home. The journey doesn't end, but I hope that this book will help you to feel well-resourced to continue to walk this motherhood path, no matter what it entails for you (see note for more).[44]

- You can't do this wrong. There is no right or wrong way to experience this process. I stand by bell hooks's assertion that frameworks and theories should be used as "liberating structures," not as a set of oppressive dictates you feel pressured to conform to.[45] I invite you, wholeheartedly, to use the Four Elements to the extent that this model serves you—to take what is nourishing and useful and leave the rest behind. The variations with which I've seen women engage in this are infinite, just as there are an infinite number of ways in which you may experience matrescence. My experience as a woman who was ambivalent about motherhood before getting pregnant will be very different from that of a woman who has been on a long fertility journey, for example. We also bring our histories of being mothered and our nuanced and unique cultural understandings of motherhood into this transition. This path is yours to walk, and you can weave your own way through this book and this transformation however feels most aligned to you.

- All mothers can go through this process no matter how many children they've had, and they can go through it with every child. Every baby is different, and every time we bring a child into our lives, we're slightly different, too. If you're the mama of more than one and are wondering why you *haven't figured this out yet*, let this be a big permission slip to be okay with not knowing what you're doing or who you are now.

- You are *already* doing this. The fact that you're here, reading this book, is a testament to how deeply conscious you are of what the transition to motherhood means for you, and probably how implicitly aware you are of the great potential this process holds for your life. You may well have naturally traversed some of these experiences on your own thus far, and my intention is to amplify the knowledge and wisdom that already lives inside you and has already been awakened simply by the fact of your motherhood. Perhaps more than anything, my goal is to remind you that *you are not alone* and that *you are normal*. You *belong* in the great circle of women who have done this before and who are doing it now. This is all part of it, mama.

And so.

Let the coming chapters be a map for your becoming. I've been using the Four Elements model to guide my work with thousands of mamas, and I have seen firsthand the power of being able to put words to your experience and know that there is a path to follow as you traverse it. As Maia, one of the mothers I've supported, says: "I didn't realize how wholly destabilizing the shift into motherhood would be. The Four Elements allowed me to normalize my experience and also have room to find my own way into motherhood. It was hugely orienting, affirming, and gave me a lot of tools and ideas that I still employ."

Welcome to all this, mama. Welcome to the transition to motherhood, to the fullness of what this transformation might mean for your life and the deep potential it has to help you uncover more of *who you are* in the process—more of what matters to you, of what you're made of, of how you want to show up in the world.

Welcome, welcome, welcome.

# PART I

# The Four Elements of Radical Transformation

## THE MAP FOR YOUR MATRESCENCE

# 2

# **Earth**

*Orienting to the Changes That*
*No One Ever Told You Would Happen*
*When You Became a Mother*

Motherhood is often the first true test of
self in a woman's life. How much holds up,
how much crumbles, how much mutates?
—Sarah Menkedick, *Ordinary Insanity*

Welcome to Earth, mama. It's time to explore the first element in the Four Elements model and how it applies to you and your experience of matrescence.

When I'm working with clients, I describe the Earth phase as a process of unpacking the contents of your life—your relationships, your identity, your work, your body, your emotions, your spirituality, all of it—and having a good look at what has changed since you began your transition to motherhood. Earth is a phase of *orientation*. It's a beginning place, where we start exactly where you are and get *real* with what's happening for you now that you've embarked on your journey of matrescence. It's an opportunity to really *name* what has changed and how you feel about it. As they say: if you can say it, you can see it. It sounds simple, but it's a step that's often skipped over, leaving us to wail *"Nothing will ever be the same again!"* without looking more closely.

Many of the things that change because of the sheer fact of what it takes to grow, birth, and nourish a baby are perhaps self-evident, or at least well-documented. But I'm pretty interested in the things that might be changing for you that you didn't know were *a thing.* Like, those things that you thought maybe you were experiencing all by yourself. Or those things that seemingly have nothing to do with actually mothering and are more about *you* and who *you are now that you're a mother.* As I've shared, research has demonstrated that having an experience of motherhood that is different—aka more challenging—than you expected is predictive of lower levels of self-esteem and higher levels of depression, anxiety, and stress.[1] Social media has a lot to do with this: images of the "perfect mother" in action aside, even the rawest portrayals of motherhood we see on Instagram have been chosen and curated for others' consumption. And so here we are, about to do one of the things I love best: let's talk about the things *no one talks about,* shall we?

We will focus on five key shifts that happen in new motherhood that you are *probably* experiencing but no one ever told you would happen—or at least no one ever told you they'd happen in this way. They are the changes to your body, your relationships, and your values, something I call the Big Slowdown, and changes to your career aspirations. All of these are *not* your average how-to-change-a-diaper conversations and focus more on the entire constellation of relationships, roles, responsibilities, and identities you hold *in addition* to motherhood. Each subsection in this chapter will introduce these shifts and some ideas to help you think about them in relation to your own life. Then, at the end of the chapter, you'll find the first "Your Turn" section, where you'll get an opportunity to reflect on what you've read and begin the healing, transformative work of exploring what has changed in your life since you've become a mother.

## YOUR BODY

They say they're tiger stripes
or battle scars.
I don't buy it.
They are rifts in my skin; wide canyons carved into my flesh
because I had to expand for you.
Because I got to expand for you.
Because I allowed myself to expand for you.

There is nothing more viscerally *embodied* than the experience of becoming and being a mother. Whether or not you carried and birthed the baby you're raising, caring for a little human is all warm embraces, sweaty armpits, hot tears, breasts, hips, and bellies. Your body is hardly your own as you enter motherhood, and the loss of physical autonomy, sometimes beginning even just days after sperm fertilizes egg, is jolting for most women. Any mother in the early months and years of her children's lives can relate to the feeling of throwing her shoulders and head back after countless hours of hunching, holding, and rocking or nursing a tiny person or of how desperately she wishes she could *just. pee. alone.*

Mothers having this physical experience often refer to themselves as being "touched out." Feeling this way is, in many ways, a function of what it means to caregive. It can be especially jarring if you, like many of us before motherhood, have thus far lived a fairly autonomous life and are rarely beholden to the needs or schedules of others. But there's also more to the experience of being touched out. When mothers lack the support they need to take breaks from the physicality of mothering or when they're operating under the spell of "perfect motherhood," which may manifest in a contortion of attachment theory that says *thou shalt never put down the baby*, being touched out takes on a whole new intensity. Amanda Montei, author of *Touched Out*, writes, "The notion that women should sacrifice their bodies at the altar of parenting, and marriage, only extends and upholds the assumption that women's bodies are made for the taking."[2]

Another challenging aspect of the transition to motherhood as it relates to your body is learning to accept it, respect it, and maybe even love it after the transformative act of childbearing.

"I feel like I've lost myself—I don't know who I am anymore now that my body can't do the things it used to. Now that I'm not as capable as I used to be. I've always been so *capable*," my client Ellen shared in a recent conversation. An avid adventurer and outdoorsperson, Ellen experienced a birth injury that had prevented her from hiking and biking everywhere with her new baby like she expected to be able to do. She had been trying desperately to reclaim her adventurous spirit but in the process had pushed her body too hard and aggravated her pelvic floor injury, leaving her in chronic pain. She and her partner, who had always connected over a shared love of the outdoors, were feeling more and more distant from each other. Ellen was slowly realizing that her body and its abilities had changed—maybe for now but maybe for longer—and along with it, so had a key part of her identity.

The world is so quick to tell mothers, "Just LOVE your body! Look at the amazing thing that it has done!" But as we see in Ellen's story and the story of so many mothers, our relationships with our postpartum bodies are much more complicated than that. When your body has, in fact, conceived, birthed, and nourished a baby with little complication, loving your body for the amazing thing it has done might be quite relatable. But if that wasn't the case for you—if your transition into motherhood was marked by a complex fertility journey, a traumatic birth, or a difficult postpartum recovery (contexts that affect more and more women in our society than ever)—that statement might feel irrelevant at best and dismissive or even harmful at worst.

At the same time it tells us to "just love our bodies," our culture emphasizes the ideal of "getting your body back" after having a baby. One minute we're told our stretch marks are "tiger stripes," and the next minute, we're given a miracle cream to make them go away. The truth is, your body has been rearranged by the presence of your baby within it, and it's not really *meant* to return to its pre-motherhood form. But society makes this transformation challenging: as your body is doing the work of birthing and caring for a little person, it likely has also deviated from societal beauty norms more now than it ever has before.

If it feels hard or complex to love your postpartum body, know that it's not just you. In fact, it's probably not you at all. It can be challenging to love your body in a culture that doesn't always love it back.

When I was newly postpartum with my first baby, and then again with my second, I remember feeling as though my body were foreign territory. My hips and thighs felt different when I ran my fingers over them subconsciously; my constitution could no longer tolerate caffeine; everything from my hair to my body odor was just *different*. I experienced a feeling of deep *disorientation*, as I imagine a teenager with new breasts and fleshier hips and "hair where there wasn't hair before" might.

We have a choice in our experience of our motherbodies: we can work like hell to try to reattain the body we had before it was radically shifted in motherhood—a feat that a baffling number of women attempt well into their elder years—or we can explore what it might be like to learn about and live in a new body, like Ellen is being invited to do. It's important to remember that *this is an identity shift too.* You might be—*even if subconsciously*—asking: *Who am I now that my body looks like this? Who am I now that my body no longer does this thing it used to do? Who am I now that my body is different from what our culture has applauded me for in the past? How do I find my sense of value and self-worth if my body doesn't look like the kind of body society deems worthy?* In this way, it's not as simple as wishing you could "just love your body" again: your *relationship with your body*, just like your body itself, has to completely transform. We'll explore this more in the second half of the book.

## YOUR RELATIONSHIPS

Motherhood also represents a significant change to the dynamics of many women's relationships. In fact, a longitudinal study by R. Chris Fraley and colleagues shows that life transitions in general changed attachment styles temporarily for half of their research participants and that one-quarter of participants experienced enduring shifts to their attachment styles.[3] That means that when *we* change, it disrupts the ecosystems of our relationships in a way that *all* affected parties can feel. As a result, we often find ourselves having to renegotiate the terms of those relationships. The most common, and often most dramatic, of these are a woman's relationship with her intimate partner, if she has one; her relationship with her own mother; and her relationships with her friends and community. Let's dive deeper, shall we?

### *The Equality Trap: How Intimate Partnerships Shift*

Relationship expert Dr. John Gottman found that marital satisfaction and happiness decline by 67 percent in the first three years after having a baby and that this is one of the most vulnerable times in a partnership—a time when it is most likely to fall apart.[4]

One of the key causes of these experiences of relational strife, especially for heterosexual couples, is that parenthood often widens the gender gap. Having a baby can careen us right back into marriage circa 1953, otherwise known as: everything we've ever been taught to avoid as modern-day women.

Before kids, a great many of us pride ourselves on having relationships that are predicated on complete and total equality and gender neutrality: you do the dishes, I do the dishes; you manage the finances, I manage the finances; you fix the car, I fix the car. Our values around this type of equality come from the hard work our feminist foremothers did to assure women's ability to "do anything a man could." This dynamic usually works well—until a baby enters the picture.

Illustrating this, Kimberly Ann Johnson, author of *The Fourth Trimester*, writes: "However nontraditional our roles may have been with partners before, having a baby places different demands on a woman than it does on a man. Most women certainly recognize that intellectually, but the lived experience of this inequality can still be disarming for many women."[5] In fact, Elly Taylor in her book *Becoming Us* shares research that shows that the more equal a relationship is before a baby, the bigger the shock may be after the baby is born.[6]

Indeed, you might be freaking out right now, or you might be nodding your head ruefully or your inner feminist might even be seething a little. Stay with me here. We're going to take our *time* with this topic, because it's nuanced as hell. Grab—or, ahem, reheat—yourself a cup of tea, and let's begin.

Biology is a key factor in the way that gender roles change when a baby is born, and so we'll start there—but know that if you are a mother who has not birthed or breastfed your baby, your journey might look a little different, and I want to acknowledge that.

Let's begin by leaning on the examples of other species and of other cultures to provide some context, and then we'll dive into some of the physiology that can underpin the gender divide among new parents.

While the mother is almost always involved in the care of infant animals of other species, the involvement of fathers is contingent on a wide range of factors, including their presence, the strength of the bond between parents, and the support of other caregivers.[7] Similarly, in cultures around the world, mothers are more likely to do most of the childcare in their families and communities. In her book *All the Rage: Mothers, Fathers, and the Myth of Equal Partnership*, Darcy Lockman reports: "There is actually no known human society in which men are responsible for the bulk of all childrearing. Cross-cultural anthropologists report that in every part of the world, across a wide range of subsistence activities and social ideologies, mothers are more involved than fathers with the care of their young."[8] These contexts are important to note because they give us a clue as to why sharing caregiving equally between partners can be such a challenge: there may be little evolutionary or cross-cultural precedence for it, reinforcing that there may be some biological foundation for mothers' role as primary caregivers.

Indeed, carrying and birthing a child result in massive changes to a woman's physiology that prime her to be an attentive, attuned caregiver from the moment her baby is born.[9] In addition, if she breastfeeds her baby, a woman's body surges with a cocktail of hormones that makes nurturing almost addictive.[10] We're only just beginning to learn about the dramatic changes to a mother's brain as a result of pregnancy and caregiving, but author Sarah Menkedick puts it best: "What women enact in pregnancy and early motherhood is no less than the development of the mammalian brain. . . . She has been made into a mother like a factory is made into lofts, a church into a concert hall, a barn into a house. The beams or bricks may be the same, but the interior energy is distinct, reprogrammed."[11] Though physiological changes have also been documented in fathers and other alloparents, these changes are not a given and remain dependent on repeated, daily caregiving.[12]

The result of all this physiological restructuring is profound. For example, research reported by Hrdy found that mothers are more attuned to their infant's cries and it takes more urgent-sounding cries to rouse a father out of sleep to attend to his infant than a mother.[13] Obsessive-compulsive disorder researcher Dr. James Leckman found that, at two weeks postpartum, mothers reported thinking about their baby for fourteen hours a day—twice that of fathers.[14]

There is a Swahili word that refers to a mother and her baby in the first two years of life: *mamatoto*. *Mamatoto* literally means "motherbaby"—all one word, all one biological and psychological *unit*. Interestingly, the first two years of life during which the term *mamatoto* is used coincides with the two- to three-year transformation of matrescence. This term doesn't mean that there aren't other caregivers in the picture, but it acknowledges that there are particularities of a mother's skin and breath and consciousness that make her especially bonded to the little human she grew—a little human who, incidentally, happens to have an evolutionary drive to survive that's dependent on their ability to develop a strong bond with an attuned caregiver.

The preceding paragraphs might tell a story of the biological imperative of maternal caregiving, but the story of *nature* is never complete without the story of *nurture*. Like it or not, from a very young age, many women who are now in their childbearing years were socialized within our patriarchal culture to be nurturing and maternal. They may have had hours of "practice" on stuffed animals or younger siblings, or at the very least, they have been the recipients of messages that, for girls and women, relationality reigns and they should care about the feelings and experiences of others. In fact, as early as two years of age, little girls are more likely to comfort others in distress than little boys are—and it takes stronger signals of distress to elicit the sympathy of little boys.[15] Once they become mothers, women receive strong cultural messages about what a "good mother" looks like and does, and these social expectations tend to shape their caregiving behavior significantly. Mothers are more likely to be the ones to take time away from work to care for their babies, while partners, especially in our current economy and with our current postpartum leave policies, usually must return to work soon after the birth of a baby. This means that mothers are spending hours and hours more time learning the nuances of how to care for their babies, leaving their partners or other caregivers in the dust. Expectant and new mothers are also more likely to engage in regular conversations with others about parenting—both the ostensibly helpful conversations at mom and baby group and the sometimes not-so-helpful conversations with random strangers at the grocery store. All of these interactions give women more opportunities to further hone their conceptualization of what it is to be a mother in our culture.

Both the nature story *and* the nurture story are true, and there's also this: all of today's most compelling evidence about caregiving indicates that though there are myriad physiological shifts that might *prime* a birthing mother for nurturing, ultimately caregiving is likely a *learned behavior*. With ongoing, daily repeated exposure and practice by any caregiver of any gender, caregiving produces changes in brain physiology and hormone balance similar in many ways to that of mothers.[16] In her book *Mother Brain*, Chelsea Conaboy writes: "There could very well be sex-based differences . . . yet, at a very fundamental level, the parenting circuitry may be something that exists universally and is regulated differently across sexes, from individual to individual, and depending on the social context of the species. It is not written only onto the brains of females."[17] This is *great news* for nonbirthing parents and alloparents. But also, birthing mothers who have been socialized as females may have already had twenty or thirty or forty years of learning how to caregive as well as ten months of subtly attuning to the presence of a baby within their body. That's a *lot* of learning to catch up on, even for the most engaged nonbirthing caregiver.

In her book *Matrescence: On the Metamorphosis of Pregnancy, Childbirth, and Motherhood,* Lucy Jones writes of her own experience of this nature-nurture tension:

> Our daughter seemed to demand more from me than her father, and I seemed to feel her needs, her pain, her desires in my body in a different, visceral way. She wanted to be held and touched and carried by me to a degree which sometimes pushed my nervous system to the brink of what I could tolerate. . . . And I found being away from her in the early years physically uncomfortable in a way my husband did not. Even when our work situation changed and my husband took on more childcare, though from the outside it might've looked more equal, I remained the primary source of care.[18]

*All* of this is to say that the story of how the gender gap may be widening in your partnership right now is *really* complex. And I want to be clear: by proposing that, especially if you birthed and/or are breastfeeding your baby, you might have an amplified role as their caregiver in early life, I am not by *any* means suggesting that you must be your baby's *only* caregiver. This is an idea that stemmed from some of the early thinking (ahem . . . by men) around attachment psychology that often gets whipped up into the intensive parenting ideologies I described earlier.[19] The vast majority of us in modern society rely on others—secondary caregivers, relatives, and day care, for example—to help us raise our babies. The vast majority of us have to return to work at some point within those first two years of our babies' lives during which they—and we—are so biologically and socially primed to be connected. But to *ignore* the biological and social influences and the monumental amount of learned behavior that shapes a mother's caregiving role is to suggest that the imbalanced division of labor in the household of a new family is a result of a mother's or partner's *personal shortcomings*—a lack of ability to communicate, the gatekeeping of caregiving tasks by the mother, a deadbeat partner, not enough chore charts, or no one in the relationship being *feminist enough* (see note for more).[20]

So what is the solution? My experience—both personally and with the mothers I've worked with—is that trying to shift this unequal caregiving load to a more equal one in the early weeks, months, and sometimes years of parenting is often more challenging and strife-filled than surrendering to it. "Equal" suggests that everyone is treated in the same way regardless of their differences. When I think of how this sometimes manifests in our culture, I think of breastfeeding, which is one more thing that you, as the birthing mother, can do that your partner *likely* can't (see note for more).[21] In the search to reclaim a sense of equality in the relationship, many mothers decide they will pump breast milk and have their partner feed it to the baby, leaving them free to, perhaps, try to reclaim the parts of their lives that allow them to feel like themselves again, like going to yoga class or coffee with friends or sleeping more than three hours at a stretch. The part that most new mothers don't realize is that (a) you will usually have to pump while at yoga class or out for coffee with friends or in the middle of the night *anyway* to maintain your milk supply and (b) nursing is about so much more than nutrition, and so the presence of the nutrition minus you and everything *else* you offer your baby isn't necessarily going to cut it. Many a mama who has gotten a frantic phone call from a well-meaning partner or mother-in-law that the baby is *still* crying even though they've attempted to give them a bottle will be nodding their heads in agreement right now. And so it is that trying to achieve "equality" in a breastfeeding relationship, and many other circumstances in the first years of a baby's life, is *still* a heck of a lot more work, actually, for the mother.

Instead, *equity*, by definition, recognizes difference and distributes resources and support accordingly. It is with equity in mind that I propose what I call the concentric circles of support model—one that looks a lot like the way motherbaby dyads are cared for in other cultures that revere the tender postpartum time.[22] This model of support is ideal for the early weeks, months, and even years of parenting in partnerships where the mother is breastfeeding and/or the person who spends the most time caring for the baby.

Picture a target. In the bull's-eye position is your baby—the recipient of care. The next ring of the target is the primary caregiver—you, perhaps. That caregiver is providing *most* of the direct baby care. The next ring of the target? Your partner. They are responsible for caring for *you*. This means, in short, taking responsibility for tending to your well-being and to the ecosystem around you. On a pragmatic level, it means paying the bills, taking out the garbage, and making sure you have snacks and water within arm's reach. It also means, perhaps, having the hard conversations with well-meaning visitors who only want to hold the baby or friends with unwelcome advice. In this way, the partner cultivates a safe space within which the mother, still vulnerable in her healing and in the learning curve of being mama, can feel really well supported (see note for more).[23] And no, this structure of household roles and responsibilities isn't *equal*, in the way we've come to think of it. At least, it's not "same-equal." It's different equal: equitable.

The truth is, our lives, including our parenting lives, go through cycles and seasons of intensity when sometimes we take on more of the household labor—the physical, mental, emotional, and spiritual load—and sometimes we cannot. For example, as the years go by, perhaps you will experience an illness or a profound loss that renders you unable to take on much or any of the work of family life, and your partner will need to take on the bulk of the work. Taking a few giant steps back and viewing our partnered lives—and our lives in general—with this seasonal, cyclical lens can help to normalize times when we're stretched thinner and need to shift the dynamic of our relationships.

The important thing is this: matrescence is a *season* of our lives. The gendered division of labor during this time is one of the many reasons why I assert that though we will always be growing and developing in our motherhood, matrescence is a two- to three-year span of time after which most parents will see a shift in many areas of their lives, including into a more equal division of household labor. Herein lies the problem: this is often not the case. Mothers of children of all ages routinely take on more of the household labor than their male partners.[24] In the United States, women perform an average of four hours of unpaid work per day compared to two and a half hours for men. According to Oxfam, if women all around the world were offered minimum wage for the amount of unpaid hours of care and household labor they do, they would have earned $10.9 trillion in 2019 alone.[25] Mothers know when the library books are due, exactly how Junior likes his scrambled eggs, how many toilet paper rolls are left, and when summer camp registration starts (including how freakin' quickly you have to click "register"). We have been deeply socialized by our patriarchal culture to take on the bulk of this mostly invisible labor, and that role continues to be reinforced every time the school calls mom instead of dad or blames mothers for their myriad shortcomings but holds fathers only to the standard of being "present." The cost to mothers' well-being, career, and identity is massive, the cost to their relationships devastating, and the cost to our society incalculable.[26]

This is where our work comes in. And it is *big* work indeed—some of which feels like valiantly trying to overthrow hundreds of years of patriarchal conditioning and thousands of hours of caregiving practice and learning with *a whiteboard chore chart*. Which is to say: this is hard. Bell hooks writes: "Certainly many women in relationships with males often found that having a newborn baby plummeted their relationships back into more sexist-defined roles. However, when couples work hard to maintain equity in all spheres, especially childcare, it can be the reality. The key issue, though, is working hard. And most men have not chosen to work hard at childcare."[27] Darcy Lockman, in her book on the myth of equality in couples with children, writes, "Women's greater relative comfort with under-benefiting juxtaposed with men's greater relative comfort with over-benefiting sets the course for men to refuse responsibility and for women to comply with their refusal . . . including adherence to inferior standards, passive resistance, strategic incompetence, strategic use of praise and flat-out denial."[28] Lockman argues *against* the concentric circles idea of equity that I propose, further stating, "The veneer of 'complementary but equal' in the gender system casts acceptability on sex roles that mostly benefit men. It serves a palliative function. Social psychology calls this 'role justification,' and it contributes to the perceived legitimacy of the status quo by characterizing cultural divisions of labor as not only fair but perhaps even natural and inevitable."[29]

Though the early days of parenting do often necessitate an equitable-but-not-equal distribution of caregiving and household labor, Lockman makes an important point, and so I would add: let us not become complicit in our own oppression by allowing the pattern to continue beyond the season of its usefulness.

So how do we know *when* to shift the gender-role dynamics as the intensive postpartum and matrescence period comes to a completion? This may happen as a result of the natural waning of the *motherbaby* dyadic bond, which could unfold after a mother's return to work, the completion of breastfeeding, or some other milestone in her or the baby's life. Unfortunately, for many mothers (raises hand), this shift comes as a result of burnout and the subsequent rage we feel at the *unfairness* of it all. Though our rage, when we have the courage to voice it, can be a powerful catalyst for change, my hope for you in reading these paragraphs is that the redistribution of gender roles in your household comes about more peaceably.

The next question is *how* do we shift the gender-role dynamics as the intensive postpartum and matrescence period comes to an end? The truth is, it takes time, and it may be weeks or months or years, depending on your context, before your partner begins to find their footing as a caregiver. Remember, whereas a mother usually undergoes a very visceral (often nauseating!) experience of motherhood right from the moment she is pregnant, parenthood and the fact of having a little baby in the house can remain a pretty abstract idea for many partners until the moment of birth. And then, our partners often have to make sense of their role in the parenting relationship *on their own*—not necessarily guided by the same strong biological and social imperatives that we mothers are. In fact, male partners may have been socialized to believe that parenting *isn't* their role, and they may have had little modeling of male nurturance to support them in finding their way. This can be really frustrating and confusing for partners who are encouraged to and want to be involved but don't know how—and it's obviously frustrating for mothers. But just as it takes us mothers two to three years to transition to motherhood, we can expect that it takes our partners as long or even longer to transition into their own identity as parent, that this process may not begin until the baby's birth or later and can perhaps be confounded by the requirements of full-time work outside the home which limit the amount of time they have to learn the role and reality of caregiving.

It's important to have lots of compassion for each other during this time, and it's also important to remember that if caregiving is a learned behavior, your partner needs as many opportunities to learn as possible. So even while you, the mother, may be providing the bulk of direct baby care, your partner needs to find their way—their niche in the caregiving dynamic, if you will. Perhaps they are the baby-wearer in the family, or perhaps they do baths or all the diapers or spend hearty amounts of time with your baby while you nap.

As the time of your motherbaby dyad wanes and the caregiving work in your household rebalances, it's important to have models of what fair might look like. We can learn so much about subverting traditional gender roles from queer parents. Researcher Samantha Tornello, PhD, in a study of 163 transgender parents, found that participants divided labor based on ability and personal preference rather than gender roles.[30] We can take this a step further by diving into the discourse around "queering motherhood," an endeavor that challenges gendered social and political norms. The researcher Margaret Gibson, PhD, shares that "to queer motherhood is to re-think, re-shape and re-establish notions and practices of normative motherhood."[31] On a practical level, Eve Rodsky, author of *Fair Play*, outlines a pragmatic and even fun(!) method of making invisible household labor visible and dividing it up between couples in a way that is conscious, actively communicated, and effective.[32]

Aside from the division of labor in your household, there are other intimate relationship dynamics at play during matrescence as well. If you, as a mother, are wondering who *you* are now that you've had a baby, so too is there an identity shift in a *couple* when they are now a family of three or more. *Who are we now that we're a family?* Many of the things that bonded you, like nights at your favorite wine bar or yearly whitewater rafting trips, may no longer be possible. *Who are we when we're not doing the things we love to do?* Childbirth educator and cultural mythologist Britta Bushnell, PhD, writes in her book *Transformed by Birth* that mothers are quite often the ones who have been responsible for the emotional labor of tending to the relationship.[33] What happens when they are no longer able to do that? Mamas are often preoccupied with learning the role of mother, with sleep deprivation and a lot of the emotional labor that comes with mothering, and may not have the capacity to contribute to fostering intimacy and connection in the relationship. So it is that another key shift in our intimate partnerships is *Who are we when we're not connecting in the same way, or as often, as we used to?* And, as we'll talk about in the pages to come, it's very common for a woman's and a partner's values to shift as they enter parenthood. *Who are we now that different things are important to us than what bonded us to each other in the first place?* Finally, in a relationship whose nurturance may be predicated on physical intimacy, a mother's changed body, energy, and life may result in a shift in the way she feels about—and how often she wants—sex. *Who are we now that we are being called to show our love, connection, and intimacy in different ways?*

All of this can be daunting, and so if you feel a little uncomfortable right now, that's okay. In this book, I endeavor only to speak truth and to talk about the things that *no one talks about* so that, at the very least, you might feel less alone, and perhaps a little more *normal*. I believe that when you can name something, you can face it head-on. And so that's what we're doing here. Motherhood changes everything: it changes you, and it definitely changes the relationship you have with the other parent of your child. And, in my experience, it is often easier to accept that and begin to reclaim a new way of being together than it is to swim against the tide and try to force things back to the way they were.

My partner and I are still forging new ways of being together as parents to this very day, even twelve years since our first child came into the world. We've probably gotten it *wrong* more often than we've gotten it *right*, and I think what matters most about that is that we're still willing to try.

## ✳ BIRTH OF A MOTHER ✳

My new ring reflected the light, and I caught a glimpse of it as I turned the page in my book.

Every time I looked at it a rush of familiarity and rootedness warmed my heart.

My first ring was beautiful, too. It was many years ago now that my fingers fished into a bag of Scrabble letters and pulled it out. I looked at you and didn't say yes so much as "of course."

It was, somehow, identical to a ring I had picked out for *myself* one day in a fit of restless anticipation—even though I had never told you about that ring or how much I daydreamed about the moment you'd finally ask.

It was, within the standards of what engagement rings typically look like, *so me*. A simple, single diamond, strongly held in a sleekly designed setting. Nothing that would catch on a scuba tank or a backpack strap and break.

Fast-forward seven years.

My fingers had swollen twice with pregnancy, and although I still loved my ring, I rarely wore it anymore. It felt confining, and I would be overcome with a sense of claustrophobia when I put it on. I would quickly pull it off again and put it back in the drawer with my other jewelry.

*I worried that this was a bad omen for our married life.*

In truth, being parents *was* stifling at times, for me and for us as a married couple. We had stopped playing Scrabble or scuba diving and were subsisting on air, strong coffee, and the laughs of the two little beings we had created.

It was not enough sometimes, if I'm honest. Becoming a mother had rocked my world. My transition into motherhood had shone a laser beam of truth at some of the choices I, and we, had made: my boring, unfulfilling job, the house in the suburbs, the people we paid to look after our kids so that I could go to that boring, unfulfilling job.

I'm not sure if you felt the misalignment of this as viscerally as I did, but you held fast in solidarity and support while I questioned *everything*.

*The roots to my tree. Grounded and running deep and strong while I reached and reached.*

\*

We both hovered over the koa wood rings, slipping them on and off our hands to test for size.

Normally, I would have ventured alone into a boutique like this, full of sacred and delicate Hawaiian handicrafts, while you got the kids a shave ice or played with them outside. But somehow all four of us wandered through. I'm not sure what made us so brave as to bring our three-year-old and five-month-old into a place with such precariously balanced breakables.

Normally, I might have quietly tried on a ring or two, remembered our budget, and herded the family out the door.

Normally, you probably would have rolled your eyes a little at me, ogling yet another piece of jewelry to add to my enormous collection. *But here you were, trying on rings, right next to me.*

*I think something shifted between us that day.*

Or rather, something had been shifting between us for quite some time, and that day, we decided to honor it.

We now knew what our marriage was made of: not just the fluttering hope and excitement we felt on our wedding day but a solidness that had seen us through two births, a six-month deployment, career changes, and the sleeplessness and vulnerability of new parenthood.

And now we were traveling again, after the long hiatus demanded by work and finances and childbearing. I was growing a business with the dream of one day being able to leave my cubicle behind forever. We were talking about downsizing and what it would be like to live near the ocean.

It was as though we both knew that we had crossed a threshold of some significance and that what we had was *rooted*. Rooted in what it takes to hold a person as they bring new life into the world, in what it takes to support another's dreams, in what it is to ride out the hard times with steadfastness and good faith.

And so now, when I see that little piece of sacred tree on my finger as I turn the pages of my book, I feel you wearing *the very same ring*, the one I catch a glimpse of as you parallel park the minivan or hold our son close after he's bumped his head. And I know that there is something deeper to what we have than sparkle and hope. We have been through the first of what may be many more life transformations together, and we've become stronger for it.

## Mother of a Mother

I remember the day like it was yesterday. I had just taught an infant massage class, and a few of the mothers lingered afterward, chatting as they packed up diaper bags and had one last nursing session before heading home. These conversations were where so many of the seeds of this book were planted: it was often not until we were finished talking about the things we were *supposed to* talk about—*sleep patterns, breastfeeding frequency, diaper brands*—that the mothers who lingered behind would really open up and begin bringing up the things *no one talks about.*

I was sharing with the women the ways in which my relationship with my mother had shifted since I had become a mother myself. Many parts of our new relationship dynamic were beautiful—I got to witness my mother transition into grandmotherhood and begin to choose how she would manifest this role in my children's lives. But some parts of it were challenging.

Although every mother-daughter dynamic is different, the common theme as we transition into motherhood and our mothers become grandmothers is that there is a direct parallel—and often a direct comparison—between the way *she did things* and the way *you're doing things.* And in a world where there is more information at our fingertips than ever, many women are choosing *very different things* than their mothers chose. More and more often, we're asking Google for advice, not Grandmother. The motherhood sociologist Sophie Brock, PhD, elucidates this phenomenon further, sharing that "how motherhood is socially constructed—and how we're socialized into being mothers—changes over time. The current cultural rules of 'good motherhood' we're living within are different to the rules of good motherhood for other generations. Social norms change. Values shift. Evidence evolves. 'Expert opinion' changes. Economic circumstances change. Social policy changes. Technology develops. How community is formed changes. Definitions of what is considered 'family' can even change."[34]

There is something more to this than just the generational differences between mothers and daughters and grandchildren, though, and it is something that has been garnering more attention and consideration in recent years. It's called the Mother Wound.

The Mother Wound originates with the challenges our mothers experienced of living, mothering, and having to survive in patriarchy and other systems of oppression that were perhaps even more insidious and unquestioned than they are now. It can show up—in both mothers and daughters—as the suppression of emotions, passive-aggressive behaviors, martyrdom, and approval-seeking, to name a few.

The Mother Wound often emerges, sometimes for the first time, in our early motherhood, regardless of our mothers' actual physical presence and our interactions with them. It's because there's never a time when we look to or compare ourselves more to our own mothers than in early motherhood. Perhaps we have expectations of our mothers—expressed or unexpressed—to be a certain way or, in our village-bereft culture, to help in a certain way. Motherhood is a time when we examine the conditions of our own upbringing—how we were loved and how our parents showed that love. It's also a time when we're more emotionally vulnerable, and our capacity to navigate those emotions healthfully depends powerfully on how our mothers navigated *their* emotions and taught us to experience ours.

It's important to have a lot of compassion for our mothers, who did their very best to adapt in a society that routinely undermined their worth as human beings. The author Adrienne Rich writes: "When I think of the conditions under which my mother became a mother—the impossible expectations—my anger at her dissolves into grief and anger for her. [It is] easier by far to hate and reject a mother outright than to see beyond her to the forces acting upon her."[35]

The Mother Wound has an even more complex way of playing out for mothers who come from strong cultural beliefs about family and grandmotherhood. I remember realizing my bias around this experience when working with Emma, a Black mother who, just days after having her baby, was finding herself in deep conflict with her mother. My suggestions to create boundaries in the relationship or even ask her mother to leave illuminated my lack of understanding of Emma's family's values. In her book *We Live for the We : The Political Power of Black Motherhood*, Dani McClain writes:

In taking [a] village-oriented approach to child-rearing, Black Americans might be out of step with mainstream white middle class American culture, which became more centered on the nuclear family at the middle of the last century and the advent of mass suburbanization, but we're fully in step with how the rest of the world has functioned throughout history. Most humans across time and space are cooperative breeders, and depend on adult women and older children in the extended family to care for the young.[36]

Needless to say, navigating the Mother Wound may be especially challenging if you come from a lineage with strong values around the interdependent relationships between children, their mothers, and their mothers' mothers.

If you *are* able to interact with your mother during this time, know that she, too, is experiencing a vulnerable period in her life as she navigates the transition to grandmotherhood and, perhaps with it, feelings of loss, uncertainty, or anxiety about aging and death. She may express—or *not* express—these emotions in ways that are a result of the deep cultural conditioning her own motherhood was impacted by. Know that it's also okay to feel disappointment, sadness, or a sense of loss in your relationship with your mother. In time, as all wounding does, this pain also offers *potential.* Tami Kent, in her book *Mothering from Your Center*, phrases this beautifully: "Becoming a mother means stepping into the lineage of motherhood: renegotiating the lines that define it and making your own mothering imprint."[37]

You have an exquisite choice here, mama. You have the capacity to look at how you were shaped by the way you were mothered, and you have the potential to begin healing the Mother Wound in your family line. But go gently here: the narrative of being a "cyclebreaker," increasingly common in today's motherhood lexicon, can also be a source of tremendous pressure for new mothers—another way the "perfect mother myth" can manifest. Healing generational wounds is big work, and old patterns run deep. But with the right support, this healing work can most certainly inform the way you choose to mother.

## *Friendships and Community*

As if shifts in your intimate partnership and in your relationship with your mother weren't enough, motherhood is bound to shift your relationships with your friends and the community of people you surround yourself with. Research shows that women's social networks and the frequency of contact that they have with the people in those networks diminish significantly in the early years of parenting.[38] And so perhaps you're the first person to become a mother in your group of friends, and after the baby snuggling is finished, you're not totally sure what to make of each other. Or, perhaps, you have been inducted into a resplendent group of friends who are already mamas, and you find yourself not seeing eye to eye with them now that you share the common ground of motherhood.

I remember, after having my first child, thinking I was supposed to "find my village." So I set about, in typical type A fashion, to do just that. This was, literally, on my early postpartum to-do list. I started out by attending a mom and baby yoga class. *These will surely be my people*, I thought. *We love yoga. We have babies. What more is there to have in common?*

It turns out: a lot. And you might find this too: being a mother may bond you in certain ways to all mothers out there, but there will be ways in which you will realize that "just" having children won't necessarily be enough commonality upon which to forge a friendship. I remember, in the early days of mothering my first child, having a really hard time being with the decisions of other mothers. While I normally pride myself on being welcoming and nonjudgmental, I still felt very vulnerable in the choices I was making, seemingly on an hour-by-hour basis, about what felt good to me as a mother. I was pouring my heart and soul into topics such as birth intervention or no birth intervention, swaddling or no swaddling, formula or no formula, cloth diapers or no cloth diapers—and on and on, as you well know. I questioned my choices and myself so very often in those early, fumbling months that I found it challenging to be in a room with mothers who were making vastly different choices.

While some of this experience is quite natural—we gravitate toward people who have shared values—some of it can be influenced by the perfect mother myth: that shadow that bears over our mothering choices, telling us how to be "good."

When we are in those confusing early days of motherhood, it can feel really good to locate sources of certainty and identity, which are often readily available to us in the myriad mothering ideologies to which we are exposed. In a 2018 article for the *Washington Post*, Leslie Davis writes:

> We had our second child, our daughter, in 2004. I further embraced motherhood, adding modifiers to claim it as my new identity: I'm a homeschooling mama of two, a SAHM and a part-time freelancer. I'm a breastfeeding mom. A home birth mom. A Buddhist mom. I'm a vegetarian natural mama who rejects fast food, plastic toys, screen time and mainstream everything. There were times when I hugged my new adjectives tighter than my babies—maybe because I couldn't hold on to who I used to be. Everything was slippery. We want to be good moms, to succeed, to do it right, so we erect towers for our new identities. Buy products. Start blogs and Instagram accounts. Crafting our shrines to the self. I know because I do it, too.[39]

So how does this impact our friendships? Mothering ideologies like the ones Davis mentions can offer us not just a sense of what we feel to be the "right" way to mother, but also a community of friends that mother that way, too. But when we begin to shape our *identities* around these ideologies it can create an "us and them" dynamic among mothers and cause us to "other" mothers who are making really different choices—just like I found myself doing.

*All* of this is to say that your friendships have very likely changed since you've had a baby. You may be grieving old friendships or the way you connected with those friends, or you may be realizing that "finding your village" is a more complex endeavor than you expected—especially while you navigate a fledgling new sense of your identity. Go gently, mama: this isn't easy territory to traverse. And don't worry, we'll keep exploring it even more throughout this book.

As I've touched upon in these paragraphs, part of the reason our relationships sometimes shift so dramatically after having a baby is that motherhood tends to shift and clarify your values and what matters most to you. Let's explore that next.

## WHAT MATTERS MOST

Probably the one unifying experience of motherhood—beyond changing poopy diapers and wearing spit-up on the left shoulder of your favorite shirt—is the fact that it brings your life into sharp focus, either clarifying or shifting what matters most to you. This may seem paradoxical, given that matrescence usually comes with a significant amount of identity confusion, but I see this time of confusion as a precursor to and a part of a massive *reorientation* to the new values and ways of being that begin to emerge as you traverse motherhood.

I like to think of this as a circle that we draw around ourselves to say "this is in—this is what's important to me; this is what matters now" and "that's out—that is no longer serving me, it's no longer important to me." This priority reorientation can manifest in myriad ways, and I hear stories of women's sudden and uncompromising clarification of their values in motherhood every single day. I think this phenomenon occurs in part because motherhood makes us realize that we only have so much time and energy to go around now that there's Someone Very Important holding a monopoly on those personal resources. In her book *Nurture the Wow*, Rabbi Danya Ruttenberg writes: "The urgency of being part of my children's lives, of raising them, of kissing their sweet cheeks, has brought to the fore the question Mary Oliver asks in her poem 'The Summer Day': 'Tell me, what is it you plan to do / With your one wild and precious life?' Both professionally and socially, having kids has been something of a refiner's fire, a burning away of the things that are not essential. If someone's going to compete for my time, there better be something real there."[40]

Indeed, motherhood can bring out a fierce strength and a fortified courage of conviction that helps us to see more clearly what attitudes, behaviors, roles, responsibilities, occupations, and people are positive in our lives and which badly need to be excised. Matrescence researcher Athan corroborated this experience in her 2005 paper about mothers' spiritual awakenings, writing that the mothers she interviewed for her study "experienced a change of values in which the trivial and unsubstantial was replaced by a bigger picture." She goes on to report that these mothers spoke about "welcoming a new [self] that felt more authentic, more honest, integrated and with a newfound agency."[41]

Interestingly, the process of becoming clear on one's values, particularly independent of or even in spite of what others may think, is a key marker of adult human development. I've touched on the concept of adult development and matrescence as a *developmental process* earlier, but it bears elucidating. While it was once thought that our psychological development stopped after adolescence, we now know that it continues throughout adulthood, growing us up into mature humans and offering us the potential to become wise elders and leaders in our families and communities. I use the word *potential* here for a reason: the adult development literature shows us that growing into increasingly deeper levels of maturity over the lifespan isn't a given. But in my experience, well-supported mothers quite often very naturally develop, and often in an accelerated time frame, this deeper maturity during matrescence.

In one model of adult development psychology conceptualized by Harvard professor Robert Kegan, PhD, this process of moving from defining and conducting oneself according to social norms and relationships to—how shall I say—*not giving a shit about what other people think* is called "self-authorship," or the ability to be the *author* or *authority* of one's own life.[42]

And it's kind of badass.

There's also this: it's *normal* to begin to feel differently about some of the strong convictions you may have had before becoming a mother. It doesn't mean you're "losing yourself." It means your priorities have changed, and also that you're going through a massive developmental shift and growing and maturing as a human being. But it takes time to reorient yourself to what matters most in your life now and perhaps make changes to reflect those shifting values.

## THE BIG SLOWDOWN

It is true that the satisfying, somewhat predictable
march of "progress" in one's life without children is
replaced, when children arrive, by a messier, more
ambiguous process of "becoming."
—Daphne DeMarneffe, *Maternal Desire*

There's this thing that happens when a woman has a baby that I call the Big Slowdown. Days blur into nights, and the healing process, a dramatically adjusted sleep schedule, and the massive learning curve of new motherhood mean that not a lot else gets *done* during the first days, months, and maybe even years—yes, years—of motherhood.

The Big Slowdown is distressing and disorienting for a great many women. Mothers I've worked with ask: "Why can't I just manage to have a shower every so often?" "My house is a mess and the laundry is piling up, and I haven't gotten out of my pajamas in days." If they have returned to work, many mothers talk about feeling like they're unable to keep up with—or tolerate—the demands of the workplace. They share that though they may manage to function at work, they have little capacity once they get home at the end of the day. Author and motherhood scholar Trudelle Thomas, PhD, articulates the Big Slowdown well: "In the career culture, time is measured and standardized and seems to move at a faster beat. The career culture is ruled by the clock, with time demarcated into schedules meant to measure productivity and commitment. The home culture, like preindustrial societies, is by necessity based on seasonal and biological cycles.

That doesn't mean schedules are always leisurely, but they are more in touch with real human needs—rather than the needs of industry."[43]

We can—and should—certainly point the finger to the lack of institutional, community, and family-based support mothers receive to meet the high demands of our capitalist culture, but there's also the issue of the high demands of our capitalist culture itself.

Our modern-day lives are defined by a frenetically paced existence where our worth is predicated on the sheer size of our to-do lists and how quickly and efficiently we can cross tasks off of them. And so the Big Slowdown is not *just* about a messy house and no clean clothes and not *just* about not having the support to keep up with it all: it's also about not being able to do as much and hustle as hard for our worthiness as we used to. It's nothing less than a challenge to our identity as worthy human beings within capitalism.

*(Also this: Of course, raising the next generation of humans is an inherently worthy endeavor, but society doesn't value motherhood in that way. And so it would make sense if you may not be able to fully convince yourself that mothering your baby equates to doing "enough.")*

So at the same time as we forget to brush our teeth for days at a time, we resist the Big Slowdown with tremendous fervor. I hear from so many women who say they are "trying to keep busy" in the early days of motherhood—often citing that keeping busy will be protective of their mental health. I usually see this as a red flag: What happens to your sense of self-worth, or even your sense of self at all, if you don't or can't *keep busy*?

I also often see "keeping busy" as a mother's way of coping with the dramatic identity shift that comes with motherhood in a culture that hasn't yet recognized that having a baby is *irreversibly transformative*. While getting out of the house and doing things that you enjoy can certainly be healthy, it's also true that, especially in the early days of motherhood, it may be wise to surrender some of these activities so that you can rest and allow your body to heal. So often women try to muscle their way back into their old life, dieting so they fit back into their old jeans or busting out of the house to meet friends for coffee even after having only just gotten to sleep a few hours previous, for example. It's easier and more societally accept-able to do this than to let yourself completely fall apart for a while and allow the transformation of matrescence do its work on you.

I remember first witnessing this when I visited my client Cather-ine at about ten days postpartum. She had had a strapping ten-pound baby who was now losing more weight than would normally be expected for a newborn. No one could figure out what was happen-ing. Intuitively, rather than asking the usual questions about nurs-ing frequency and effectiveness, I asked Catherine what her life had been like since she had her babe. The answer to the weight gain problem became abundantly clear. She described a week that was filled with driving to and from appointments and errands as well as several coffee dates with friends who wanted to meet the new baby. The baby was falling asleep happily in the car seat, seeming as though she was just a "very good baby." But actually, she was not waking to nurse like she normally would, and Catherine was also missing some of the baby's cues to nurse because she was driving or between appointments and didn't want to pull over to breastfeed. Through no fault of her own, the stretches of time between feeds began to draw further and further apart without Catherine noticing.

As I inquired a little more, I learned that few of the outings she described were necessary, and most of them, I noticed, looked like attempts to "get back to normal" as quickly as possible. She had felt pressure from others to do this, to be sure, but a lot of the pressure was internal. As we continued to talk, Catherine shared that time spent resting and recovering was so drastically different from what she had become used to in her day-to-day life that she felt like she was losing her sense of identity in the world.

Ah. There it is. The Big Slowdown.

I often see difficulties mothers experience with the Big Slowdown present as problems with breastfeeding—and also with sleep—because those are the two primary things that slow us down as new mothers. With breastfeeding, every two to three hours and some-times more often, a mama needs to stop what she's doing (at least usually!) and nurse her baby—sometimes, in the case of a newborn, for up to an hour. That is a *lot* of time spent breastfeeding. That is, essentially, a new full-time job—*or two*. It is *always* more of a commitment than a mama thinks it's going to be. The same goes for sleep. Most babies following a very normal, evolutionarily adapted sleep pattern will wake every two to three hours, sometimes more often, all through the night for as long as one to two years. *That* slows a mama down, too. *All* of this is normal, but when it slows us down enough to dramatically change our lives and challenge our identities as busy, productive humans, we often *make* these perfectly natural behaviors a problem. This is where I have found women begin to struggle, attempting to change infant behaviors adapted over hundreds of thousands of years through sleep training, schedules, pumping breast milk, and bottle-feeding. Sometimes these things work, but more often I hear from women who are *deeply distressed* because their babies won't sleep through the night or won't take a bottle or can't sleep alone. So very, very often, these things are a sign of a happy, healthy, normal baby and a mother who is struggling with the Big Slowdown.

If we widen the lens on the Big Slowdown, we can look at it as a shift from a state of *doing* to a state of *being*. Motherhood, especially in the early days, forces us to *be* instead of *do*. There's very little we can *accomplish*, in the capitalist patriarchal sense, you know? Despite the fact that the laundry piles and the email lists keep growing, we are almost jolted as mothers into a state of complete and utter presence, just as our babies experience only *the now*. There are a great many hours spent nursing in the middle of the night, staring out the window, rocking, shushing, or gazing into your little one's eyes waiting for the first glimmer of a smile. As our babies grow, they continue to invite us into the present as they begin to explore the world, crawling and walking and climbing, asking us to play peekaboo or build Lego towers ad nauseam.

For so many of the women I work with and speak to, motherhood is an *initiation* into this more slowed-down, deeply present way of living. That is, though we may not choose it for ourselves, priding ourselves on our ability to "make it" in a world that is often harsh and demanding, motherhood will choose it for us. And so it is that sometimes this initiation into the Big Slowdown is a trial by fire. It's possible that you've been fighting it tooth and nail. It's not hard to imagine why: if, in our culture, our value as human beings is predicated on our productivity, so too is our sense of belonging and even safety in the world. As it was for my client, the slowed-down pace of motherhood may not just feel foreign, but even dangerous.

Nevertheless, here you are.

Your life will slow down, and you will be initiated into the discomfort—*and yet also possibility*—of this season of your life where you are being asked to be a human *being* not a human *doing*. You will be asked to find a new sense of self-worth, one that is rooted in the *fact* of you and who you are, rather than what you achieve.

Let me pause here and delineate an important point: though the imperative to slow down when we have a baby is, in some ways, a universal one necessitated by what it takes to meet a baby's needs, the *actual ability* to heed this call to slow down is one that often only comes with privilege. In these paragraphs, I am focusing more on the personal experience of slowing down and some of the resistance we may feel about it due to our internalization of capitalist ideals, and less about the systemic forces that prevent a mother from being able to divest herself of a busy culture. As feminists have long said, however: the personal is political. Tricia Hersey, founder of The Nap Ministry, teaches that "rest is resistance," affirming that rest *shouldn't* be a privilege—that slowing down is an act of "deprogramming, decolonizing and unravelling ourselves from the wreckage of capitalism and white supremacy." She goes on: "Our bodies are portals. They are sites of liberation, knowledge, and invention that are waiting to be reclaimed and awakened by [rest]."[44] I know more than anyone that having a new baby definitely isn't "restful," but I also know that mothers' refusal to keep up with the demands of the work of the "good mother," "good woman," and "good employee" has the potential to disrupt those oppressive norms. McClain, in her book *We Live for the We*, writes about slowing down as a radical act: "I am claiming this time with my daughter as something bigger, something historically meaningful, and due me and Black women as a whole. I am claiming for myself and my child time that was historically denied Black women and children that needed time to bond."[45]

The refusal to comply with the demand to keep up with capitalist norms must start with those who have the privilege and resources to disrupt systems without risking harmful consequences to themselves or their families. Those of us who can must insist that slowing down in the early years of mothering is a necessity, not a luxury, and that our systems and institutions must undergo a paradigm shift in order to support us.

I will share more in final section of this book about how the countercultural nature of mothering has the potential and power to change systems. But for now, let's talk about one of the biggest challenges to slowing down in new motherhood and often one of the most universal and dramatic shifts in matrescence: the change to your work.

## LEANING IN AND LEANING OUT

There is no such thing as Supermom. Lots of
women may appear to have their cake (as mothers)
and be eating it too (as paid workers), yet the net
result feels suspiciously like emotional bulimia.
—Susan Maushart, *The Mask of Motherhood*

Michelle Obama has become well-known for her response to author Sheryl Sandberg's concept of "leaning in." Sandberg, like second-wave feminists everywhere—women who I secretly imagine wearing the classic 1980s white shoulder-padded power suit—says that women should lean in within the workplace, taking on bigger and more powerful leadership positions wherever possible. Obama, in describing her life as first lady, mother of two, and all-around Very Powerful Woman, responded: "That shit doesn't work all the time."[46]

Many of us who are currently of childbearing age were raised by second-wave feminists and have internalized the message that we should *lean in* and that motherhood shouldn't stop us from pursuing our career goals. Hell, I am one of them, wholeheartedly. Never in a million years did I think that becoming a mother would change the trajectory of my career ambitions. For me, so many mothers I know, and our wider culture, "allowing" motherhood to impact our careers is considered the Least Feminist Thing We Could Do.

But let's explore that narrative further, shall we?

The tension between work and motherhood began to brew in the early stages of capitalism. Before this, women always worked alongside men and other family members in and around the home. In *Of Woman Born*, Rich writes:

> From the earliest settled life until the growth of factories as centers of production, the home . . . was a part of the world, a center of work, a subsistence unit. In it, women, men, and children as early as they were able, carried on an endless, sea-sonal activity of raising, preparing, and processing food, pro-cessing skins, reeds, clay, dyes, fats, herbs, producing textiles and clothing, brewing, making soap and candles, doctoring and nursing, passing on these skills and crafts to younger people. A woman was rarely if ever alone with nothing but the needs of a child or children to see to.[47]

Capitalism saw work shift outside the home and into factories and businesses, and over time, the ideology of the nuclear family and the "cult of domesticity"— where parents and children lived isolated from other family members and the father was the breadwinner while the mother took care of domestic chores and caregiving—took hold.[48] Our second-wave foremothers did hard work to reject this ideology, insisting that women be able to enter and have the same opportunities in the workforce as men.

One of the massive blind spots of the second-wave feminist move-ment was that it ignored the realities of Black mothers. In her essay "The Meaning of Motherhood," Patricia Hill-Collins, PhD, writes: "The assumption that mothering occurs within the confines of a private, nuclear family household where the mother has almost total responsibility for child-rearing is less applicable to Black families. Racial oppression has denied Black families sufficient resources to support private, nuclear family households."[49] Bell hooks elaborates on this: "Had Black women voiced their views on motherhood, it would not have been named a serious obstacle to our freedom as women. Black women would not have said motherhood prevented us from entering the world of paid work because we have always worked. In contrast to the labor done in a caring environment inside the home, labor outside the home was most often seen as stressful, degrading and dehumanizing."[50]

However valiant white feminists' efforts to reject the cult of domesticity and insist that women have the opportunity to claim the power and worthiness once only afforded to white men through paid work, their activism did not result in the systemic changes that would actually make this possible. Rich writes: "[Women] had not found [themselves] entering an evolving new society, a society in transformation. [They] had only been integrated into the same structures which had made liberation movements necessary."[51] Feminists' claim to power in the workplace without the addition of social supports to lighten women's domestic workload was the birthplace of the idea that mothers could "have it all." But "having it all"—as in, specifically, leaning in to your career and being a mother (and doing both really, really well)—is not *more fair* or *more equal*; it's profoundly *unfair*.

The result of the impossibility of the "having it all" narrative has been that women have been encouraged, subtly and not so subtly, to deny the impact and demands of motherhood at all costs so that they can keep up in a world that has never had to be up all night breastfeeding, too. Mothers in our culture are stretched thin, expected to work as hard as and harder than their male counterparts while still performing a second shift of carework, including but not limited to pregnancy and birth, breastfeeding, night waking, vast quantities of emotional labor, and being the one the school calls when Johnny or Janie pukes on a teacher's shoe. These roles and duties are magnified by expectations rooted in intensive parenting. With this ideology at play, mothering becomes a 24/7 endeavor of researching and learning parenting philosophies, packing perfectly appointed bento box lunches, and chauffeuring children to various enrichment activities.

What happens as a result is what, for many women, feels like an irresolvable tension of opposing roles. As Rich alluded to, lack of supportive social policy adds to this tension, making scarce the supports a woman needs to perform both her mothering *and* her cog-in-the-capitalist-machine roles even remotely well. In the United States, a great many women have a mere six weeks of maternity leave—sometimes much less. In Canada, known for its yearlong, partially paid maternity leave, women who are self-employed find themselves needing to return to work at three months postpartum. Additionally, a woman returning to work is faced with childcare fees that are often unaffordable—and yet *still* underpay childcare workers. All of these injustices were magnified during the early years of COVID-19. In her book *Screaming on the Inside: The Unsustainability of American Motherhood*, journalist Jess Grose reports that during the pandemic, "while some mothers were laid off, others made the 'choice' to leave paid work, a choice made under duress when there were no other options for childcare or education. In March and April 2020, forty-five percent of mothers of school-age children were not working. That percentage had declined by January 2021, but there were still 1.4 million more mothers out of paid work than there had been before the pandemic, in January 2020. Non-white single mothers were hit the hardest."[52] As Anne-Marie Slaughter wrote in an article in the *Atlantic*: "The world as it is currently structured cannot accommodate the needs of women who are both ambitious in their professions and their home lives. Social and economic change is required."[53]

The impact of this "care-career conundrum" is devastating.[54] Psychologist Jennifer Hahn-Holbrook, PhD, mapped rates of postpartum depression, finding the highest in countries with the greatest numbers of women of childbearing age working more than forty hours a week.[55] According to a study of men and women from their late twenties to midfifties, work is protective of the mental health of men and of women with older children, but working women with young children suffer higher rates of poor mental health.[56]

Once again, there is important nuance to be noted in the experience of BIPOC or other racially marginalized mothers. Racial oppression has meant that many of these mothers have always had to work, and so their experience of the care-career conundrum is unique. Hill-Collins writes that, among Black mothers, work is often not seen as a conundrum or in opposition to caregiving, but as a *function* of caregiving.[57] Additionally, in part because of the necessity of work and the impossibility of the nuclear family ideology, Black families may have vastly different values and practices around caregiving and alloparenting. Hill-Collins affirms that "African and African-American communities have recognized that vesting one person with full responsibility for mothering a child may not be wise or possible."[58] This may shift the relationship that many BIPOC or other racially marginalized mothers have with the tension between the responsibilities of work and caregiving.

When I made the choice to leave my nine-to-five job, I did it for many reasons, including the fact that I didn't truly enjoy the work—but I also left it because working an eight-hour day where someone with a clipboard dutifully peeked into my cubicle at precisely 9:00 a.m. to make sure I was there felt impossible to me given the demands of motherhood. It felt radical to give that kind of unforgiving capitalist ideology the finger, but now, many years later, I realize that (a) doing so was only possible as a result of my privilege and (b) leaving that job wasn't exactly the empowered choice I thought it was at the time; it was the only power I could claim in a system that dehumanized its workers.

So why am I telling you all of this?

If, as I posit, the transition to motherhood takes two to three years, then surely that process will be impeded by the requirement to integrate back into a work life that at best ignores and at worst actively discriminates against the fact of your motherhood. The narratives about work and motherhood you've likely grown up hearing and continue to hear are not set up to see you succeed. Sure, some women try to "do it all" and manage it—usually with a lot of extra, often-hidden, often privilege-dependent supports. Many women try to "do it all," burn out, and find themselves needing to seek another way. Some women experience that massive priority shift I wrote about earlier and have the privilege to be able to lean way, way out while they're in the most intense years of early motherhood. Others have that postpartum laser clarity about what's important and what's not and make a huge change to their careers. Some of us (raises hand) fumble their way through every single one of those permutations of career shift. But suffice to say, especially until we have social policy that doesn't require mothers to deny their motherhood to achieve "success," having a baby might change the way you think about how you make your living or the support you need to do so.

## ✳ BIRTH OF A MOTHER ✳

Although I don't remember the year, exactly (*those early days are all a blur*), I remember that I was driving down North Street.

In my mind's eye it was late fall, because the sky was darkening as I drove home from work, giving me a sense of urgency as I waited in traffic on my way to pick my daughter up from day care.

It had been dark when I dropped her off, and now the sun was winking through the ever-baring trees once again.

I was listening to the public radio station I always listen to, and a new song by a local artist soared across the airwaves and changed everything.

> You've got to hold on, it goes so fast
> these early days, well, they don't last
> Got to enjoy them, they go so fast
> the baby days, well, they don't last.[59]

Though I'd heard these words of advice—treacly and sometimes impossible to fathom though they are—from a million well-meaning grandmothers before, This Was It.

My heart shattered and I wailed. Sitting there in traffic, my eyes blurred with tears and I gasped with sobs.

It wasn't so much my little girl's particular anxieties about being away from me or that my daughter came home each day smelling of the perfume of the other women who had comforted her and played with her. It was that I had to leave her so that I could stare longingly at the gray walls of my cubicle (as if my escape route were somehow encrypted in the fabric, if only I could decode it) sitting in one Sisyphean meeting after another and trying to muster enthusiasm for my inbox.

It wasn't what I thought life would look like.

*(I want to say, also, that the flow of my tears came with the ache of guilt. I had a great job with benefits and a fair wage, a home that was safe, loving care for my daughter, and enough privilege to even consider leaving my career.)*

But also.

There it was.

The longing and uncertainty had simmered long enough, quelled by my placations: *be grateful for what you have* and *all in due time.*

A torrent of maternal instinct and desire—a rallying cry for what might be possible—tore forth from me that day as I shifted into first gear, inched down North Street, listened to the sweet plunk of banjo music, and knew that nothing would ever be the same again.

## THE CHANGE THAT CHANGES EVERYTHING

And so here you are, mama. Everything has changed.

Although you may have known that having a baby would certainly change your life, it is truly hard to comprehend just how and how much. While for some of us, change like this is a welcome shift, for others it's a shock. Usually, it's both.

One of the most common questions that mothers ask me is *"Will I ever get my old self back?"* Following right on the heels of that question often comes *"Will I ever get my old relationship back? My old body? My energy? My career ambitions? My hobbies? My friendships?"*

My answer to this is always the truest thing I can possibly say, which, in the beautiful complexity of motherhood, is also always the most frustrating:

*"You might. But if you do, it won't happen on your time line. It won't happen as quickly as you'd like it to."*

Indeed, some of the changes you'll experience as a new mother will be temporary, like diaper changing, perhaps breastfeeding, and hopefully the sleepless nights. Other changes, like shifts to the way you spend your spare time—or your lack of spare time altogether— and changes to your relationships with your family, partner, and friends, may feel more likely to stick around.

If this brings up feelings of sadness or anger or disappointment in you, that doesn't mean that you're broken or a bad mother or not normal. In fact, it means you are *profoundly* normal. Matrescence requires you to leave your old self behind so that you can explore who you are as a mother and as a woman who happens to be a mother. In aspiring, in this book, to open up conversations that *no one is having*, it stands to reason that you might not have realized (or agreed to!) what you were signing up for when you chose motherhood or when motherhood chose you. It's so very, very much more than learning how to change diapers and make really strong coffee. We're going to dive more deeply into some of the more complex feelings that might be coming up for you in the next section of the book, but for now, I want to offer you a way to begin to make sense of the shifts that have occurred in your own life since you began your motherhood journey.

## YOUR TURN

In each part of this book, you will find a section titled "Your Turn." This section is an opportunity for you to begin to explore your personal transition to motherhood. These questions are meant to be a catalyst for your own process, but also take kindly to being shared with the people around you. This is a beautiful way to build relationships and a sense of community as you traverse your mothering journey.

And so grab your journal and a pen, and maybe brew yourself a cup of your favorite hot drink while you're at it (*or, let's face it, reheat the same cup of coffee you've been nursing all day*).

The work of Earth in the Four Elements model is to get real with the seismic shift that is happening in your life since you became a mother and to really, really name it. I want to invite you to do that here.

Some of what you will uncover might feel obvious. My invitation to you is to keep writing until you start uncovering the shifts that feel less obvious.

Some of what you will discover will feel exciting and new, and some of it might bring up feelings of sadness and loss. As much as you can, sit with the full spectrum of these emotions, knowing that they are normal and okay and that you will be supported to begin to more deeply explore them in the next chapter of this book.

## Lifestyle

Motherhood changes our lifestyles dramatically. Sometimes those changes reflect a simple shift in what we have capacity for in our lives; sometimes those changes are a reflection of shifting values.

*What changes in your lifestyle—the way you spend your time, the activities you enjoy—have you noticed since beginning your transition into motherhood?*

### Relationships

Changes to our relationships during matrescence can be unanticipated. Sometimes we have expectations of the people closest to us—our partners, our family, our friends—that don't get met. Sometimes people you didn't expect to receive support from come through for you in surprising ways.

As you explore the next question, think broadly about the relationships in your life, not just the relationships with the people closest to you. Consider what your expectations of these relationships were/are; think about how your role within these relationships may have or might be shifting, about how you connect with the people closest to you and how that might be changing, too.

*What changes in your relationships—in your intimate partnership, your family connections, or your friendships—have you noticed since beginning your matrescence?*

### Self

Probably most dramatically, you are likely noticing changes to yourself and your identity as a result of your transition to motherhood. Your body is changing, your ways of knowing and being in the world are changing, and perhaps even your values are shifting. This can at times be both incredibly distressing and incredibly liberating. I want to invite you to sit with that now.

*What changes in your self—your identity, your ways of knowing and being in the world—have you noticed since you've become a mother?*

*How do you feel about the changes in your life since you became a mother?*

*What has been the hardest?*

*What has been surprising?*

. . . . . . . . . . . . . . . . . . . . . . . . . . . . . . . . . . . . . . . . . . . . . . . . . . . . . . . . . . . . . . . . . .

# 3

# Water

*Traversing Grief, Anger, Ambivalence,*
*and Losing Yourself in Motherhood*

> Grief plays an essential role in our coming undone
> from previous attachments. It is the necessary current
> we need to carry us into the next becoming.
> —Toko-pa Turner

The next stage of the transition to motherhood, even when it involves the birth of a happy, healthy, very much wanted baby, involves traversing feelings of grief and loss.

We are so acculturated to see birth and becoming a mother as a happy occasion, you might find yourself taken aback by this statement. We, in our culture, give ourselves permission to grieve the death of someone, not the birth of someone. But it's true that with the joy of motherhood also comes a significant amount of loss and grief. It's an uncomfortable fact that is woven into the fabric of what it means to become a mother, for to truly step into *any* new identity in our lives, we must leave an often-cherished former identity behind. In this way, we *are* grieving the death of someone: ourselves.

*Birthing from Within* author Pam England phrases this so eloquently: "In a lifetime a human being experiences countless las muertes chiquitas, little deaths. The deaths of hopes and dreams, beliefs, relationships, careers and status in the family or society. In the childbearing year, every woman experiences las muertes chiquitas."[1]

And so I am here to tell you that if you're feeling sadness, grief, ambivalence, or even feelings of regret about motherhood, it is *normal*. You are *normal*. If I've written this book to have the conversations about motherhood that *no one else is having*, then grief, loss, and ambivalence during matrescence is *where it's at*.

As you were reading and working through the previous section on all the shifts that have happened in your life since becoming a mother, you were probably beginning to notice those pangs of grief quite acutely, if you haven't already. You may have observed a sense of loss as you downshifted into the Big Slowdown and had to contend with what it meant for your life and your sense of self-worth to be challenged to live up to the demands of capitalism. Now that the reality of motherhood has fully sunk in, you may even be feeling a sense of loss over the fantasies you consciously or unconsciously held about how you would parent—that you would travel or breastfeed effortlessly in public or only feed your child organic food. Definitely one of the biggest sources of grief for mothers in the first handful of years postpartum centers around the loss of their "old self." Your pre-kids self—her values, ways of being, relationships, and career ambitions—may feel *gone*. The physical and emotional autonomy, full nights of sleep, hot cups of coffee, and other luxuries that you *didn't even know* were (a) luxuries and (b) part of what made you feel like *you*, are also gone—for now and maybe, in the case of some aspects of your life, forever.

As always, there is also a systemic, cultural dimension to the losses we experience as new mothers. Perhaps you are feeling as though you've lost yourself because the lack of social supports like adequate maternity leave and affordable childcare mean that you're having to sacrifice more than you would have if you had a village to share caregiving or household responsibilities with. Maybe you've found yourself caught in the snare of the perfect mother myth and have been spending more time researching cloth diapers and baby sign language than tending to your own well-being. It's difficult to grapple with whether the losses you may be experiencing are because the rite of passage into motherhood has *always* necessitated them or because we live in a society that is profoundly unjust for and unsupportive of new mothers. But the impact of those losses is the same: complex and deeply mixed feelings about motherhood.

It's hard enough to experience these feelings, but our society takes it to another level: the idea of "losing yourself" in motherhood has become taboo in our culture. And so, in addition to living with unprocessed grief about this, we also hide it in a cloak of shame rather than talking about it openly.

## YOU WILL LOSE YOURSELF IN MOTHERHOOD

We give our children life. How, then, can we expect to keep our own intact afterward? But we do. At first, out of innocence: Let me get back my looks. Let me get back my energy. Let me get back into the swing of things. Then with ferocious will: Let me get back to my own life! So goes the battle between the old and the new, the giver and the taker, the parent and the child. I'm talking about something more than just the gauzy cycle of life. Sure, you're older now and one day you're going to have to die, but before that, you have to die. Your child has arrived and the battle has been joined. It is the battle to the death of your ego. The demise of your selfishness and impatience. The end of your idle distractions and carelessness. The decline and fall of Numero Uno.

—Karen Maezen Miller, *Momma Zen*

"It's not like I'm going to let motherhood change *who I am*," I remember saying, with unintended smugness, hand hovering over my resplendent belly when I was pregnant with my first child. I felt beautiful and powerful, and morning sickness was only a temporary limitation to my life as an avid triathlete and surfer.

Somehow, I was certain that I had the *key*, some mysterious alchemy of ambition and a supportive partner and a really great baby carrier: I would not *lose myself in motherhood.*

Many of us try mightily not to lose ourselves in motherhood. Of course, lots of us have less-than-ideal maternity leave and childcare circumstances which jolt us back into our pre-baby realities whether we like it or not. But we also hear stories of celebrity mamas hitting the gym to achieve their pre-motherhood shape. We talk about striving for a "new normal," which, for so many of us, looks a lot like the old normal. We secretly, or not so secretly, applaud women who are meandering through the farmers market with a baby who appears still wet behind the ears. Women who admit to losing themselves in motherhood have become the target of pitiful glances, life-hacking life coaches, and motivational Pinterest memes.

To me, all of this seems as though our culture is saying that motherhood, being one of the least valued roles a woman can occupy in our society, is to be denied at all costs. It should certainly not *define* a woman.

Should it?

In my work as a doula for the last fifteen years, I have seen the behind-the-scenes truth of thousands of new mothers' lives, and I want to say it's often the women who seem to have picked up right where they left off before birthing their babies who are secretly struggling the most. So often, they are pushing through exhaustion or fighting the demands of breastfeeding, desperately clinging to the behaviors of their pre-motherhood lives.

And I get it. Because this was me, too.

But the truth is, motherhood *will* change you.

You *will* lose yourself in motherhood.

Before you start breathing into a paper bag, let me also say this: It's *supposed* to.

Creating an entirely new human with your body, birthing it, perhaps nourishing it with your breasts every two to three hours all day long, and then having this little creature *need* you in the most primal way known to mammals for the next eighteen-or-so-ish years *changes you.*

You *will* lose yourself in motherhood. And though that might seem terrifying to you now, let me say the next part, the part we all keep forgetting: you will find someone entirely new.

I feel like I want to say that again.

*You will lose yourself in motherhood.*

And:

*You will find someone entirely new.*

You may find a woman whose body made an everyday miracle. You will find the paradox of knowing this while also knowing that your body has been made less societally acceptable in the process, and you might find a way to respect the skin you're in more deeply than you ever did before.

You will find an empathy for your baby, and possibly for the world, that takes your breath away. You will find a gut instinct, a *knowingness*, when it comes to your child and maybe to other things, too, that guides you like a compass that lives somewhere within your newly expanded heart.

You will find a cadre of other women who *get it,* whose messy buns and Lego-strewn floors look a lot like yours, and you will find smiles and knowing glances to assuage every grocery store meltdown.

You will find a new understanding for your own mother and the mothers before her.

You might find a way to slow down. As you care for your child, you will find your needs pared down to the basics: sleep, water, food, repeat. Everything else falls away, because it often has to, and sometimes what you might find underneath it all is *freedom.*

You might find yourself with an entirely new set of priorities in your life, with laser discernment for any career path, person, or way of spending time that doesn't feel worthy of your now more-divided energy and attention.

You might.

But first, you have to lose yourself in motherhood.

That is, you have to surrender to what motherhood is here to show you.

As for me? I don't care very much about competing in triathlons anymore, and I am just now, twelve years into motherhood, contemplating the idea of surfing again. I shower *almost* every day, and I drink hot cups of coffee—*not reheated or choked down cold while saying the Motherhood Mantra of "No really, it's an iced coffee! So good!"*

All of this took much, much longer than what felt comfortable to me, trust me. But also? I left the job I hated and started a business. I started writing poetry again. I have found a sense of deep permission in surrendering the parts of myself that motherhood has made irrelevant or impossible or, at the very least, not-right-now.

I have begun to trust that the parts of me that I was meant to reclaim, eventually, after becoming a mother would return to my life with a force that I have found to be almost gravitational—even if it doesn't happen on *my* time line. It never does. And I have found a reverence for the woman I've become since I've brought two little humans earthside. It's a reverence for myself, for all mothers now, and for the mothers before me.

And so, mama, if you're feeling lost in motherhood, let me remind you: It's okay. You are okay. This is normal; you are *supposed* to feel like a different person. Finding your way into who you are as a mother will take time and may be uncomfortable. Discovering the woman you're becoming is like following the trail of a wild animal in the woods: walk soft, listen close, and be patient. She is waiting for you.

## BUT FIRST, CRY

*"You can't do the growth without the grief."*

This has become one of my favorite things to say to the mothers that I work with. Grief, sadness, and a sense of loss are messy, snotty things to deal with, and most of us would rather bypass the process altogether. But I have a theory that ignoring or bypassing grief that is showing up in your life is like eating carrots when you're really craving a chocolate bar. The need to grieve—or eat chocolate—goes unmet, and so it returns, often with a fierce vengeance.

There is evidence to back my theory. A 2003 study by researchers Denise Lawler and Marlene Sinclair interviewed new mothers about their postpartum depression, finding that "it was after they had experienced a cycle of grief that they were able to accept their new self and new role as a mother. These women came to accept their experiences as normal. They felt they had to experience the death of their former self before giving birth to their new persona."[2]

The challenge is that we have lost the skills and spiritual literacy that our ancestors had for being with and integrating grief. In our culture, grief is something that happens behind closed doors and should be resolved as quickly as possible—we have few meaningful rituals to help us hold the bigness of our grief. Grief, like motherhood itself, is also deeply countercultural, requiring us to slow down and tussle with complex emotions that don't always have "right answers" or even any resolution at all.

In my years of exploring grief in the context of life transition, I've come to know that grief usually wants four things: to be felt, to be honored, to be metabolized, and, sometimes, to be released. Grief wants to be felt fully through your tears, through your body; it wants to be honored with deep self-compassion and validation. It wants to be metabolized and moved through you, with journaling, sharing, and meaning-making with a trusted friend, coach, or therapist. And finally, it sometimes wants to be released—for the past to be given permission to live in the past, or at least to take up its "right size" in your life.[3]

It's important to note that feeling and expressing grief may be additionally challenging for BIPOC or otherwise marginalized mothers. When I was employed at a nonprofit providing prenatal education, doula support, and breastfeeding support, I worked with many mothers whose marginalized identity put them at greater risk for being flagged by child and family services. One mother in particular shared with me her concern that after having a C-section, she couldn't take her garbage to the garbage chute. She worried that her caseworker would certainly consider having full garbage bags in her apartment a strike against her. Under these circumstances, how could this mother—and so many others like her—feel safe to express feelings of grief or ambivalence about her motherhood? For Black mothers, the "strong Black woman" archetype may limit the ability to tap into feelings of grief about motherhood. Helena Andrews-Dyer, author of *The Mamas*, writes: "I've learned through my own experiences—and those deep ones swimming in my blood—that you should never under any circumstances be vulnerable. Why not admit to the whole damn world that I had no clue what I was doing with this baby in my belly and just hand my phone over with Child and Family services already dialed?"[4]

Beyond the permission, skills, and privilege required to experience and express grief in motherhood, so many of the mothers I work with deeply fear the idea that they might lose themselves entirely in a pit of despair. They worry that allowing themselves to feel grief at all might cause them to slip into postpartum depression. Indeed, for this reason and others, we have a great fear of grief in our culture. We tend to metaphorically—and sometimes literally—ask ourselves *Are you done crying yet?* rather than *Have you cried enough yet?* One of my teachers, death doula Sarah Kerr, PhD, talks about the importance of "touching the bottom" of your grief—of actually allowing yourself to *go there*. She says, "Coming up the other side of your grief, there's a kind of ferocity to what's true, to being true to who you are."[5] This is important to remember, and also, as Martin Prechtel, author of *The Smell of Rain on Dust: Grief and Praise*, teaches, believing that grief might swallow you whole is a good sign that you need "someone to pull you out of the water" if and when it's required—the anchoring accompaniment of a friend, family member, or wise guide on your grief journey.[6]

As it relates to grief in matrescence, we are so attuned to the existence of postpartum depression that, in a double-edged sword kind of way, we're quick to diagnose and treat women who *may* just be feeling the full spectrum of emotions that are perfectly normal in motherhood. Scholar Paula Nicholson, PhD, posits that "some degree of postpartum depression should be considered the rule rather than the exception. [It is also] potentially a healthy, grieving reaction to loss."[7] But when we as a society don't have language for and the skills to work with the very normal *las muertes chiquitas* of motherhood, our well-meaning efforts to support new mothers may actually be pathologizing and bypassing this crucial phase of the transition into motherhood.

All of this is to say that if you find yourself feeling sadness at this stage in your transition to motherhood, it's okay.

I want to invite you to take time here to feel how you're feeling. Cry if you need to.

Cry enough.

Ask for help if you need it: you don't need to do this alone.

## AND SOMETIMES, SCREAM

It starts in my fingertips
an energy that shoots into my forearms, retracting muscles and
drawing my fingers into fists
it flies up to my shoulders
and they jerk toward my earlobes as if magnetized.
The effort leaves me trembling.
The sinew in my neck bulges
as too-big energy passes through
strategically placed filters
First, it squeezes through Not Right Now
and more easily bypasses Not Here.
It jumps the hurdles of Bad Motherhood and What Will People
Think
and before I know it
my Primal Scream

rattles my teeth and my ears.
The faces of the people around me,
the pillow I've used to dampen the sound
reveal their shock at my outpouring.

While we have an increasingly prevalent discourse about postpartum depression in our culture, we most definitely lack a fulsome acknowledgment of mothers' rage. We have reason enough to feel angry given the impossible social conditions and expectations under which many of us mother, the devaluing of motherhood, the sheer magnitude of the transformation becoming a mother represents for our lives, the daily frustrations of caring for little humans, and the fact that most of us are doing the lion's share of that work—and are expected to feel satisfied doing it.

Maternal anger may be the fiercest taboo of them all—and yet so many mothers do experience anger, citing that, in fact, they had never been an angry person before motherhood. But, as Dr. Barbara Almond, psychiatrist and author of *The Monster Within: The Hidden Side of Motherhood*, wrote about mothers' rage: "This aggression is both psychologically inevitable and socially unacceptable."[8]

Read that again.

*Psychologically inevitable.*

And so, if part of the emotional landscape of your motherhood includes anger, know that you are far from alone—it's yet another one of those things that *no one talks about* when it comes to their mothering experience.

Maternal anger expert Christine Ou, PhD, shares that although anger can be a subtheme of postpartum depression, it may also occur independent of depressive symptoms. The biggest predictors of mothers' anger are violations of autonomy and unmet expectations.[9]

My sense is that these sources of anger have a lot to do with our society's failure to support mothers, to be sure, but just as much to do with our failure to speak honestly and openly about the realities of motherhood. I cannot help but see mothers' anger at their loss of autonomy as a function of our inability to grieve that loss and our society's constant reassertion that we shouldn't have lost ourselves in the first place. I cannot help but see mothers' anger at the violation of their expectations as a function of the fact that we are consistently inundated with portrayals of idyllic pregnancy, birth, and motherhood online. So many of us are unconsciously steeping in the perfect mother myth that *of course* the often (usually!) gritty reality of motherhood catches us off guard. *No one told me. No one told me. No one told me:* the anthem of modern motherhood.

More and more often, I find myself working with mothers who feel frightened of their own anger and unsure of how to metabolize it. They are desperately seeking quiet corners to cry or to scream, lest anyone—especially their children—witness the full spectrum of their emotions. However, as Almond asserts, "Denying ambivalence and the hate that engenders it denies a mother her personhood."[10]

Yes, hate.

Knowing that anger is a normal feeling in motherhood, I hope you feel bolstered in your ability to express it somehow. But know that "anger privilege" is certainly at play here: there is a hierarchy of People Who Are Allowed to Be Angry in our culture, starting at the top with white men whose anger is often perceived as power and moving on down the lines of gender, race, class, and marginalization from there.

Brave spaces to share your rage might include with a loved one, skilled coach, or therapist. You might run or swim it out; you might, indeed, scream into a pillow. And if your rage—or any of the big feelings you might be having about motherhood—surfaces at a time when you are with your little ones, know that the most important thing is that they know they are safe and loved and that the emotion you're feeling is not directed toward them. In this way, you can model for them what it looks like to be a whole human and take responsibility for your emotions in a courageous and healthy way.

And there's also this: anger and rage are almost always a reaction to injustice, to the ways our needs as humans are being overlooked or dismissed.[11]

In my life I've learned that anger can do one of two things: it can eat you alive from the inside or it can become what I've come to call a "holy anger"—an assertion of one's humanity that has teeth and muscle and *energy* to move toward a better way. The former results in what motherhood sociologist Sophie Brock, PhD, calls the "anger-guilt trap," wherein mothers express anger, feel guilty for expressing anger, and so try to suppress it, resulting, of course, in even more anger.[12] A holy anger, however, calls out injustice and works for change. A holy anger, as Rich wrote, *threatens the institution of Motherhood.*[13] In the oppression of motherhood, I located a holy anger that catalyzed me in a way that I may never have otherwise been catalyzed. And so, the paradox is that only by feeling in my bones how tightly I was held under the thumb of patriarchal motherhood did I find the ferocity to want things to be different.

## THE UNDERBELLY OF MATRESCENCE: WHY FEELING COMPLEX FEELINGS ABOUT MOTHERHOOD IS SO HARD

It's likely that this may have been the first time you've thought about the idea of emotions like grief and anger in the context of otherwise normal, healthy motherhood. And yet these are *absolutely* a normal part of *most* women's experience of matrescence *and* their mothering years beyond that initial time of transition. But we have limited exposure to the deepest truths of motherhood, and I have an idea as to why that is.

I've touched on the impact of social media on modern motherhood already, but it bears exploration in a bit more detail because, like it or not, it is one of the vehicles that carries the narrative of our culture into our everyday lives—and vice versa.

In recent years, the cultural narratives around the transition to motherhood, postpartum self-care, and postpartum mental wellness have changed dramatically. The rise of the "mommy blog" in the early 2000s saw a revolution in the way mothers were "allowed" to talk about the reality of their role. These blogs were confessional and raw, full of "real talk"—and sometimes a hearty amount of snark—that invited mothers to feel less alone when their experiences of motherhood didn't meet cultural expectations.

I call this portrayal of motherhood the "Scary Mommy narrative." Admittedly, it's a slight dig at *Scary Mommy,* a well-known blog started in that era. Although the forum has been of great service to many mothers, including myself, the bread and butter of its content has often been self-deprecating stories about the misery of motherhood and the "hot mess mom." Amanda Montei, author of *Touched Out: Motherhood, Misogyny, Consent, and Control,* writes:

> Especially in White women's America, the image of the hapless mother bereft of herself—the hot mess mom struggling with her own desire to have it all and her related inability to keep up with her maternal and domestic labor, full of loss and always on the brink of breakdown—has become an almost revolutionary anti-ideal. . . . She is the motherly spinoff of the new American cult of busyness. She is also funny, I guess, because she looks like shit, drinks a lot of coffee and wine, has no sense of style, loves Target, and either DGAF or shares her struggle because, well, the struggle makes her likeable and honest. [See note for more.] [14]

Intended, I believe, to give women permission to fall well below their own—and society's—expectations of the "perfect mother," the Scary Mommy narrative also sometimes serves to make motherhood seem like the Worst Job in Town.

In many ways, this Real Talk is a response to what Susan Maushart, author of the book *The Mask of Motherhood,* calls the "conspiracy of silence" around mothering. She writes:

> Mothers delude each other by wearing a "mask of motherhood," an assemblage of fronts—mostly brave, serene, all-knowing— that we use to disguise the chaos and complexity of our lived experience. The mask of motherhood keeps women from speaking clearly what they know, and from hearing truths too threatening to face. That for every woman

who "blooms" in pregnancy there's another who develops root rot. That childbirth—however transcendent or revelatory it may or may not be—still hurts like hell . . . that your child's physical demands will diminish at only a fraction of the rate at which her emotional ones will multiply and intensify. That getting the knack of combining motherhood with career is like getting the knack of brain surgery: nice work if you can get it, but 99.9 percent of us never will. That having a "joint project" called a baby drives most couples further apart, reducing intimacy as it reinforces gender-role stereotypes.[15]

Maushart also claims that "this mask silences, divides, isolates and devalues mothers."[16]

But even years after the mommy blog era, in so many ways, we're still wearing the mask.

Of course, there are the aspirational images of motherhood we see on Instagram. In her blazingly insightful book *Momfluenced*, author Sara Petersen describes the rise of the "momfluencer" that eclipsed the "mommy blogger" movement once Instagram became more popular.[17] Now, beautiful images rather than raw narratives became the social capital of the online space for mothers—both for those who were using those images in sponsored content to sell products and also those who were inspired, or pressured, by those images to discover, assert, and perform their motherhood identity online. The perfect mother myth is alive and well on the internet. I call this the "Sacred Mommy narrative." This is the curated Instagram feed of motherhood, where our babies look up at us with milk-drunk smiles and we have never been so grateful for the miracle of our bodies, and we've managed to bake a loaf of bread and meditate while Junior was down for a nap. This imagery, writes Menkedick, "has created a society full of brittle, too-good mothers who . . . feel they must not only do everything right but must also love doing it."[18]

Though the mask of motherhood may be obvious in the Sacred Mommy narrative, performative vulnerability is a new, rather insidious antidote that we've sourced, in the post-mommy-blogger years, to too often portraying the image of the perfect mother. Enter the now-classic postpartum Instagram post: the side view of the brand-new mama with her still-round belly, wearing the universal diaper-like combination of giant mesh underwear and an absorbent pad, usually with her hair in a messy topknot, always with tired eyes. Enter also the myriad images that I seem to be served in my Instagram feed of mothers' tear-stained faces, crying in their minivans as their babies nap in the back seat. But many of the mothers in these posts show their vulnerability in a very specific way, sometimes couching it with a bite-size "lesson learned" and assurances to the reader that they've somehow overcome the source of their struggle. Additionally, the "vulnerable share"—inspired in no small part by the ubiquity (and I would argue misuse) of Brené Brown's research on vulnerability—has become currency. "Authenticity" gets a lot of likes, hearts, and shares, and so it is that performative vulnerability functions as the commodification of the same relatability mommy bloggers offered us with the hot mess mom trope. The problem is that even the most vulnerable of shares curate what parts of our motherhood experience we expose—including the "messy" ones. But the *real* messiness? We keep that to ourselves.

The truth is that though women's experiences of motherhood and all its paradoxes are more and more available to us online, these complexities are ones that women have been wrestling with for decades—likely since becoming a mother transformed from something women *just did* (read: without complaining) to something that women could choose and then had the freedom to reflect upon publicly (see note for more).[19] As Kate Figes writes in her book *Life after Birth*, "Motherhood is riddled with contradictions. We can relish the domesticity one minute and feel trapped the next. A mother is never alone with her child present, and yet she can feel deeply lonely. She has gained a new identity, yet paradoxically there is also a sense of loss of her former life."[20]

Maternal mental health specialists have a name for the incredibly complex feelings we've been talking about in this chapter: *maternal ambivalence*. Maushart articulates maternal ambivalence poetically:

"The private experience of motherhood unmasked is quite another matter—infinitely more profound and meaningful, more joyous and transcendent, yet more vexed and ambivalent, more downright dangerous, than we have yet dared to voice."[21]

Anyone who is a mother knows that *both* the Scary Mommy and Sacred Mommy narratives are true. But we humans in today's world have an excruciatingly hard time holding paradox and complexity. We much, much prefer hard distinctions: one thing or the other. And so we decamp to the motherhood narrative that most resonates with our experience and deride the alternative. If I choose to live a Scary Mommy narrative, then I do not have the capacity to see the sacredness of my own motherhood while, likewise, if I choose the Sacred Mommy narrative, I experience dissonance and pain when my motherhood feels anything but sacred. In doing this, we not only oversimplify our lived experiences but also perpetuate a feeling of "not-belonging" to the collective of mothers as a whole.

And here's the thing: remember how I've shared that just like our babies and children go through developmental leaps, so do we as adults? The ability to hold paradox and complexity is another key marker of adult development and maturity. Here's what Athan has to say about it: "Maternal ambivalence is natural and purposeful. The joy and pain inherent in the day-to-day experiences of mothering are designed to be fruitful and growth inducing."[22] In short, holding our complex emotions of grief, rage, and ambivalence has the potential to grow us up and grow us inward, into a richer and deeper understanding of motherhood, ourselves, and life as a whole.

Motherhood is so much more complex than our society has space for. We do women a disservice by asking them to contort the full spectrum of their motherhood experience into a box of irresolvable dichotomies. Motherhood is always both/and all at the same time, and mothers are some of the most exquisitely capable humans in our society at living in and being with that paradox. If you've been silently suffering under the illusion that you're experiencing motherhood "wrong" somehow because your complex feelings don't fit into a neat package, join me in the both/and. It is excruciatingly joyful over here.

## SACRIFICE AND THE POWER OF SURRENDER

As we explore the territory of grief, loss, anger, and ambivalence in motherhood, it's important to address the idea of *sacrifice*—the root meaning of which is "to make sacred"— and its companion *surrender*.

Surrender is inherently tied into the feelings of loss and grief that are so common in early motherhood because the trappings of our former life—the hot cup of tea and the crossword puzzle in the morning, or the time we used to spend curled up with a book, for example—are often ceded in a series of small surrenderings.

Surrender gets a really bad rap in our culture, which is hard-driven toward accomplishment and loves a good story about never giving up. Menkedick writes:

> I have been devoted to the American religion of realizing my potential, my possibilities, and then creating more potential, more possibilities, in a perpetual froth of ambition. I have absorbed the cultural definition of "settling" as an unfortunate compromise, particularly one made by a woman. There is an implied "for less" at the end of the term, with home, family and rootedness comprising "the less." Less than intrepidness, less than rugged individualism, less than risk. To settle, to not push as hard and as far and as much as one can, to not roam, accumulate and discover is a particularly American defeat. It is to reconcile oneself to the here and now, to be imperfect, the triumph of the banal over the exceptional, the inward turn as opposed to the outward gain, and as such has always seemed to me like a type of giving up. But the primary definition of settle is to resolve or reach an agreement about . . . to become or make calmer, or quieter.[23]

Surrender gets a bad rap in motherhood, especially, because we have a challenging time separating the idea of surrender from the idea of martyrdom. The truth lies, as it so often does, somewhere in between. Brock writes:

> While I do challenge the cultural narrative of the "selfless" mother . . . if we recoil at "sacrifice" and see it as the betrayal of our own empowerment, then we can end up replacing one cage of conditioning with another. In many ways, caretaking does require what can be framed as "sacrifice." But what if instead of being self-less (the depletion of self), we saw it as "self-giving" (giving from the self to others). To self-give means an offering, rather than the depletion of self-less. It means we need to have something to give, which honors the need for Mothers to be supported, valued and nurtured, in order for them to continue mothering. The act of mothering can be a part of our self-creation rather than experienced as self-erasure.[24]

This possibility for "self-creation" is corroborated in a study of new mothers by Athan. In this research, mothers shared that while sacrificing things like their autonomy and independence in new motherhood was challenging, they felt that doing so was an important part of their growth and development through the process of matrescence.[25] Indeed, sacrifice asks us to decenter ourselves in our hyperindividualistic culture. Though we must still remain attuned to our own well-being, this is also the kind of inner shift that makes community, interdependence, and revillaging *possible*.

Like the ability to tangle with the both/and of motherhood, the ability to know when to surrender—and to know when to fight for what matters—is another marker of adult development. Lisa Marchiano, Jungian analyst and author of *Motherhood: Facing and Finding Yourself*, writes: "A key developmental task of growing up involves sacrificing our youthful experience of endless potential for the limitation and fixity of adulthood. If we make this sacrifice we become changed. We grow in ways that may be surprising even to ourselves. In the psyche, when we cannot let something die, the result is that we cannot fully live."[26]

Let me be clear: there are plenty of things about the conditions of modern motherhood in our culture and in our homes that we should *very much* fight for. Advocating for paid and lengthy maternity leaves and a fair (or fairer) division of labor within your home are causes deeply worthy of time and energy. So how does one know the difference between surrender that is "making sacred" and surrender that perpetuates the idea of "mother as martyr"?

There is a thin, wavery gray line between the two, and the distinction is one to be made solely by *you*. My guiding principle?

*When pushing for what you want causes more suffering than surrender itself, it's time to consider the latter.*

Though we often associate surrender with a sense of *powerlessness*, I think surrender can also be *deeply empowering*. Because true surrender happens when there is *nothing* we can do to change the situation at hand—at least not in the moment.

When I think of the power of surrender, its opposite comes to mind: I think of a toddler who is having a massive tantrum because the sky isn't green or any of the other wild reasons toddlers have for freaking out. They expend a massive amount of energy screaming and yelling and stomping their feet and pounding the floor . . . all about something that *just is*. We all know times when we've effectively done the same thing: trying to get your baby to sleep on a schedule, wishing breastfeeding didn't take so much time in the early days of mothering, trying to accomplish the to-do list when our babies need us to just *be*. We put an enormous amount of time and energy into trying to control things that simply defy controlling.

It's a tough place to be, especially in this day and age, especially if you're a little type A, or just, you know, like to know what's going to happen next.

But imagine if you took all the explosive energy, the energy you're using trying to fight what's already happening or to know that which can't be known, and redirected it.

That is, essentially, what surrender is all about: letting go of the fight that you're not going to win to focus on the challenges you *can* face or on what you're going to do in the aftermath or to just bring your loved ones in close, gather your strength, and ride out the storm.

Truly, when you think about it, surrender is something we do almost constantly, every single day—especially as mothers. But we do two things to surrender when it shows up on our doorstep, asking us to throw our best laid plans out the window: We label it "giving up," "giving in," or some other unsavory act, and either get angry about it or shoo it under the rug, hoping it won't happen again. When we do this, we don't give ourselves the opportunity to learn and grow from it. The other thing we do with surrender is we don't necessarily notice all the moments it's happening. You might forget your meal plan and surrender to ordering pizza, or you might forfeit your desire to watch movies with your partner one night because your kid gets sick. When we notice those moments and then label them surrender, we can begin to think of surrender as a muscle that can be flexed and strengthened. We can get better and better at inviting grace in those challenging moments. We can witness our own adaptability and resilience in the face of a changing situation and changing expectations, and we can even consider what it might be like to *celebrate it.*

When we really notice moments of surrender, labeling them as such and seeing them as positive opportunities to grow and as something to truly be celebrated, it's a way to recognize our ability to be with what is and make the most of where we've landed.

### SWEET RELEASE

Though motherhood may ask you to leave behind, either temporarily or forever, parts of yourself and your pre-motherhood life, there is a beautiful bright side that accompanies the aching feeling of letting go of the old and greeting the new.

This time of letting go also gives you the exquisite opportunity to release the things that *you're not going to miss at all*. There might be a wise woman emerging in you who has laser-sharp clarity on who and what matters most and doesn't have time for bullshit, toxic relationships, and oppressive societal norms. She is here to help ease the process of letting go of what's not working for you in your life.

This is also a time when you have permission to decide what's *just not meant for you* when it comes to your own mothering. We often have a lot of our own expectations about motherhood or experience the expectations of others. Now is the time to begin charting your own path and leaving those expectations behind. You can decide not to do the things "everyone else is doing" and start to listen to your own intuition instead.

## WHEN WILL IT END?

No kidding right? The feelings we feel in the Water element of Radical Transformation are some of the toughest to ride out. The thing about feelings of grief and loss is that they chart their own course. And, as I've touched on already, grief really, really wants to be *felt* and *acknowledged*. You can imagine your grief as being like a little child within you, not unlike your own little one: the sadness you might be feeling about the many, many shifts happening in your life right now wants to be validated and wrapped up in a warm embrace of acceptance.

And, amazingly, it's when we are finally able to embrace the enormously complex—and definitely not *one-tone joyful*—feelings about motherhood that their edges begin to soften and they slowly dissolve.

Don't get me wrong—twelve years into motherhood, there are still some days when I wish I could go to the bathroom by myself. And this brings me to the most important nuance about feeling sadness in and among all the joys of motherhood: it involves a good dose of self-compassion when this transition feels hard and you long for the days when life felt a little easier or just different. With compassion, you can say to yourself, *Honey, I know. Those old times were so, so wonderful. They're over now, but they were important to have experienced. What could happen next?*

And that's just the thing: what *could* happen next? Trust me, I know from firsthand experience that forcing yourself to "snap out of it" and get back to normal won't allow you to evolve into the kind of mother—and human—you have the potential to be, wholly and compassionately.

Remember that although you're feeling sadness and grief and a lot of complexity right now, there *is* enormous potential in all of this. Truly *going through* this process of letting go and releasing some of the pre-motherhood parts of yourself that no longer fit your new life allows you to move forward rather than living in or yearning for a life that is no longer your own.

Sometimes, it can help to honor your sadness with a little bit of ritual. It's kind of like a way of validating and embracing the tiny little child of your grief in a meaningfully symbolic way. For example, you could take slips of paper and write down what you are feeling sad about or what you are being asked to release and surrender and throw them into a fire—or write these things down on rocks and toss them into the ocean. Engaging the five senses and the body in your ritual—the heat and smell of the fire you release into, for example—creates a visceral memory associated with the idea of letting go that helps to consolidate that intention in your brain and allow it to live on in your very cells.

Sweet mama, it's okay to feel sadness in this time of also-joy. It's okay to long for the days when you could sit in silence or see the world outside of your house after dark. It's okay to wish some days that you weren't a mother at all. It's even okay to wake up seven years from now and have a little knot of sadness in your heart for your pre-motherhood life. None of this makes you a bad mother: it makes you a human. And, in fact, it makes you a human who has *loved* her life and who is on the path to creating a life that encompasses the enormous love you have for your baby. Consider this your giant permission slip to feel *all* the feelings that come when you embark into matrescence, even the gnarly ones. Consider this your permission slip to speak those feelings aloud to someone who can hold you and the fullness of your emotions in reverence and respect.

## YOUR TURN

Earlier I shared that many of us in Western society have lost touch with the skills and cultural rituals that support us to move through grief and loss. It stands to reason, then, that you might be wondering how to navigate the emotional landscape that we've been exploring together in this chapter.

Remember how I shared that grief wants to be felt, honored, metabolized, and sometimes released? Let's start at the beginning, by *naming your grief* so that you can actually work with it in these four ways.

To name your grief, it helps to use what I call a "grief lens." A grief lens is a way of looking at your life experiences and wondering: Is there something I'm being asked to let go of here? Is it possible I could be feeling grief about that? Using a grief lens means that even with life transitions like motherhood that seem to be positive ones, I'm always quick to ask: What are you leaving behind? What is no longer? What are you releasing? What might you be experiencing untended grief about? Grief might feel like a strong word for the experience of never being able to sit down with a hot cup of coffee, but I'm inviting you to stretch your imagination a little here, acknowledging that sometimes these "little" things mean a lot and deserve to be honored rather than dismissed as insignificant or foolish.

You may feel hesitant to give yourself permission to name and feel grief for things you hope will return. There is an experience elucidated by therapist and author Pauline Boss, PhD, called *ambiguous loss* that I like to borrow to talk about the way that these losses feel in motherhood.[27] Boss's original application of *ambiguous loss* referred to the unique emotional experience of having a loved one go missing. Sufferers of ambiguous loss do not get closure in their experience: they don't know whether to grieve or to hope against hope that their loved one might return.

I think new mothers can experience the same kind of loss. Especially when you're in the thick of the early days of motherhood—and especially with your first baby—you might truly wonder if those hot cups of coffee are ever coming back. Am I grieving or am I hoping against hope that one day life will return to "normal"?

I always tell the mothers I work with to remember: this may be "goodbye for now" rather than "goodbye forever" for some aspects of your former life. For example, if you love to run, you may be bidding farewell to running as you knew it, wild and free along a wooded trail, and inviting a new practice of running with a jogging stroller along a side-walk or forgoing running altogether until you are comfort-able leaving your baby in the care of someone else. I think it's also important to remember something that I often find myself telling the women that I support: the return of some parts of your former life will not happen on your time line. Part of surrendering to the fact of your own motherhood and how your life is right now is letting go of the "when" when it comes to the return of your "old self," in addition to letting go of the "exact old self."

*Naming* your grief helps to ease this sense of over-whelming and sometimes ambiguous loss that can happen in early motherhood—and, for that matter, in most life tran-sitions that unmoor us from a large number of our identi-ties, roles, and responsibilities. And so that's what I want to invite you to do now. But before you do, I encourage you to read all the way through the suggested exercise *before* you begin. This is deep work, and I share some of the things

I recommend so that you can take care of yourself and your nervous system as you do it.

I use the concept of the "fearless and searching inventory" of twelve-step program fame to think about how we can start to name our grief. A fearless and searching inventory is an exhaustive list of something you want to bravely take stock of in your life. In the context of grief, this practice involves taking stock of everything you're being asked to release—everything you're grieving or feeling a sense of loss about—including identities, behaviors, thinking, or ways of being that you're leaving behind. For example, you may be feeling a loss of identity as you navigate who you are now that you're a parent, but you may also be navigating feelings of sadness or loss around the changed shape of your body, changing relationships, changing values or career goals, or a changing sense of belonging to your community of friends. A fearless and searching inventory helps because it allows you to more fully recognize and acknowledge what you're being asked to let go of or grieve rather than allowing it to continue on as a vague sense of amorphous and ambiguous loss.

Fearless and searching inventories are what I call Cardigan Lists: the kinds of lists that do well to be tucked away into the pocket of your favorite cardigan—or jeans or purse!—for you to carry around and add to as you continue to unearth this aspect of the transition you're in. And also there's no need to feel like you have to *do* anything with these griefs now that they're named. Acknowledging they exist is the potent first step.

There are a few important things I want to invite you to keep in mind. I shared that I often hear from women who are afraid that allowing themselves to grieve will cause them to tumble into a dark hole of unrelenting sadness or depression. And so, whenever you're doing grief work, it's important to remember to create a strong container for your work—like a way to open the door to grief, to feel it and to work with it, but also a way to say, "I can close this door when I need to for my own wellness" or "I can get help with processing this." That isn't to say that you can control your grief, that grief won't show up on a random Tuesday afternoon in the grocery store or that it requires closure. All of the recent grief research shows us that grief needs to live in us and through us and can't be quashed down or compartmentalized into a linear experience of progress. But creating a strong container in the form of a ritualized engagement with grief can help you feel like you have some agency in your grieving process and can assist you in feeling a sense of safeness as you dance with grief, for as long as that dance needs to continue. You can do this by, for example, speaking to your grief, saying, "I welcome you now" and "I am complete with my time with you for right now, but I will be back." Regular therapy appointments or times set aside for journaling can also be a form of creating containment for your grief.

In addition, it's important to engage in some aftercare once you've spent time with this exercise. It's quite likely that you will experience some big emotions as you write your inventory, and some of those emotions may still be lingering and want to be felt and moved fully through your body before you transition into the rest of your day. Grief is inherently dysregulating to our nervous systems, and I invite you to do what you can to find a sense of regulation again. If you already have a practice that helps you do this, now's the time for it. If you don't, I find that embodied practices are a great place to turn after engaging in work like this. Simply taking a moment to feel your feet on the ground and to look around the space you're in can be a powerful way to come back into your body and orient to safeness. You might also lie on the floor for a few minutes and take some deep breaths, go for a walk, or run a bath.

One of my wise teachers, grief worker Shauna Janz, always says, "Grief needs ears to hear."[28] And so it is that if and when you're able, I encourage you to find someone you can share the results of your inventory with, someone who can hold space for and witness the emotions you're experiencing. If you don't have someone to share with or you're not feeling ready to share just yet, the "ears to hear" might simply be the act of coregulating with someone you love—receiving nurturing touch from them or laughing about something together can be brilliant ways to allow your nervous system to match that of someone who is relaxed and attuned to you.

Tread softly, mama. This is important but challenging work.

> *Write a fearless and searching inventory of what you are being asked to leave behind or grieve in your journey through matrescence.*

.................................................................

# 4

# Air

*Navigating the In-Between:*
*What to Do When You*
*Don't Know What to Do*

Welcome to the liminal space, mama.

Liminal space is the space between. Imagine that the slate of your former identity has been wiped clean—or at least seriously rearranged—and you are being invited to begin anew.

But before that happens, you are in a space of not-that-anymore but not-this-yet. You are no longer a woman who isn't a mother—or a woman who is a mother of one or more children—but not yet a woman who is fully embodied in her motherhood or in the expansion of her family.

Liminal space is filled with unknowns. Everything has changed, and you have yet to begin to explore "what's next" in the wake of those changes. You might be asking: *Who am I now? What is important to me now? What will happen to my relationship, my career, my friendships, my body, my community, my spirituality, to the great many things I love that ostensibly have nothing to do with mother-hood at all?* Being in liminal space doesn't imply that we're sitting around twiddling our thumbs—life certainly continues life-ing in the in-between times—but the overall sense of this time is of being suspended between an old life and a new one.

Though feeling a sense of liminality is a perfectly normal, natural phase of *any* massive life transition, this is the stage of matrescence where most of us get *really* uncomfortable.

This discomfort can be traced back to a few key causes. First of all, we live in the era of Google—aka being able to find out anything we desire at the tap of a button and never having to be in the unknown for very long at all. Our culture makes it difficult to traverse the unknown as well: we deify certainty, goal-setting, and Pinterest-worthy vision boards, and the liminal space is the opposite of any of that.

The second reason liminality feels so uncomfortable is somewhat more primal. In traditional cultures, the liminal space was thought to be dangerous, because the time between identities is also almost always the time between belonging.[1] For our ancestors and for today's subsistence cultures, belonging means survival, because they rely on community and kin for provisions and safety. But this isn't only true for our ancestors and other cultures: belonging *still* keeps us safe, and we need coregulation and communion with other humans in order to feel human ourselves. In addition, in traditional cultures, the people traversing liminal space were themselves thought to be dangerous because not quite belonging meant they could operate outside of social norms, and therefore could be disruptive to a community's ways of being.[2]

This, dear reader, makes my rebel heart sing, and I do dearly hope that you might see the liminal space as a time when you're especially equipped to disrupt oppressive social norms. But often, the opposite happens. As I touched on earlier in the book, in our desperate search for belonging and certainty, new mothers can find themselves gravitating toward mothering ideologies which, in addition to easing our sense of not-knowing with a set of Rules For How To Be, often offer us a community of other people who are also following those rules. In this way, we can begin to shape our identities around ideologies. We *become* "attachment parents" or "gentle parents," "supermoms" or "crunchy moms."

But any ideology held too dear becomes a prison, even if it looks like freedom. And so it is that we might follow an ideological path beyond what is healthy for us. We may take "attachment parenting" down a path of intensive motherhood that has us never alone, over-functioning for our children and anyone else they encounter, and dangerously sleep-deprived. We may turn ourselves inside out with guilt and anguish if, as a "crunchy mom," we find ourselves with no option but to feed our babies formula. The truth is these ideologies only feel good as long as we live up to their standards. Underneath our ideology-informed identities and communities comes the threat of losing those identities or sources of belonging. What happens when we stray? What happens when it turns out that we are, inevitably, *human* and complex? Your mothering choices do not make *who you are*—but in liminal times, I'll be the first to say: it's near-impossible to resist the belonging and sense of certainty and "rightness" that mothering ideologies engender.

Because of how uncomfortable the liminal space in matrescence feels, this time is one that many of us try to bypass. We do this in one of two ways: we'll either scramble to recreate the circumstances of our past, trying to fit ourselves into a former self or a former life that no longer exists or we can no longer occupy (cue suffering), or we'll try to "do" our way out of liminality, setting goals and plowing ahead blindly (cue finding yourself in a job or relationship or location that *still* doesn't feel like you, because you were unsure who *you* were when you sought them).

The result, no matter how you look at it, is that you avoid engaging with your own process of evolution. You might bypass discomfort, but you'll also bypass the opportunity to learn and grow deeper into who you are and closer to what matters most to you.

I liken the liminal space to the winter season. You've gone through this massive change and released so much of your pre-motherhood life. This release, by the way, is a bit like autumn, when the leaves of the trees drop to the ground. Over winter—and during this liminal time in your life—everything seems to have gone fallow in a period of dormancy.

And here's the thing about that: it *looks* like nothing is happening. The snow blankets the earth, and you may have forgotten what the plants underneath it even look like. But, in reality, the earth is going through a magnificent process of composting all the old growth and preparing for spring.

So, too, is the liminal space in your transition to motherhood a preparation for "what's next." The compost—the parts of yourself and the trappings of your life that motherhood has asked you to leave behind—is slowly, but surely, becoming fertile ground for the woman you are becoming.

And so it is that if you can become comfortable with this time of not-that-anymore but not-this-yet, you make space for all the potential that your life as a mother, and as a woman who happens to be a mother, holds for you.

I promise.

Because when nothing is sure, everything is possible.

## ✳ BIRTH OF A MOTHER ✳

I lingered in the shower this morning, mama.

And I did it without sneaking from bed before my children were awake, without hurriedly stepping into just-a-little-too-cold-yet water, without shampooing my hair first, just in case that's all I could squeeze in.

Mama, it wasn't that long ago that I had to *make plans* to have a shower, too.

And, I know you know, that inevitably meant that I would *not* manage to make it happen, day in and day out.

Mama, it wasn't that long ago that I had to sit down and have a *conversation* with my partner about *how I could shower more often.*

It felt ludicrous and necessary all at the same time.

Mama, it wasn't that long ago that I went about my daily activities feeling not-so-lovely, feeling ever-so-frumpy, and some days even *gross*. It wasn't that long ago that, as I walked down a crowded downtown street, I caught a sidelong glimpse of my greasy, wayward bedhead in the reflection of a shop window and felt shame. I hoped that no one I knew would see me.

Disheveled. Not-together. Not even able to care for my *own* body; caring for the bodies of my two children instead.

But mama, despite all the *conversations* and the *sneaking* and the *agonizing* over the simple feeling of warm water cascading down my rounded mother-body, showering was still. not. happening. Not on my schedule. Not *whenever I wanted*. Not when I needed a pick-me-up or a few minutes of solitude.

And there was certainly never any lingering.

And so mama, like I imagine you do, too, I railed. I railed against the fact of my motherhood some days, and against the nearly incomprehensible and yet-undeniable fact that *showering* had become my mental preoccupation.

Until this morning.

This morning, I lingered.

Yes, I *finished soaping my entire body*, and *my hair*, and then instead of grasping for a towel and slipping across the floor to prevent my toddler from climbing on top of the toilet tank *again* . . . I lingered.

The moment was made sweeter as the sounds of my two kids cuddling and tickling each other with early morning camaraderie filled the bathroom.

*They had hardly noticed I was gone!*

The moment was made sweeter, too, for all the struggle of these last few years. All that struggle seemed to evaporate in the steam that billowed around me.

This moment, you see, didn't happen on my schedule. It always takes much, much longer than any of us wish it did or would care to admit. It takes much, *much* longer than society leads us to believe it will, and that, mama, might just be the *reason* for the struggle: we live in a world where our expectations of how motherhood impacts our lives are totally, utterly skewed.

*Becoming* unfolds in its own time.

And so I lingered in the shower this morning.

The moment was fleeting, and yet it was a sign.

It was a sign of my *self* growing back as my children's *selves* grew, too.

And it was precious and cleansing and delightful and a little bittersweet, as well, believe it or not.

Even after all the struggle. The bargaining and the *conversations*.

But on the days that it was hard to have patience for my transformation into motherhood, something told me this shower would come. This moment would come.

And it will for you, too.

## YEAH, BUT WHAT DO I *DO* NOW?

If you can find a way to hold your feet to the fire of the discomfort you're feeling—to find a way to *stay* here in the messy middle—the liminal space can be a beautifully fruitful time. You've probably had an experience of coming up with an amazing idea while on vacation, in the shower, or during a long walk in the woods. These are liminal times too—moments when your brain is engaged in a different way, when you're resting. They often, ironically, result in greater productivity and more clarity about the way forward.

But because most of us still long for something to *do* during this space between, I'd like to offer you Six Things to Do When You Don't Know What to Do. They're a way to hold yourself tenderly in the liminal space, avoid the temptation to bypass it, and reap the benefits of this incredibly rich time. They are make space, be still and know, ancient remembering, engage in the art of the possible, create ritual, and rest + tend.

## Make Space

The liminal space is often accompanied by literal spaciousness in our lives. The spaciousness we experience in early motherhood is paradoxical: though we seem to never have enough time to, say, brush our teeth, the days are also often inexorably long and mundane, involving much staring at the ceiling while breastfeeding or chirping at our babies as they kick their feet on a playmat. In our society, we can feel pressured to try to fill up this spaciousness in our lives with productivity—to *do* our way out of the discomfort of the liminal. Now is the time to actually *attend to* and *make sacred* the micromoments of liminality that are woven throughout your days. So maybe, rather than opening Instagram the minute your baby latches, consider waiting for a little while and seeing what it might be like to sink into the moment. Tending to moments of spaciousness allows for rest and also for new ideas, thought patterns, or inspirations to come through. In fact, I've become convinced that these moments are the birthplace of two of the most exquisite MotherPowers that we mamas have access to: creativity and intuition.

## Be Still and Know

Though we'll explore this more in the next section of the book, it's worth noting here that the in-between time is ripe for learning to cultivate your intuition. Intuitive nudges don't happen in an overfull brain and a body that's locked into rigid routine: intuition flows in the space between. And because you'll need your intuition to hear the clarion call of what's next when it finally arrives for you, now is the perfect time to begin to listen to it. Intuition may show up as a visual image, sound, or word that pops into your consciousness, as an embodied feeling, or as a fierce but mysterious sense of "just knowing." The best way to reconnect with your intuition? Begin following the seemingly random urges in your life—to turn left instead of right, to eat oatmeal for breakfast rather than eggs— and see what happens. Those urges are often the whispers of your inner knowing, waiting to be attended to.

## Ancient Remembering

Matrescence is a time that is ripe with opportunities to step into a more authentic expression of yourself. It may seem paradoxical, given the sheer number of social norms that also tug at our selfhood when we enter motherhood, but there it is. I will unpack this further in the following chapter, but for now? One of the things we can explore during the liminal space—and one of the ways we can begin to unearth that sense of authenticity—is in a practice I call *ancient remembering*. Ancient remembering is a look back to who you were, what you loved, and how you lived as a child or during some other time in your life when you felt most authentic and alive—perhaps before you began assimilating ideas about who you should be or what was expected of you. As you think back, you may remember that you loved to paint, adored classical music, or couldn't go a day without having some kind of adventure. Explore these as a map back to who you are and what matters most to you during this time of transition in your life.

## Engage in the Art of the Possible

Once again, we'll dive deeper into this in the following chapters, but the liminal space is the perfect time to start playfully and creatively exploring what might be *possible* in your life now that it has completely transformed. Do some thought experiments: Without judgment, imagine what it might be like to open that café you always said you wanted to own, to quit your job, or to move to a new place. Take it one step further and draw up a business plan, experiment with a new budget, or look for real estate. These are small, safe actions you can take to begin exploring what's possible and what might be waiting for you on the other side of the unknown.

## Create Ritual

Remember how I described traditional cultures thinking of the liminal time as being quite dangerous? According to anthropologist Mary Douglas, this danger was often mitigated through ritual and rite.[3] Again, I'll dive more deeply into the role of ritual in matrescence in the coming chapters, but know this: ritual has a way of creating structure in our lives, of grounding us. Even the tiny rituals of making your morning coffee or whispering a few gratitudes before you fall asleep at night have this effect. Ritual creates *containment* in a time when we can feel utterly unmoored.

## Rest + Tend

Because the liminal space of matrescence is so uncomfortable, the best way we can meet ourselves well in this time is to care for ourselves deeply. In fact, I think motherhood is a time that necessitates that women *finally* really learn the art of resting and offering themselves *truly meaningful self-care*.

Because of this, the ability to truly rest and tend to your own good care is one of the first *MotherPowers* that we can learn to access as new mamas.

I'm going to tell you all about MotherPowers in the final section of this book, but, in short, they're the amazing capacities women *gain* when they become mothers. They are abilities and propensities that become heightened and can be nurtured and developed into a wealth of *possibilities* for your life—and *the world*.

Yes. the world.

I've already talked about the adjacent experience of the Big Slowdown, and I'll dive deeper into the art of *self-care* in the MotherPowers section, but let's focus for a minute on *rest*. It's important to learn to rest in the liminal space not *just* because we become more well-rested versions of ourselves (*eventually, eventually*), but also because rest's companions, spaciousness and presence, are actually pretty rare commodities in our fast-paced culture.

And so, sweet mama, if you are able to take some time to "just rest" these days, remember that you're not only lying there, you're actually engaging in a totally countercultural act of defiance and good self-care, as well as carving out a new identity—a new way to be, as a mama and as a human who deserves the gifts that space and rest bring. You are doing a tremendously monumental thing by nurturing this little baby of yours. And so even if you're not *sleeping* much these days, it's important to *rest* as much as possible: To stop. Sit. Stare out the window. Put the eldest children in front of the TV for a while; catch a nap every so often, even. Drink a cup of tea. Know that, especially in this time in our world, rest is a skill, and it's one you've never had a better opportunity to learn. And know that your ability to learn to rest well will actually open up a whole realm of possibilities for you.

### YOUR TURN

This space of liminality—of not yet feeling fully embodied in your motherhood but no longer being "not-a-mother"— is one that can be deeply uncomfortable. During this time, most women have a sense of not really knowing who they are anymore and perhaps not knowing what will happen in some of the areas of their lives that have shifted since they became mothers. The role of mother may still feel new and uncomfortable—like it's a title you can't quite fully wear with confidence yet or you feel like it's a role that perhaps *other* women occupy, but not you, not yet.

So I want to offer you some ways you can work with those Six Things to Do When You Don't Know What to Do in order to support yourself during this in-between time of matrescence.

## Make Space

*Imagine five ways you could make more space in your life right now. Perhaps you could take your baby for a walk in the woods instead of doing another load of laundry; perhaps you could just stare out the window for a few minutes while your baby nurses. Perhaps there are some moments in your day when you could journal or engage in creative practice or movement.*

## Be Still and Know

*Think of a question you really want to know the answer to. Now spend five minutes freewriting a response to it in your journal. If it helps, imagine your wisest self is writing a letter to you, through your hand.*

## Ancient Remembering

*Make a list of five ways you could reconnect with a former version of yourself or your life that feel authentic, energizing, or exciting. If scuba diving in the Red Sea doesn't feel doable right now, ask yourself what it was about that experience that enlivened you and made you feel more like yourself. Perhaps there is a way to access a sense of adventure, accomplishment, or discovery in your life that touches into that ancient part of you but feels doable, given your tiny little circumstance, right now.*

## Engage in the Art of the Possible

*Write five things you could do, try, think about, or experiment with because everything is up in the air right now. Maybe you could haul out your old water-*

color paints or look for jobs that are way outside your normal milieu. Don't censor yourself here!

## Create Ritual

*Imagine five tiny rituals you could do that might help you feel more grounded as you navigate these early days, weeks, and months of motherhood. One of my favorite of these kinds of rituals is something I call #firstsipoutside. (Yes, it has its own hashtag now.) In the chaos of the year that I homeschooled my kids, I made a ritual of heading out on the back deck and taking the first sip of my morning tea outside. I would close the patio door behind me, and the kids knew these two or three minutes were off-limits. I would try to listen to the birdsong, take great gulps of the cool air, and sink into this micromoment of self-care. What ways could you offer yourself and ritualize some tiny moments of good care?*

## Rest + Tend

*Grab your journal, set a timer for ten minutes, and freewrite your response to these two prompts:*

*If my body spoke to me, it would say . . .*

*If my heart spoke to me, it would say . . .*

*Sometimes all our needs require is the opportunity to be voiced. Notice how it feels to pause long enough to hear your innermost longings. If you can make a move toward meeting them, that's great, but know that even just attuning to yourself for a moment is big, important work.*

# 5

# Fire

*Exploring Who You're Becoming*
*Now That You're a Mother*

> Motherhood is meant to overwhelm us. It's meant to slow
> us down and remind us of what matters most. It's meant
> to expand us in order to make room for the children we're
> (briefly) given to guide. It's meant to reshape us into fuller,
> more well-rounded women. It reminds us of our inter-
> dependency, shows us where we still need to grow, and
> strengthens our capacity to connect from the heart.
> —Beth Berry, *Motherwhelmed*

I probably don't need to say it again because you're beginning to
know it in your very marrow: becoming a mother is no less than a
change to your identity.

It's not just that someone calls you "mom" now or that your primary occupation seems to be washing cloth diapers or being awake
all night—although that's certainly part of it.

As Mother, you have been asked to leave behind some aspects of
yourself. Perhaps you used to be career-driven, and now you can't
imagine going back to work. Perhaps you harbored negative feelings toward your body, and now you respect it deeply for its ability
to grow and nourish a baby. Perhaps you're too tired to stay up late

drinking wine and playing Scrabble with your partner (no? just me?) and so that important way to connect in your relationship is gone.

Granted, there are some things that may return to your life: one day, but maybe not as soon as you'd like, wine and Scrabble might be a more distinct possibility than they are now.

But other aspects of yourself will change forever.

Some of the things you've left behind you may happily and heartily surrender, and others, it seems, are harder to let go of. You may want to, but you feel frightened and maybe a bit unmoored by what happens or who you are in their absence. Or you may *not* want to let certain aspects of your pre-motherhood life go but find them incompatible with your new role.

No one said this was easy.

We do ourselves and all mothers a disservice when we try to "get back to normal" or fight against the fact of our own motherhood and all the life changes that entails when, in fact, motherhood is asking us not just to shift our day-to-day routine but the way we operate in the world, how we think, what we prioritize, and what we want for ourselves and our families.

Matrescence truly is an identity shift that finds us saying "I am no longer who I was before. I leave the expectations I had for that former life behind."

When we say, "I am different now. I am no longer the person I used to be," it begs the question:

"Who am I, then?"

Though this question might seem like a daunting one to be faced with, it is also a question that is absolutely *full* of possibility. We get a sparse few chances like this over the course of our days: our early mothering time offers us a divine opportunity to take stock of our lives. In this way, motherhood might not take you further away from the woman you are, but actually more deeply within yourself.

In the Four Elements model of Radical Transformation, you have reached the Fire phase. You've traversed the initial phases of orienting to the shifts that have occurred since you became a mother and grieving the parts of you that are on pause for now, or that no longer serve you in your motherhood. You've navigated the vast unknowns of the liminal space, and you are ready to ignite your imagination and explore what is possible for you, your life, and your motherhood. In this chapter, I'll share more about the cultivation of authenticity through matrescence and then dive into *how* you can start exploring who you are now that you're a mother (or a mother again!).

## ON IMAGINAL CELLS AND AUTHENTICITY

Have you heard of imaginal cells?

Well, somehow I've managed to write a book about transformation and have gotten more than halfway through it without *ever mentioning butterflies.*

I know—the *masters* of transformation.

The story of the butterfly is a lot like the story of your transition to motherhood. You were hanging out in your pre-motherhood life, a little caterpillar, munching on leaves and unaware of the changes that were coming your way.

*(If you were like me, and you want to extend this metaphor into the realm of the* Very Hungry Caterpillar, *sometime in your pregnancy you may well also have eaten one piece of chocolate cake, one ice cream, one pickle, one slice of cheese, and one slice of salami in the process, too.)*

Eventually, you enter the cocoon of late pregnancy and early motherhood.

And then, you turn to goo.

The goo phase is otherwise known as the liminal space, or Air in the Four Elements model, which we explored in the last chapter. In my experience, the goo phase happens sometime between the moment you place your baby on your chest for the first time, all slimy and wonderful, and the moment, sometimes two to three years later, when you feel this subtle but distinct feeling of "Ah, okay. I'm here. I'm a mother. I think I've got this. Mostly. Ish." Of course, everyone's individual experiences vary dramatically, but it's safe to say we all spend a wildly uncomfortable amount of time in the goo phase.

But what most people don't know about the goo phase is that the caterpillar isn't *completely* goo. Inside that caterpillar, inside the goo, *and* inside the butterfly are these things called *imaginal cells.* Even when the caterpillar completely disintegrates in the process of transformation, the imaginal cells are *still there.*

Imaginal cells are comparable, in my opinion, to what some people call "the essential self," or "authenticity," or, even, "the soul." They're the part of you that is *you*. Not the *trappings* of you—the job or the house or the clothes or the friends or the skills—just *you.* Who you are, in your heart of hearts.

You see, motherhood has this way of bringing us to our knees at times, yes, but it also has this way of bringing us back home to ourselves.

Research by Elizabeth K. Laney, PhD, corroborates this idea of imaginal cells in new mothers. In a 2015 study, Laney and her team found that "women redefine themselves in a variety of ways through motherhood, yet once they emerge from their children's infancy, women also demonstrate a level of continuity within their identities because they maintain a core sense of self as achieved prior to motherhood."[1] Laney described that, in many ways, motherhood *intensified* her study participants' personalities.

Earlier in this book, I wrote that one of the key shifts that happen for women when they become mothers is that even through the disorientation of matrescence they become clearer about and often reorient toward their values. A great many of us become unwilling to tolerate anything in our lives that doesn't align with those values and receive a bolt of enhanced courage that gives us the fierce capacity to quit, unfriend, unfollow, undo—just as much as it also gives us the capacity to nourish, nurture, and bring forth.

As you birth and care for your baby, you are also birthing a new version of yourself. Or, perhaps, you are growing the capacity to unearth yourself from beneath the roles, responsibilities, and societal expectations that have been heaped upon you since girlhood. In the process, you may become more of who you are.

The idea of this return to the "authentic self" is one that will have most mamas reading this nodding their heads, but it's something that has only in recent years been documented in the growing literature around matrescence and the transition to motherhood—file it under: *conversations no one else is having* and *stuff no one told you would happen in motherhood.*

Taylor-Kabbaz writes beautifully about this *return to self* in her book *Mama Rising:* "Since [my daughter's] birth, I have given birth to my true self. Although I felt at the time that I had lost myself in the overwhelm of new mamahood, in hindsight I can see that I never really knew myself. I thought I did. I thought I had it all figured out. But the reality is that it is only through the years of births, babies, and toddlers that I have glimpsed who I am at my core. That is the gift of matrescence."[2]

Here, mama, is where you can begin the exploration of who you are now that you're a mother—or perhaps of who you have always been, with the plumb line of truth that runs within you, no matter what life has in store for you, no matter how much you change and shift and transform.

## EXPLORING WHO YOU ARE BECOMING

One of the questions mothers always ask me is: How do you know it's time to explore "what's next" and who you are now as you traverse matrescence? My experience is that most women just begin, without thinking about it very much and with a sort of gravitational pull toward their own becoming. They pick up a set of charcoals or reconnect with an old friend. They, perhaps finally managing to piece together a few more hours of consistent sleep each night, decide to use nap time to write poetry instead of catching z's alongside their baby. They decide that they are totally done with their cubicle job and start brushing up their résumé.

Before I begin our deep dive into *what's possible* as you begin to find your footing in motherhood, I want to divest us all from the perfect mother myth when it comes to finding a sense of deeper self-actualization in motherhood. What I describe in the following paragraphs is not about *optimizing* motherhood, not about another thing you must *accomplish*. A great many of us experience motherhood in harsh realities that feel anything but potential-filled. Welcome to yet another paradox of modern mothering: it is an experience that is both deeply empowering and harshly oppressive, both full of possibility and limitation. As Brock posits, "The social construction of motherhood sets us up to perceive becoming a mother as being the way to self-actualize and become complete, but then asks us to self-erase and self-sacrifice in order to be the 'good mother.'"[3] I will expand on this more in the next section of the book, but for now, I want to invite you to unearth the ways in which your motherhood may bring you closer to who you are and what matters most to you—perhaps not in spite of, but in fact *because*, it's an experience so richly appointed with challenges. As Rich writes in *Of Woman Born*, "No one mentions the psychic crisis of bearing a first child, the excitation of long-buried feelings about one's own mother, the sense of confused power and powerlessness, of being taken over on the one hand and of touching new physical and psychic potentialities on the other, a heightened sensibility which can be exhilarating, bewildering and exhausting."[4]

And so here you are, bewildered and exhausted, perhaps, but also feeling the tug of your own selfhood, ready to be renegotiated in light of your new reality. But how? How, after becoming utterly *undone* in the process of matrescence, does a mother become *remade* anew?

This is a time when I advocate for women to engage in a practice of Tiny Experiments.

Mind if I geek out on you for a few minutes?

The idea of Tiny Experiments comes from something called *complexity theory* or *complex adaptive systems theory*.[5] In short, the theory says that complex systems—like governments, ecosystems, or *human beings*, for example—are tricky to understand, and therefore even trickier to change. In a complex system, there are a lot of ever-transitioning, mutually dependent, individual working parts that make up the whole.

We, as a society, really don't love complexity. We *adore* simplicity. We love the idea that we could wave a magic wand and transform, that there's a quick fix to our problems. For example, simplicity is the axis upon which the diet industry rotates: "Just eat less food and move your body more, and you'll be thin! Let's not think too hard about why you eat your feelings or the cultural persistence of fat-phobia and whether or not you might actually be healthy already . . . just . . . just . . . have this paleo muffin! Please!" Simplicity is also the premise of a great majority of our health care system. It goes kind of like this: "Here, take this pill! You'll be more of this and less of that! Never mind that you can't pay your bills and your marriage is falling apart . . . just . . . just . . . this will cure you! Promise!"

And so it is that approaching the transition to motherhood from a lens of simplicity is awfully tempting, too. "If only I can learn how to change diapers and make really strong coffee, I will be fine. I just need to get a postpartum doula to help for the first few weeks. Then I'll be fine. I just need to get out of the house . . . to get eight hours sleep . . . to find a playgroup with other mothers I actually like . . . to go on a date night with my partner . . . then I'll be fine."

You've made it this far into this book, so I know you know this is mostly always untrue. Motherhood is one of the biggest—*if not the biggest*—transformations you'll ever experience in your life. Stronger coffee and an eight-hour sleep aren't going to make it okay.

I know, it seems like it.

Okay, it might. A little. It might be a little more okay with strong coffee and eight hours of sleep.

But I digress.

You are becoming someone new. That is a *complex* change.

Usually, when we modern humans want to experience change in our lives, we set goals. Goals can work really well in many life circumstances, but in a *developmental* process like matrescence, goals are pretty useless. In a developmental process, you are, by definition, growing and changing at the very marrow of who you are. The self that creates a goal will *not even be the same self* that reaches it, thereby likely rendering the goal itself irrelevant.

Enter: Tiny Experiments. Tiny Experiments are the opposite of broad sweeping changes, the opposite of On Monday Things Will Be Different, the opposite of a pill that fixes everything. Tiny Experiments are just that: little incremental changes and explorations that *might* inch you closer to the shift you're trying to make.

Notice I said *might*?

Tiny Experiments are also known as "safe-to-fail experiments."[6] That means they're small and low-stakes enough to not matter in the slightest if they go sideways. It's like writing a business plan and chatting with an entrepreneur or two before quitting your day job. It's writing a few articles on the Notes app in your phone before starting a blog.

And here's the thing: Tiny Experiments are *only* about learning, *not about success*. We learn a lot more from failure, actually, than we do from success. If our Tiny Experiments are safe-to-fail, then our potential to learn who we're becoming magnifies tenfold. We also know that most adults learn best through *experience*, and so Tiny Experiments allow you to actually embody the changes in your identity that you're exploring and consolidate your learning about who you are becoming.

And so it is that Tiny Experiments can support you when you're beginning to explore who you are now that you're a mother and a woman who happens to be a mother. Everything is changing—*we've wholeheartedly established that*—and now it's time to begin to ever-so-gently nudge at what's next.

The beauty of Tiny Experiments is that they keep you true to yourself. You get to explore new ideas, discover new parts of yourself, and experiment with new ways of being in the world and *constantly* ask yourself: *How is this? How does this feel? Do I love this? Is this for me? No? Okay, let's try something different. Yes? Okay, let's do more of that; let's take the next step; let's dive in deeper.* And with a strong self-tending practice and the cultivation of intuition, as we'll talk about in the next section, you'll have the inner dialogue and sense of self-trust to be able to really listen for what feels authentic and true for you, not someone else's ideas of what you should do, what success looks like, or what a "good" mother would do.

So how do you start your Tiny Experiments? Well, it's possible, if you're the mama who's picked up a set of watercolors on her last Walmart run, connected with an old friend, or started writing poetry during nap time, that you already have. But if you haven't, you'll get to explore where you can begin in the "Your Turn" section of this chapter.

## ✳ BIRTH OF A MOTHER ✳

I remember the morning as though it were yesterday.

My daughter was just a handful of months old, and she had a propensity for long, wakeful stretches of nursing through the wee hours of the morning. I found that it was hard for me to fall asleep between nursing sessions and difficult to find a way to slide my light-sleeping baby (she is *still* a light sleeper) out of my arms and onto the bed beside me without waking her. I wouldn't master the art of side-lying nursing until four years later when my son came along, and so I spent great swaths of my night reading by the light of my e-reader, occasionally lifting the sweet, dimpled little arm of my baby girl to see if it was floppy enough to indicate the potential for a possible transfer.

Usually, it wasn't.

This particular morning, I had, in a fit of restlessness, decided to sit in the giant papasan chair tucked by the window in our master bedroom for what I hoped would be the final nursing session of the wee hours. The chair was deep and oh-so-comfortable, and it was large enough that I could nurse my sweet girl on my lap with one arm and perch my journal on the side of the chair and write with my other arm.

Though writing is my catharsis, my way of making sense of myself and of the world, I hadn't written in my journal in months. The day-to-day tasks of mothering and the giant learning curve I was on had completely subsumed me, and without writing my way through the experience, I felt as though I was adrift.

I was deep in the liminal space of motherhood, spending my nights in almost total sleeplessness and my days changing diapers, nursing, and catching naps where I could.

But something flickered in me that day when I decided I could nurse the baby in that comfy chair in the darkest predawn hours and begin to put words to paper once more.

I know now it was the flickering of "what's next" as I began to contemplate what was on the other side of this deep liminality I was experiencing—even though my process of matrescence would continue for a few years yet.

At the time, it was just a great relief. *Aha! I've figured it out! I can meet the needs of my baby and myself* at the same time.

*Mama, I know you know that this always feels like a triumph.*

What I found myself writing that morning was not what I expected, however. Instead of the usual rambling on about what was great and what was frustrating and what happened last week, I began to write a list.

The list was a declaration of sorts. It was a statement of *how I wanted to be* as a mother, now that I had begun to experience the fledgling days of what that new role meant. And it was also a statement of *who I wanted to be* as a woman who *happens to be a mother*—as a woman with very strong values and beliefs and preferences and ambitions, still, shifted and tempered though they had become by the fact of my motherhood. The list said things like:

I am committed to an adventurous life. I will find new and surprising ways to incorporate adventure into my motherhood.

I am committed to being present for my daughter. I will spend at least some time completely focused on her every single day.

I will allow motherhood to change who I am. I am open to whatever might happen to my career and my goals and dreams as I navigate my first postpartum year, and I will actively begin to take an inventory of my passions and desires to guide me along the way.

I jokingly called the list my Momifesto, but the power of that list was no joke. I referred back to it many times throughout that first postpartum year and beyond, checking in with myself and my intentions often. My Momifesto became like a compass for my motherhood and a map back home to myself in those early days.

It can be hard to know where to begin when you're just emerging from the cocoon of your earliest mothering days and into what's possible for your life. You might love the idea of writing a Momifesto, or perhaps you'd like to begin with some Tiny Experiments, but don't know how to start. In the following "Your Turn" section, you'll have the opportunity to explore both of those things as the spark of who you're becoming ignites and begins to grow into a steady flame.

## YOUR TURN

### Your Momifesto

After creating my own Momifesto, I decided to create a Momifesto Workbook to help the women I was working with begin to find their way in their postpartum years. What follows are a few of the journal prompts from the Momifesto Workbook. They are designed to help you begin to remember yourself, both as woman and now as mother. It will probably surprise you: there will likely be many, many aspects of yourself that actually haven't changed at all. Hold fast to these and remember that even when everything is changing—when the ground under your feet literally seems to be shifting—there is an essential self, a fundamental you full of beautiful, sparkling imaginal cells that remains.

These first questions are designed to help you explore who you are, as a woman.

*What do you know about yourself? Nothing is too seemingly unimportant or frivolous to write here. Start with the color of your eyes and your favorite foods, if you'd like. What makes you smile? What is the best way to spend a day? What feels really, really good? Make a list of twenty-five items— or a list as long as your arm, if you like.*

*What matters to you? Again, here, think big or think small—from environmental activism to only ever eating the best chocolate, these are the things you care about. There are no wrong answers, just exploration.*

*What are your loves? As in, who do you love, what do you love, how do you love to feel, what do you love to do, where do you love . . . you get the picture.*

*Make a list of things that make you awesome. Do you make a mean risotto? Are you great at breaking the ice with strangers? Have a way with spread-sheets? Don't hold back here, SHINE!*

*What words describe the ways you'd like to show up in the world? Examples might be: grateful, joyful, authentic, in service, honest, in awe, nurturing, reverent . . . you get the idea.*

The next section is designed to help you articulate who you are as a mother. Take some time here to find clarity—rooted in your own values and inner knowing—about how you'd like to show up for your kids, your family, and yourself as a mother.

*What do you know to be true about motherhood so far?*

*What messages or stories have you heard or received about motherhood—from your family of origin, from our society, or from friends and acquaintances? What of those messages would you like to embrace? What do you resist or hold in curiosity?*

*What matters most to you as it relates to motherhood? You can explore this question with regard to the "little things," like time for hot coffee in the morning, or the "big things," like raising your children with an understanding of social justice.*

*What strengths do you have that will support you in motherhood?*

*How would you like to meet with the challenges of motherhood? What resources, support, or tools do you need to accomplish this?*

*What words describe the ways you'd like to show up in your mothering role? How do you want to feel as you navigate motherhood? Examples might be: grateful, joyful, authentic, honest, in awe, nurturing, reverent . . . you get the idea.*

## A Week of Tiny Experiments

Hopefully some of the questions in the previous section have helped you begin to remember who you are becoming now that you're a mother. Now you have the opportunity to actually *reclaim* some of those aspects of who you are and who you are becoming. Maybe you have an inner artist who stopped painting when she entered the corporate world. Perhaps you've always wanted to start a business but thought you could never make a living from your passions. So many of us, by the time we reach our childbearing years, have shed a great many parts of ourselves in order to fit in to what society dictates are the behaviors and occupations of a "good woman." So many of us have lost ourselves along the way.

It's time to begin to reclaim the woman you truly are. This is one of the first of many opportunities motherhood will give you to live your truth. It's time.

The first step on this path is to take an inventory of the areas of your life that feel most—and least—aligned with that inner authentic self. You see, many of the women I've worked with actually feel deeply connected to themselves in some areas of their lives as they traverse matrescence, but not others. The areas of your life in which you are not living from a place of deep self-connection may feel really clear to you. You might be able to pinpoint, for example, your career or your physical body as the source of your discontent. Sometimes, though, these feelings can show up less obviously, as just not feeling like yourself or feeling lost or out of integrity in some way.

So it's time to do a check-in with your life.*

To do this exercise, set aside some quiet time.

---

* The exercise described in the following paragraphs is an adaptation of the "Wheel of Life" exercise popularized by the Co-Active Training Institute.

Sometimes starting out with a few deep breaths or any other brief practice that centers you will help you to think most clearly about your life.

Take a piece of paper and draw a big circle on it. Now, divide it up like a pie into six to eight slices and label each slice with key elements or categories that make up the most important areas of your life. These labels are up to you, but some ideas are: career, health (both physical and emotional), relationships, money, physical environment, spirituality, social life, family, or personal development.

Now consider how you feel in each area of your life.

You might start by asking: *How am I honoring who I am and what matters to me in this area of my life? How am I neglecting who I am and what matters to me in this area of my life? Does this area of my life feel nourished and nourishing or untended and draining?*

Feelings of being at home with and deeply connected to yourself might show up as satisfaction, pride, or happiness or as a physical sensation, like a grounded feeling in your feet or a lightness in your chest.

Feelings of discomfort with some aspects of your life might show up as disappointment, sadness, or unease or, physically, as a flip-flutter in your chest, a pit in your stomach, a lump in your throat. You might feel a sense of loss, as though you've forgotten who you are or have lost touch with what you love.

Now shade in each wedge, starting at the tip, in accordance with how you feel about yourself and this particular area of your life. For example, if you are feeling as though your career reflects you, your values, and what you want for your work, you would color in the majority of your "career" wedge. Other areas may be shaded halfway or perhaps not at all.

*This is half the work.*

Sometimes even sitting with the awareness of how you've become disconnected from the woman you know yourself to be can begin to create shifts.

*Know that you're on the right path.*

Now, I want to invite you to identify the area of your life from your circle in which you feel least connected to yourself.

The next step in this process is to brainstorm ten tiny, safe-to-fail experiments you can do to explore and honor who you are, who you are becoming, and what matters most to you in that area of your life.

For example, perhaps you feel least aligned in and connected to yourself within your career. A great, tiny, safe- to-fail experiment might be to brush up your résumé or have coffee with someone whose job you think you'd really love. Tiny Experiments can be "thought experiments" too: you could brainstorm what qualities your ideal career would have, what skills and capacities you want to bring to your next role, or what your family budget might look like if you had a change in salary.

Before you begin, a note of compassion: the part of your brain responsible for the creativity, curiosity, play, and learning that you will need to bring to this exercise can't work at the same time as the part of your brain that is responsible for sympathetic nervous system activation—the fight, flight, freeze, and fawn responses. When we are stressed, burne-dout, or otherwise experiencing nervous system dysregulation, we tend to zero in on the negative, and it's hard to see possibility or ways in which we have choice and agency. If you know that you're feeling a little crispy lately or if you find it hard to come up with ideas in this next section, that's a good sign that tending to your needs right now is paramount. To explore this further, move ahead to learn about self-tending in the MotherPowers section of the book. This work of creating Tiny Experiments will always be here when you're ready.

> *List ten Tiny Experiments you could do to explore how you could honor who you are and what matters most to you in your chosen area of your life. (Hint: These should feel fairly easy to do and involve little to no risk. They should also include some parameters that help you to know when you've completed the experiment and to keep it tiny—like time limits or outcomes. For example, you might start some kind of regular practice, like ten minutes of movement per day or perhaps thirty minutes of research into a career option that you've been considering.)*

> *Now, circle one to three of your experiments that you'd like to try over the course of the next week. You can always return to the list and do more another week! If your experiment is a daily practice, that might be enough for now. If it's more of a "one and done" activity, choose a few things to try.*

Note: What these experiments are intended to do, first and foremost, even if they don't end up turning into regular practices or the beginning of something bigger, is to allow for exploration and curiosity to spark your imagination and to make room for the possibility that something new—a new way of thinking, a new identity, a new practice or behavior—might emerge.

Even though these experiments are designed to be fairly safe and easy, you may feel resistance to some of your new explorations. As coach and author Danielle LaPorte says, "Procrastination is a form of intuition."[7] The goal here is not to tick off a bunch of accomplishments, but rather to notice how these experiments *make you feel*, what happens for you when you do them. There is as much wisdom in the not-doing as in the doing, so don't be hard on yourself if you don't "accomplish" what you set out to. Instead, get curious about why that happened: perhaps what you're exploring just isn't right for you, or perhaps feelings of self-doubt are creeping up as you venture into new territory in your life. Either way, you're *learning* more about who you are, what you might want to explore next, and what's possible for you.

> At the end of your week of Tiny Experiments, reflect on how they went. How do you feel—Physically? Emotionally? Consider if you'd like to continue implementing these or other Tiny Experiments. If so, how can you build on what you've started?

Over the last four chapters, we've explored Earth, Water, Air, and Fire—the Four Elements of Radical Transformation—as a way to understand your matrescence and as a map to guide you along that journey. In Earth, you explored the changes you've experienced to your *whole* life as you've made this transition. In Water, you dove deep into what you've had to let go of during this transformative time in your life and allowed yourself to grieve parts of yourself and your identity that are no longer—or at least not-right-now. In Air, you learned how to support yourself during the discomfort of the liminal time and that it's normal to feel a little unmoored and unsure of yourself during this phase of matrescence. Finally, in Fire, you began your exploration of *who you're becoming*, as a mother and as a woman who happens to be a mother, through exploring some of the Momifesto journal prompts and trying some Tiny Experiments. This is *part* of the work of the Fire phase. In the next section of the book, we will step further into Fire, exploring and reclaiming the power and potential of your matrescence and unearthing your

*MotherPowers*—those skills and gifts that motherhood allow us to develop which unlock the deep potential to become more of who we are and to become leaders and advocates in a world that needs empowered women and mothers more than ever.

# PART II

# Reclaiming the Power and Potential of Matrescence

# 6

# Motherhood as Revolution

*Mothers as Change Agents*
*in a Broken World*

I recognized motherhood as a deeply frightening,
potent source of power: a recognition that came five
years into my experience of motherhood, largely because
I had become so conditioned to assume that motherhood was more of a dull hindrance or a cute aside than a
world-shattering awakening. Becoming a mother is one of
the few experiences in life that really re-makes a woman,
that dramatically unsettles her center of gravity. And
there is opportunity here, to connect, to collaborate,
elucidate new visions, and change the status quo.
—Sarah Menkedick, *Ordinary Insanity*

We know that the transition into motherhood is deeply challenging. It shakes our very sense of who we are in the world; it asks
us to transform and adapt and surrender every step of the way. Not
only that, but modern-day mothers are navigating this transformative process in a global social, economic, and political context that
makes it *even more* difficult. I have already outlined some of the

many, many ways in which motherhood—specifically that "capital M" Motherhood filled with unfair and outdated cultural norms—oppresses mothers. As a result, so many mothers are suffering.

And, as with so many of our mothering experiences, these truths about motherhood are not the *only* truths. It's also true that we often forget the *potential* and *possibility* that exist for mothers—and the world we live in—in spite of, or perhaps because of, the challenges they face in matrescence.

This is not just another gratitude list or a way of bypassing real challenges. We *must* find ways to see this power and potential if we are to fully embody and value our motherhood *at all* and, arguably, to fight for social change that also values motherhood.

You see, I have come to truly believe that matrescence is so challenging for so many women in part because becoming a mother is considered a demotion in our society. It represents a decrease in our value as humans—sometimes quite literally, as we become less able to stay productive in our capitalist society. It's no wonder that mothers everywhere don't want motherhood to change them or define them; it's no wonder that we try, often despite the well-being of our bodies and our health, to *do it all*. To become a mother and to let that process have its way with you and completely transform you can often feel like becoming invisible in our culture. Perhaps, in fact, the unspoken fear behind losing yourself in motherhood is in fact a fear of *losing your worth in society*.

And so *of course* we fight matrescence every step of the way.

My vision for you in the coming chapters, mama, is to begin to see the many things motherhood has *given* you. And I don't mean adorable baby snuggles and milk-drunk smiles. No. I mean that motherhood has given you access to a realm of potential and a depth of power that are both deeply personal and radically political.

## MOTHERS AND POWER

The story of mothers and power is a complex and often extremely paradoxical one. It's important to begin unpacking it a little bit here in order to offer you some context from which to explore your MotherPowers in the next chapter.

There are two historic ideologies that were important in shaping our thinking about how mothers do or don't hold power. The first is called *maternalism*. Maternalism first started in the late nineteenth and early twentieth centuries and advocated for mothers' values and rights in the social and political sphere because mothers were thought to be the moral compass of society and held particular skills and experiences that made them well-suited for leadership and positions of power. Sounds good, right? The thing was, maternalism implied that women's *only* potential source of power was through motherhood—implying also, then, that women couldn't hold power simply because they were *humans* and that women who weren't mothers were *less valuable* in society.

Enter *momism*: the backlash to maternalism. In the midtwentieth century momism asserted that women's path to power could and should be paved with professional achievements—not through motherhood. This allowed nonmothering women to hold more power, but it also relegated motherhood to the private, domestic sphere and ended up devaluing the experience completely. In her book *Ordinary Insanity*, Menkedick writes that momism "marginalized motherhood to the extent that women could no longer derive real power or authority from it. . . . Mothers, then and increasingly now, were damned if they did and damned if they didn't: they couldn't fully and autonomously function in a world that pretends motherhood doesn't exist, nor could they expect support, rights, or sympathy for their work as mothers, which, they were reminded over and over, is a simple and beautiful privilege and nothing very special, difficult or interesting."[1]

There is also an important racialized dimension to the way mothers have and continue to hold power in our culture. Maternalism and momism were concepts formed around white women's experience of motherhood. Both historically and in current times—due to slavery and residential schools in the former and, in the latter, the disproportionate numbers of young Black and Indigenous children and youth in the criminal justice and foster systems—the ability to mother their children wasn't a given for Black and Indigenous women. For many, mothering was and is considered a privilege and could in fact be an act of defiance against oppressive systems of power.

To illustrate this, bell hooks writes, "Early feminist attacks on motherhood alienated masses of women from the movement, especially poor and/or non-white women, who find parenting one of the few interpersonal relationships where they are affirmed and appreciated."[2] In her essay "Homeplace," hooks goes on to assert that "one's homeplace was the one site where one could freely confront the issue of humanization, where one could resist. Black women resisted by making homes where all black people could strive to be subjects, not objects, where we could be affirmed in our minds and hearts despite poverty, hardship and deprivation."[3] Motherhood studies scholar Patricia Hill-Collins, PhD, confirms, in her work and writing, that motherhood has been and is a site of self-actualization, status, and power for many Black women.[4]

Indigenous scholar Jennifer Brant, PhD, writes about the matriarchal worldview held by her own and other Indigenous cultures. Women and mothers were—and are—held in reverence as the life-givers of the community, both in the physical and spiritual sense.[5]

There is a middle ground here in this question of mothers and power. Sociologist Andrea O'Reilly, PhD, coined the term *matricentric feminism*, which seeks to reject the oppressive, "private, non-political undertaking" that is patriarchal motherhood and uplift mother-work as a "socially engaged enterprise and a site of power, wherein mothers can and do affect social change through childrearing and activism."[6]

The through line in all of these articulations of motherhood and power is the tension between the sometimes-challenging but also profoundly meaningful work of mothering and the fact of doing that work within an oppressive cultural, political, and economic system. The question at the heart of it all is: Can mothers change the conditions under which we mother, and, perhaps, in doing so, change the conditions under which we *all* live? Can mothers change the world?

## MOTHERS AS CHANGE AGENTS IN A BROKEN WORLD

My answer to that question? I think so.

I hope so.

Thankfully, I'm not alone.

Rich, in *Of Woman Born*, writes of those who *mother against motherhood*. She articulates that these mothers must reject the "good mother" trope and become "bad mothers," or "outlaw mothers."[7]

I love the idea of being an outlaw mother just as much as the next rebel mama, but I also think there's more to empowered motherhood than this. So much of where we've gotten so far with our ideologies of motherhood has been a reaction to the currently oppressive paradigm, and then a movement as far in the other direction as we can get—only to find that the view from there is just as distorted, but in different ways. What I am curious about is a motherhood that is generative and creative—that comes from a place of "what about this?" rather than a place of "not like that."

This is the question at the heart of Alexis Pauline Gumbs, China Martens, and Mai'a Williams's anthology *Revolutionary Mothering*. They ask how we can get from a conservative definition of mothering to "mothering as a liberating practice that can thwart runaway capitalism."[8] Angela Garbes, in *Essential Labor: Mothering as Social Change*, imagines a world where the work of mothering can be "our most consistent, embodied resistance to patriarchy, white supremacy, ableism, and the exploitation that underlies American capitalism."[9]

Damn. Are you as fired up as I am?

"Mothers transmit culture," Dani McClain writes in *We Live for the We*.[10] I couldn't agree more: I think mothers and the work of mothering have a lot to teach us about how to be more human in a society that is often dehumanizing.

We mothers are asked, over and over again, implicitly and explicitly, to deny the fact of our motherhood in order to participate in a world that values moneymaking over caretaking, productivity over presence, and individuality over relationality.

But last I checked, most of us don't *want* to live in a world that values moneymaking over caretaking, productivity over presence, and individuality over relationality. Last I checked, most of us are contorting ourselves, denying our authenticity and our most basic human needs, and often becoming physically, mentally, or spiritually unwell in our efforts to try to survive in that world.

And so it's time to change the *world* rather than trying to change *ourselves*.

Because so many aspects of motherhood are oppressive only within the context of a world that is not set up for mothers—and, let's face it, most humans, particularly those who are not white males—to thrive.

It's time to explore mothering as a countercultural act and to advocate for a society where our motherhood is not what oppresses us but is in fact what makes us *change agents* and *leaders* in a world that desperately needs mothering.

Here's the thing, mama: Remember how I said that, for a handful of specific reasons, becoming a mother has maybe never been harder than it is right now at this time in history?

Well, the other half of that equation is that the world, right now in this particular moment in history, is *waking up* to all of the ways in which our culture is broken. And there is a growing movement of people who are, in all kinds of acts of subversion both radical and subtle, speaking out and speaking up for change. For so many women that I work with, motherhood has catalyzed them to join that movement.

You see, we, as mothers, have the potential to advocate for a world that allows for the fullness of our humanity, for the acceptance of natural cycles of rest and productivity, for intuition to become a way of knowing that is just as valuable as facts and figures, and for the recognition of our interdependence. These, and more, are the skills, capacities, and *powers* that mothers often learn to *master* as they traverse matrescence.

These are your MotherPowers, mama.

The MotherPowers are the abilities and proclivities that happen to make you good at raising your babies, yes. In many ways, they're the abilities and proclivities that will keep you grounded and well during the tumultuous early years of parenting. That too. But they're also more than that. These are the superpowers, as it were, that mothers have the potential to gain that I deeply believe can change the world. They are a set of skills and ways of being that, when cultivated and wielded unapologetically, might begin to shift the power structures that have caused so much harm to people and the earth alike. The MotherPowers are as old as the hills—ancestral, really—and accessing them isn't so much about learning something new as remembering something that lives somewhere inside of you, waiting to be awakened once more.

This is motherhood-as-revolution.

Are you in?

# 7

# Your MotherPowers

*What They Are,*
*Why They're Important, and*
*How You Can Cultivate Them*

I'm certainly not the first person to posit that motherhood endows us with myriad valuable skills and capacities. It's something anyone who's assuaged a grocery-store meltdown, fished a toy out of the toilet water, or had a tricky conversation with the mother of the kid their kid punched knows in their bones. It's the assertion of maternalism and of feminist philosopher Dr. Sarah Ruddick's theory of *maternal thinking*, which refers to the "intellectual capacities [a mother] develops, the judgements she makes, the metaphysical attitudes she assumes, the values she affirms."[1] Maternal thinking was directed toward three tasks, in Ruddick's perspective: preserving life, fostering the child's growth, and shaping an acceptable child.[2]

The focus of maternalism and maternal thinking was on the child and risks objectifying mothers as producers of future (hopefully upstanding) citizens rather than as humans with their own subjectivities. But as I alluded to in the last chapter, I'm pretty interested in the kinds of skills and capacities that support mothers' self-actualization as individuals and *also* have the power to allow us to step into positions of activism, leadership, and eldership in our communities.

Though there are likely many more, in my years of working with new mamas and other women traversing radical transformations, I have outlined seven key skills, powers, and areas of potential that I have witnessed so many mothers *gain access to* as a result of their matrescence. These are your MotherPowers.

They are:

Self-tending
Creativity
Embodiment
Ritual
Community
Inner knowing
Earth connection

Many of the MotherPowers are skills we cultivate because we've *never needed them more*. If we don't learn how to tend to our needs in meaningful, doable ways, for example, we're *going to* burn out. If we don't find a supportive community of like-minded others, we're far more likely to feel isolated and lost. If we don't make peace with and get to know our new motherbodies, we will live on feeling disoriented in our own skin. Motherhood lights the fire under our asses, as it were, to cultivate these skills—*or face the consequences*.

In other ways, motherhood is ripe with *potential* to explore our MotherPowers, but we might need a little nudge to recognize that potential. Inner knowing is an example of one of those Mother-Powers. With a gentle prompting to put down Grandmother Google and ask our intuition what we should do about our never-napping baby, we can unlock an entirely new way of knowing that will guide us throughout our mothering years and the rest of our lives, too.

Creativity is another one of these: motherhood is a creative act, by definition—but it also carries an enormous potential, if we recognize it, to enhance our creativity in our day-to-day lives. Whether it's by starting to write poetry again during nap times or finding a way to create a rewarding career that allows us to be home for bedtime, motherhood can be one of the most creatively inspired times of our lives.

I'll be abundantly clear that by no means are the MotherPowers exclusive to mothers. Motherhood is certainly not the only life experience that can support us to cultivate these critical capacities. In fact, though I first conceptualized the MotherPowers in my work with mothers, I have since applied them to my work with *all women* traversing life transitions, calling them the Seven Core Competencies of Radical Transformation. So it is that, as you read, I invite you to imagine how cultivating your MotherPowers may actually represent the development of a series of *metaskills* that can be applied to many areas of your life beyond motherhood and throughout the myriad transformations that will inevitably unfold for you.

This chapter will explore each of the MotherPowers in depth. Keep reading to learn about the seven skills and capacities, why they're important, and how to continue to use the opportunity of your motherhood to cultivate them more deeply.

### SELF-TENDING

Ignoring my needs [implies] that I am either superhuman,
sub-human or otherwise exempt from the laws of nature.
—Beth Berry, *Motherwhelmed*

The first MotherPower—arguably the foundation of all the other ones—is self-care, or what I call *tending* to yourself—more on that choice of words later.* Whenever you traverse a radical life

---

* A big shout-out, here, to my friend Mara Glatzel, who I credit with the use of the term "tending" in reference to the work of meeting our needs, and whose work is paving a new way of thinking about self-care.

transformation like matrescence, the experience is inherently dys-regulating to your nervous system. One of my teachers, coach and author Carolyn Coughlin, says that "your nervous system doesn't know if it's your identity that's at risk, or if it's your *life* that's at risk."[3] Our bodies respond to change like they respond to threat, with a sym-pathetic nervous system response of fight, flight, freeze, or fawn. This response may be further magnified if you are experiencing other stressors like caring for another child, dealing with inadequate childcare or a lack of supportive alloparents, birth trauma, and more. Let me be clear that self-care isn't a cure-all for these extremely complex circumstances—but it does certainly need to be a part of a multifaceted response.

The thing about self-care is that, not unlike resting during the Big Slowdown, it is something that many of us have a *really* hard time doing.

Caring for a wee babe, whether it's your first or your fourth, requires a whole lot of your time and energy, and there's often not a lot of said energy left over for *you*. There is a lot of wisdom in the clichés that you have to put your own oxygen mask on first, you cannot pour from an empty cup, and all that, but I also think that those placations fail to take into account the complexity of engaging in meaningful self-care as a new mother.

Self-care is an area of our lives that is often fraught with lots of shoulds—and the requisite guilt and self-judgment that come with them. I also think that our common definition of self-care is too simplistic and has been co-opted by capitalism such that self-care is something that you can just *buy*. But if self-care were just a matter of drawing yourself a bath and booking a pedicure, we'd all be doing it, right? And we'd all feel deeply satisfied after doing it, *right?*

In fact, ironically, attending to our own self-care has become a source of guilt and stress for so many mothers. It's become yet one more thing we need to try to get done. It becomes yet another emo-tional labor that mothers take on, and then, in failing to execute self-care in the way our culture tells us we "should" (cue the bubble bath), we feel like shit. Not just because we *need* self-care and aren't getting it, but because we feel like we're failing at the very fundamental act of keeping ourselves *okay*.

But here's the thing: in a culture that undermines women's sense of self-worth and value—and *especially* the self-worth and value of mothers—it's awfully hard to muster up the feeling that you actually *deserve* good care. Underneath the shoulds and the "why can't I just . . . ," there's likely an undercurrent of guilt at the idea of being *selfish* or that in caring for yourself you are not caring for the needs of your family—which couldn't be further from the truth, I'm sure I don't have to tell you.

But it's there.

And here's the other thing about self-care in new motherhood: the paradigm of what we have come to believe good self-care looks like is often categorically impossible when you're caring for a tiny human.

I want to tell you a little story about postpartum self-care and some potentially wildly unpopular ideas to go with it.

My client was one week postpartum. She was struggling with breastfeeding, and she and I were both pulling out all the stops to establish her milk supply and help her baby achieve a comfortable latch. She was healing from a very long and challenging labor and birth.

And she was booked for a pedicure, just a few days hence.

Her mother had agreed to look after the baby; her friends had all encouraged her and told her that she needed to take a little "me time." She should get away from her baby every so often. It was the healthy thing to do.

Shortly after her pedicure, my client planned to go on a date night with her husband. Her friends had all encouraged her and told her that she needed to take some time to be with her husband, just the two of them. She should get away from her baby every so often. It was the healthy thing to do.

First, let me take a minute and propose that wildly unpopular idea I promised you: as demonstrated in the case of my client, when you are, perhaps, healing from birth, struggling with breastfeeding, or outrageously sleep-deprived, self-care that takes you out of your home and away from your baby can actually end up being *more* stressful and harder on your body. Second, though time away from our kiddos is absolutely necessary, so much of our paradigm of postpartum self-care sees the presence of your baby and their demands on your time and body as being the thing that's clearly the Problem. I would argue that the Problem is that our culture no longer knows what it means to support women during matrescence. We are afraid of the messiness and vulnerability of new motherhood, and so we try to fix it, to tie it up in a nice little bow with ultimately counterintuitive and unhelpful suggestions, convinced that a little toenail polish will make everything about mothering in a broken culture okay.

I also believe that many mothers today suffer immensely during the postpartum period not because they haven't had a date night in months, but because we have also forgotten how to support women to *surrender to the transformation of motherhood.* So much of our paradigm of self-care for mothers sounds a lot like recommendations for trying to get back to one's old self. As I think we've wholeheartedly established, this may be a fool's errand, at least right now, and may cause more suffering than benefit.

I want to give you permission to question what society and your well-meaning mother-in-law might assume is the best self-care you can engage in. Your early postpartum is a season in your life. It is not permanent. Your toenails can wait. This is one of those times when surrender might be the more empowered choice. Surrender to the fact that you're stuck with a nursing baby in your arms more hours of the day than you can count. Use the time to count your breaths and count your blessings, if you can. Surrender to sleeplessness. Learn how to make great coffee. Surrender to the messiness of life, of your hair, of your scattered sense of self. Learn how to sink deeply into your own chaos and get comfortable there. As a mama, at least for now, it's your new home. I can guarantee you that learning to hold tight when the times get tough and being vulnerable enough to ask for help are the most exquisite self-care you can possibly have. This is the self-care of courage, of finding your inner strength. And it lasts a lot longer than nail polish.

## A Better Self-Care

The thing is, we all need a healthy dose of *actually helpful* self-care in our lives, and during times of transition, we need it even more. Matrescence is definitely, definitely one of these times. And now that I've totally dismantled the idea of the kind of self-care you've likely become accustomed to, I want to introduce you to a whole new kind of self-care practice. In my humble opinion, it's better than bubble baths and pedicures in every single way.

I call this practice *self-tending*.

Self-tending comes about thirty-seven steps before what we commonly think of as self-care. Whereas self-care is often focused on what you *want* or desire, tending is about your *needs*—first of all recognizing that you have them, second of all affirming that they are valid, and third, learning how to meet them.

If I may geek out on you for a moment: the philosophy of self-tending is rooted in attachment theory, a paradigm originally developed by psychologist John Bowlby to describe the attachment between a baby and their caregiver. If you've done any reading on attachment parenting in your motherhood journey so far, this won't be unfamiliar to you.

The essence of attachment psychology in reference to parenting is that a baby, unable to meet their own needs for nourishment, comfort, or a diaper change, for example, will cry out or otherwise let their caregiver know that they need some help. When they cry out, ideally their caregiver comes in and figures out what the baby's need is and then meets it in the best way they know how. When this happens over and over again in a baby's young life, that baby begins to develop a sense of what Bowlby describes as a "secure base" and "safe haven." In short, this means that the baby feels like someone's got their back and that, in fact, the world is a safe place to be.

The idea of self-tending takes this fundamental psychological construct of attachment and applies it to *ourselves.* Our bodies and hearts and minds call out to us a million times a day—maybe literally—for attention. Our bodies and hearts and minds may not cry like a baby, but the language of our own needs is alive and present within each of us.

But so many of us have forgotten the language of our own needs.

And so, so often, we ignore those needs. We leave our bodies and hearts and minds crying out, unmet in their longings.

Let's take a moment to explore a little bit about *why* we ignore our needs. There are potentially dozens of reasons: we're too busy; we've been conditioned to put everyone else's needs before our own; or there's no one to take up our other responsibilities while we make the time to meet our needs. But there's also another reason that is important to share.

When our needs haven't been met well—by ourselves or others—in our lives, we disconnect from those needs as a way to keep ourselves safe.[4] We subconsciously say: my needs won't get met, so it's better not to have needs at all. It's a beautiful strategy for keeping ourselves safer in a care-bereft environment, but it has long-term consequences. When we disconnect from our needs, the volume on our attachment system turns *waaaaay* down. Those cries that our babies—and our own bodies—know to make when they have a need? They become muffled into near-silence. In addition, these unmet childhood needs can cause us to develop what is called a *nourishment barrier.*[5] A nourishment barrier is an adaptive strategy that we develop when, somewhere in our psyches, we learn that it's not safe to receive care. And so it is that even when we are offered—or offer ourselves—attuned care, we cannot land it in our hearts and minds and nervous systems. It beads upon our unmet needs like oil on water, unable to sink in.

Something similar to the nourishment barrier may also happen when our nervous systems are under duress. Under stress, we develop a stronger negativity bias. Essentially, in a mechanism that worked really well when we ran the risk of being eaten by a saber-toothed tiger, our stressed-out bodies sense that there is danger in our midst and become hypersensitive to threat. What happens as a result is that we *only see threat.* We only see the hard things, the struggle, the impossibility—as if the gratitude and pleasure and joy switch has been turned off. This also makes it hard to really allow good care to sink into our bones and nourish us properly. As a new mother in today's modern context, it's probably safe to say that your nervous system might be a little jacked up these days—and so before sharing the ways you might begin to explore how to tend to your needs, I want to offer you a ton of compassion and space for this if it feels harder than it should. There's good reason for it, and it isn't because you're not *trying hard enough.*

So gently, tenderly, let's begin.

The best way to think about self-tending and beginning to relearn the art of meeting your needs is by first noticing your very basic, physical needs, like the urge to pee or being thirsty.

We—especially those of us conditioned as women—often manage to ignore even those most basic, fundamental, and pretty undeniable needs.

If you've ever put off peeing when you had to because you were needed by someone or something else, you know what I'm talking about. I use the example of peeing when you need to pee every time I teach about self-tending, and everyone laughs because almost *every* woman I know can relate to this. It's kind of funny-not-funny though, isn't it? We somehow manage to justify our way out of meeting *even our most primal bodily requirements.*

So let's start there. Let's start by peeing when you need to pee, and gradually build up your ability to meet your needs so that maybe, soon, you can begin to meet your more complex needs, such as the big gnarly emotions that surface as a part of our very normal human experience.

There are three basic steps to learn in your self-tending practice. The first step is to *recognize* that you are experiencing a need.

Though this may sound simple, for those of us who have been living disconnected from our bodies and in denial of our own needs, recognizing that you're experiencing a need is no small feat. So start with noticing that you need to pee or that you need a glass of water, and work your way on up until you're able to notice emotional needs like *I am feeling sad*. For needs that show up in your awareness that don't necessarily have a precise name like *I need to pee*, there is also a process of exploring how to appropriately *name* your need. This is especially true with emotional needs. For example, *I am feeling anger because my partner forgot to book the babysitter for date night* might *actually*, upon closer inspection, feel more akin to *I am feeling afraid that I will lose my connection with my partner*.

The next step in your self-tending practice is to *validate* the need that is being expressed in you. It goes something like this: *It's okay to pee when I need to pee*. Once you stop giggling, think of it this way: in saying this, you might also be saying to yourself, *It's okay to put the baby down, even if she cries for a moment, to pee when I need to pee*, or *It's okay to meet my own needs before I meet the needs of my family*.

Of course, validating an emotion you may be feeling is often more complex. In my own life, this is where I imagine that there's a beautiful fairy godmother within me with a warm and soothing voice who says things like, *Oh honey, motherhood takes a lot of energy. Of course you're tired. You're doing a great job. It's okay to feel overwhelmed*.

This is empathy in its purest form. If you've ever been in the same room with a toddler having a tantrum and you're about to throw up your hands in despair, it's often this fairy godmother voice of empathy that just causes all a child's big feelings to dissolve into thin air. *Oh honey, your sister broke your Lego creation. I can see you're feeling so mad right now! It's okay to feel mad!* Try it sometime; trust me.

Just as empathy and validation are like a magical incantation for soothing toddlers, so they are for soothing yourself. Sometimes, all your emotional needs require is just a sweet dose of honest, loving validation. This is *especially* true if what you're feeling is really complex or is laced with a bit of shame. *Oh sweetheart, it's okay to feel sad about motherhood sometimes. There are lots of things in your life that have been put on hold so that you can care for this little one. You are doing a beautiful job. You are beautiful. And it's okay to feel sad.*

The final step in self-tending is to *meet* the need that is being expressed in you, as best you can. Sometimes, meeting your need is simple: you pee when you need to pee or drink water when you're thirsty. Sometimes, though, it's more complex—meeting your own needs is always unique to you, and sometimes unique to every different occasion that need arises. For example, when you're feeling sad, sometimes the best way to meet that need is to have a good cry. Sometimes the best way to meet that need is to talk to someone you love or to go for a run. It's important to keep the dialogue with yourself open and flexible so that you can respond to your own needs as best you can.

I want to emphasize the *as best you can* part. Sometimes, we meet our needs "skillfully." A skillful way to meet sadness, for example, might be to allow yourself to cry. A skillful way to meet anger, for example, might be to scream into a pillow. But let's face it, when you're a new mama—or heck, when you're a *human*—sometimes you're not feeling well-resourced and resilient enough to meet your needs *skillfully*. Sometimes, the best you can do in that moment is to meet your sadness with a bag of chips or a shopping spree.

Can I be the first person to give you a huge permission slip to meet your needs imperfectly sometimes? To do your best, but sometimes not quite hit the mark?

Attachment theory posits that it matters more that babies are responded to in a loving way *at all* than it matters that they are *responded to appropriately*. In fact, some research indicates that babies only need to be responded to in an attuned way about 30 percent of the time in order for them to develop a sense of secure attachment.[6] This relates to pediatrician Dr. Donald Winnicott's concept of the "good enough mother," which affirms that you don't have to meet your baby's needs perfectly, just well enough.[7] Can we all breathe a sigh of relief here? And so if your baby is crying because they are hungry and you pick them up and, not realizing they are hungry, snuggle them and change their diaper instead, you are *still* contributing to their sense of secure attachment. Of course, they will eventually continue to express their need until you meet it *well*, just as your big emotions will continue to express themselves until they're released in a way that is truly satisfying. But for now, both in your care of your baby and in your care of yourself, know that doing the best you can with the resources and resilience you have available to you is *good enough.*

So why does self-tending matter, and why is it so much more powerful than self-care? Because every time you ignore your needs and throw the requirements of your own body, heart, mind, and spirit under the bus, you undermine your sense of self-trust. But when you begin to learn to meet your own needs, you begin to develop a schema of "secure base" and "safe haven" *within yourself.* You begin to know, in your very marrow, that you can trust yourself with your own needs. Over and over again, you show yourself, in tiny ways and in big ways, that you can respond to those needs—either meeting them yourself or asking others to help you meet them. And so, over time, not only are you a more well-nourished mama who's resilient and has more capacity to care for her baby and herself, but you may also feel more confident and more self-assured. It's from this place that you can explore the other MotherPowers—as well as other areas of potential and power in your life.

Within the concept of self-tending also lies one of the great—*perhaps most important and definitely most overlooked*—calls in the rite of passage into motherhood. It is not just the call to become a mother to a tiny little human. It's to become a mother to *ourselves.* It is a process that, for many women, begins with unearthing their own Mother Wound—and a decision to heal that relationship and to parent from that healed place—and ends with a shifting of the maternal figurehead away from one's mother and toward *oneself.* There is a tremendous freedom in this: it doesn't mean the end of your relationship with the mother figure in your life, but it does release her from your expectations of her mothering and allow her to *just be human.* And it allows you to develop the ability to meet your own needs in the way that you may have, even unconsciously, been looking to a mother figure to meet for you.

The deep sense of self-trust that this engenders is the birthplace of your ability to have your own back and know that you have the tools and the resilience to meet whatever the world throws at you.

And it all starts with peeing when you need to pee.

Note: The "Your Turn" section of this MotherPower is covered in the "Air" chapter. Perhaps you've begun a self-tending practice of identifying, validating, and doing your best to meet your needs already. If so, how is it going so far? If not, what is a need that you can identify in your heart, mind, or body right now? How could you go about validating and meeting that need as best you can?

## CREATIVITY

My muse wears a baseball cap, backward. The minute
my daughter is on the school bus, he saunters up behind
me with a bat slung over his shoulder and says oh so directly,
"okay, author lady, you've got six hours till that bus rolls back
up the drive. You can sit down and write, now, or you
can think about looking for a day job."
—Barbara Kingsolver

You have just created a human—or you're creating the conditions for that human to thrive. And so, despite the lack of sleep and time and enough strong coffee, welcome to the most creative time in your life. Time and time again, I witness mamas in their childbearing year decide to pick up their paintbrushes again or start writing prose in little notebooks while their babies sleep. I have also seen, over and over again, women gaining momentum, somehow, during the early years of their children's lives, to start businesses or creative projects on the side.

Truthfully, I've come to believe that mothers' creativity flourishes in part *because* of the sleepless nights and the general ennui of the day-to-day tasks of childcare: breastfeeding, changing diapers ad nauseam, and a great many games of peekaboo. These are the tasks of being over doing, the very essence of the Big Slowdown that so often makes us uncomfortable as mamas. But these tasks are also fertile ground for creativity. You've probably noticed that your creativity thrives after you've gone on a long walk in the woods or when you're in the shower. From a brain science perspective, these are times when our *default mode network* is activated—the part of our brains responsible for blue-sky, creative thinking.[8] It's a brain region that doesn't come online easily in the course of our overfull, hustle-driven days, but there is something about the way we spend our time in the early mothering years that activates our default mode network and invites our creativity out to play.

There's also something about the *constraints* of new motherhood—the extraordinary demands on our time and energy—that, paradoxically, support our creative life. I will never forget attending a writer's retreat back when my kids were seven and four years old. I was out of the early years of matrescence, to be sure, but my kids were young enough to still need a whole lot from me at any given time of day. The weeklong retreat was the longest I'd ever spent away from them. There were about thirty people attending, and of the group, I was one of the only ones with young children. I was also the *only* one with a regular writing practice: a ritual of showing up to put words on a page every day. Many of the attendees felt the acute pain of *identifying* themselves as writers—and so creating a life where that was their primary endeavor each day—but *not actually writing very much at all.* They had great expanses of time in which to create and yet somehow were not creating. The thing is, creativity thrives with limitations and boundaries, whether these are of time, context, content, or capacity. And the daily act of mothering is nothing if not a constraint to creativity that drives us mothers to use the precious time we *can* carve out exquisitely well.

Lucy Pearce, author of *The Rainbow Way: Cultivating Creativity in the Midst of Motherhood,* writes about a multitude of influences that might also factor into the surge of creativity so many women experience in matrescence: "The creative renaissance in new mothers is, I believe, the result of an incredibly complex, once-in-a-lifetime shift of the woman's hormonal, emotional, physical and psychological states, along with a total shift in her social role, responsibilities and daily routine. It is something which has not been researched . . . the coupling of increased creative brain activity (increased alpha and theta waves), powerful emotions, an awakening of forgotten memories and dreams, heightened intuition, decreased physical activity and raised hormone levels . . . that place her in the biologically optimal state for creative flow."[9]

I also believe that creativity awakens in new mamas in part because of the reorganization of our priorities that happens to so many of us when we make the transition into motherhood. Simply put: we become extremely motivated to create the lives that we want, ones that will support our mothering intentions and our families, and also create a world we want to raise our kids in. This *might* involve picking up your paintbrushes for the first time in over a decade or learning how to make artisanal sourdough, but often creativity might show up in the form of creating a business that allows you to be home with your child more, for example, or establishing a community group that is taking action on a social justice issue that is important to you.

So why does this creative surge that flows through women's bodies around the time they create and nurture life itself matter?

Creativity can support us through times of radical transformation like matrescence in three key ways. The first is that creative practice can be a conduit *back home to ourselves.* Through poetry or art or handcrafting, we may offer ourselves the vital opportunity to reconnect with who we are. Creativity also helps us to metabolize change. Particularly repetitive, meditative creative work like knitting, doodling, movement, or engaging in free-form writing can allow our minds the time and support they need to process, integrate, and help us to begin to make sense of ourselves and our lives now that *everything has changed.* Finally—and I've alluded to this already—creativity can support us to dream into the life we'd like to lead and the world in which we'd like to lead it. Through vision boarding or writing or collage, ideas and intentions for *who you're becoming* might nudge their way into your consciousness.

Despite its supportive potential, a great many of us have had our creativity quashed over the years. A few times a year, I host a pregnancy retreat. During the retreat, we spend a lot of time creating together: collages, paintings, journaling, group art. It's a way to tap into the space of being-over-doing that will serve mamas so well in labor and early motherhood. But more often than not, I see women picking up a paintbrush or holding a glue stick midair only to become completely paralyzed.

*What if it's not good enough? What if what I create doesn't look like what I have pictured in my mind? I'm not a creative person. I don't know how to paint. What if I do it wrong? What's the right way to do this?*

We can be immobilized—by our own perfection and expectations, by the teacher in grade school who gently told us we'd be better off sticking to math, by the rejected manuscript from ten years ago, by a culture that confuses the perfect with the good.

But here's the thing: the creative process is deeply counterculture, resplendent with cycles of ambiguity and clarity, nonlinearity, and more concern with process than outcome. In a world of goals and targets and bottom lines and protocol, the force of creativity is like a breath of fresh air. Channeling the creativity that is flowing through your body during the transformative years of early motherhood is a radical act. Creativity questions the way we've always done things and lives in the art of the possible. Creativity recognizes beauty as fundamental, not frivolous, and is the purveyor of joy. Most of all, creativity is the life force of all transformation (*including your own, yes?*), and so it is the power by which we change our lives *and* change the world.

## ✻ BIRTH OF A MOTHER ✻

I still myself so as to feel the edges of his little body and where they overlap the edges of mine.

One small leg is slung over my thigh, resting as heavily as a few pounds of soft flesh can.

His arm is curved over my breast, holding it in that gesture of both possessiveness and comfort, and his little fingers touch, the pad of each one, to the bareness of my shirt-lifted skin.

His body is close enough to mine that I can feel each inhale and exhale, the occasional shudder in between.

To my right, his sister. She is turned to face my love, her body merely a warmth next to me. My escape will only be encumbered by the unconsciously grasping limbs of one small child this morning.

When I lie with them in the evening, the sensations of entwined legs, fluttering fingertips, the even rhythm of inhale, exhale, inhale, exhale

is so toe-curlingly delightful

it is as though my blood has been replaced by light

and I could nearly hover above my own body with satisfaction and fullness and pure unadulterated love.

But in these wee morning hours, the very same entwined legs and fluttering fingertips feel like an ocean riptide, and I struggle to make my way back to shore.

And so I begin.

Slowly . . . so slowly . . . I pull back the blanket. Legs free, blanketed instead by the coolness of the nighttime bedroom.

A tiny wrist between my thumb and forefinger, gently raised off my breast and tucked alongside a fleece-jammied body.

I wait. Listen for a settling sigh.

A shimmy that has my heart in my throat, pounding: *please don't wake up!*

Wait. Silence again. The rise and fall of breath.

I pull the edge of my tee shirt so . . . so . . . so slowly from underneath him, and then I feel the release.

I am free.

I curse my separated abdominal muscles, still not healed two years postpartum, for not being strong enough to lift me up to a seated position. I must carefully place my hands on the mattress beside me, grateful for the invention of pillowtops and my ability to press myself up to sitting without moving the sleeping bodies surrounding me.

I duck low and roll off the bed.

*Like a goddamn ninja.*

The dog awakens and shakes, her collar jangling, and her arthritic body dragging and scratching across the carpet. I drop to the ground so I cannot be seen from the bed, and I think: *They should make camo for moms. Like, with Legos and uncapped markers, so we can blend in with the floor.*

The catching of breath and a soft "Mama."

*fuck fuck fuck*

I wait . . .

false alarm.

One arm, one leg, another arm, another leg, I crawl across the floor, avoiding the spots that creak. (*I know them, after so many failed attempts. But like the prisoner digging their way free with a spoon, I am nothing if not persistent.*)

Because on the other side of that door

is me.

Warm, milky tea. Flickering candle.

And The Muse.

She knows, now, to meet me here, on the other side of that door. She comes, I think, in a nod of sisterhood and solidarity, knowing what it took, how I maneuvered my way back to myself

not defined by where I feel the edges of their little bodies overlapping mine

but just
by
myself.
By myself.
She wraps me in the colored cloak of my own imagination
and escorts me quietly down the stairs and sits patiently, next
to my desk, while I do the work of
reclaiming myself
each morning.
Each morning, when the toe-curling pleasure of writing
my words is so delightful
it is as though my blood has been replaced by light
and I could nearly hover above my own body with satisfaction and fullness and
pure unadulterated love.

## YOUR TURN

. . . . . . . . . . . . . . . . . . . . . . . . . . . . . . . . . . . . . . . . . . . . . . . . . . . . . . . . . . .

*What role does creativity play in your life? Do you
consider yourself a creative person? Has there ever
been a time in your life when you engaged your
creativity on a regular basis?*

*What are your creative curiosities? Perhaps you love
making food, knitting, painting, or writing?*

*How might you channel your creative energy at
this time in your life? Remember, creativity can
encompass a broad range of activities, including
being creative in the way you spend time with
your child.*

. . . . . . . . . . . . . . . . . . . . . . . . . . . . . . . . . . . . . . . . . . . . . . . . . . . . . . . . . . .

## EMBODIMENT

Let's figure out how to help you make peace with
your body. We've got to host a reunion. Bring back
together your body, mind, and spirit. Vote your
body back on the island. Make you whole again.
—Glennon Doyle, *Love Warrior*

Motherhood changes our bodies.

It's for forever.

Despite what the magazines say.

As I've already explored earlier in this book, motherhood often brings us into a very complex relationship with our bodies—if you didn't already have one before you became a mother. First of all, in carrying, birthing, and nourishing our children, our bodies do this amazing thing. Most of us want to appreciate our bodies for this miraculous feat. And some of us really do. But if that process has resulted in difficulty or even trauma, as it does for an increasing number of birthing mothers today, your matrescence may be marked with a sense of dissociation from or even distrust of your body (see note for more).[10] We also experience an often-jarring loss of physical autonomy in motherhood and may feel "touched out" much of the time. Finally, carrying, birthing, and nourishing babies with our bodies often means that they don't fit into societally accepted standards of what good bodies look like anymore. Many mothers, in addition to traversing the tumult of identity shift and caregiving, take on a "third shift"—a nod to Arlie Hochschild's second shift of emotional and household labor—of body work, trying to reclaim or maintain their pre-motherhood body.

You may be experiencing one or all of these things in your new *motherbody*, but at the very least, because our bodies have become so very different than we once knew them to be, most mothers experience a sense of disconnection or disorientation in their own skin in the early weeks and months postpartum. We feel as though we're living in a whole new body.

But the fact is, we, as women and as human beings on planet earth right now, have become increasingly disconnected from our bodies, whether we're postpartum or not.

We live so much of our lives from the neck up—more than ever before in history. We are tethered to devices and bound up in a sense of constant low-grade stress and nervous system dysregulation that often makes it feel unsafe to be embodied.

And also this: we who are women live in bodies that have historically and systematically been commodified, controlled, pathologized, distrusted, and shamed. Those of us who have unruly bodies—bodies that don't fit into societal norms, standard-size clothing, medical models of what "healthy and functioning" look like, or who are not otherwise normalized and validated by the culture—feel this deeply.

All of this is to say that if you feel disconnected from your body as a woman—and now as a woman who happens to be a mother—know that you're not alone, and that it's not your fault. And it's also to say that matrescence *can be* as good a time as any to undertake the radically countercultural act of reclaiming your relationship with your body. We rarely have an experience so profoundly somatic as carrying, birthing, nourishing, and caring for a baby. In early pregnancy, we are thrust into a practice of tuning in to feelings of nausea, perhaps, or to what foods feel good and which ones feel bad. We are attuned to tiny movements and kicks as our babies grow, and gradually to the feelings of our bodies opening and preparing for birth. Once they are born, we feel our babies' cries in our chests, in our guts, in that fiery jolt that leaps us out of bed to attend to them. For a culture that spends so much time in our brains, pregnancy, birth, and mothering are a time of awakening to the presence and potential of our physical selves.

Part of the process of reclaiming your relationship with your body is to just *get to know it again* in a compassionate, nonjudgmental way. This is particularly true in the postpartum time when your body may not only look different but may also act differently: you may be more or less sensitive to certain foods; your metabolism may change;

your period, when it returns, will likely be different; your hair or your body odor may change. Reacquainting and reorienting yourself to your motherbody is the beginning of cultivating the MotherPower of embodiment and below, I will outline a few of the ways that I encourage you and the mamas I work with to do this. Note that each of these ideas could be a whole book in and of itself, and so this is an invitation to begin to explore what resonates and piques your interest.

Hopefully, by now, you are learning to respect your body's need for rest, getting comfortable with the Big Slowdown, and honoring that need as best you can while juggling the needs of a baby with different ideas about what your priorities should be. Honoring rest is a beautiful place to start when it comes to reconnecting and reuniting with your body.

As you learn the terrain of the skin you're in, you can explore how your body likes to be nourished and how it likes to move, eating and exercising in a way that feels intuitive to you. This is a time ripe with the potential to use your increased attunement to your body to trust and follow its cues rather than the restrictive rules set forth by diet culture. Okay, seriously: this is my nice way of saying please, please let your matrescence be the time when you finally, once and for all, give the finger to the misogynistic patriarchal bullshit of diet culture and run, as fast and as far as you can in the other direction—in the direction, perhaps, of *yourself,* as worthy and beautiful because of your *humanity,* not because of the size of your jeans.

You could also start to explore the language of your nervous system, learning skills and practices that can help you feel more regulated and resilient. Though the theory behind them is complex, nervous system regulation practices are often quite simple. For example, to support yourself to downregulate when you're feeling activated, you can simply land your gaze on something in front of you and, in your mind, "notice and name" what is there. For example, right now, I see my mug of tea. I notice the light blue-gray color and the wavelike swirls sculpted in the clay. If I stay here in this moment of noticing, I can also name the way the light hits the curve of the mug and the little flecks of loose-leaf tea along the rim.

By doing this, I slow down and orient to my surroundings, which my nervous system registers, at this moment, as safe. As a result, my body may show signs of downregulation with the emission of an involuntary sigh, perhaps, extra salivation, tummy grumbles, or a yawn.[11]

You may, once your menstrual cycle returns, want to explore the rhythms and cycles of your body, noticing how your energy, creativity, and emotion shift over the course of the month. You might even observe the many ways in which your body is perfectly in sync with nature, waxing and waning with the moon. To take it one step further, you could start to shape some aspects of your life around your cycle. For example, I know that my energy is high when I ovulate, and so this is a good time for me to clean out the shed or launch a new program. In contrast, my energy is really low—and so is my self-esteem—right before I menstruate, so it's a time to rest more, let the kids have more screen time than usual, and stay the heck off social media.

You can also begin to listen to the messages of your body and its inherent wisdom when it comes to being intimate with your partner. Never in your relationship will sex be more of a negotiation than it is with a new baby in the house, and most women notice that their desire fluctuates significantly within the context of sleeplessness, their changing bodies, and the sheer demands of a young child. In a world that has taught us that women's sexuality should mimic men's sexuality, this cyclical, deeply context-dependent desire is an invitation to explore what *authentic intimacy* might look like: a way of relating to your partner that is authentic to your own body's needs and desires, not some arbitrary number of times per week—that is best, "experts" say, *scheduled into your calendar.*

Finally, so many of our feelings, our intuitions, and our physical and emotional experiences are held in our bodies. We get a little flip-flop in our stomachs when something feels scary, or a tightening in the chest when we're overwhelmed. We can feel expansiveness in our heart and sureness in the soles of our feet. In this way, our bodies are like canaries in the coal mine when something isn't right and barometers for what good feels like. Our bodies are rich with messages for us, if only we learn to tune in. We'll dive deeper into this in the MotherPower of inner knowing.

All of this is yours to explore in your motherbody. You have an opportunity now, perhaps more than ever, when your body feels so different and while the experience of mothering is so *embodied*, to reconnect with your body and maybe even with its inherent power.

Because here's the thing: after fifteen years of supporting birthing women, I have come to know that our bodies *are*, in so many ways, *the source of tremendous power*. Our bodies are where we birth creative ideas and babies alike, they are intuitive and resilient and connect us with the earth we walk on every day. Our bodies beg us to return home to them, to silence the loathing we feel and become enchanted with the unique language they've been using to speak their wisdom to us from the day we were born.

This is, like all of the MotherPowers, not only a move toward your own well-being, but also a radical act of reclaiming your worthiness and humanity.

Welcome to your motherbody, mama. It is your home; it is your MotherPower.

## YOUR TURN

*How has motherhood impacted your relationship with your body?*

*Exploring the MotherPower of embodiment is the perfect place to begin a practice of self-tending. Your body is resplendent with messages for you— some urgent and some subtle—about what it needs. What does your body need right now? When you sit quietly and listen, what is your body calling out to you for?*

*We often have a great many judgments or percep-*
*tions about our bodies—and those judgments are,*
*for many of us, negative. But reuniting and recon-*
*necting with your body is about learning the truth*
*of the skin you're in, not necessarily the beliefs you*
*have about it. And so here, write a list of things that*
*you know to be true about your body—not judg-*
*ments or beliefs, just truths. You can write a list as*
*long as your arm if you like, but also don't be sur-*
*prised if it's challenging, especially if you are feeling*
*disconnected from your body or if thinking in a neu-*
*tral way about your body is new for you. Start with*
*simple truths—like, what color your eyes are or*
*what kinds of movement feel good in your body.*

............................................................................................

## RITUAL

Ritual is another key skill that mothers can cultivate as they traverse
matrescence. Although ritual isn't necessarily one of those Mother-
Powers that can naturally evolve when our babies are born, like embodiment, perhaps, motherhood is still a time ripe with potential to
create ritual to support our lives—and those of our children, too. You
may already have engaged in rituals surrounding your matrescence,
like a baby shower, mother blessing, or babymoon. Or perhaps you
are engaging in tiny rituals, like the hug that you share with your
partner in the morning that reminds you both, even in the thick of
it all, that you're still there for each other, or the way that you put
your baby to sleep. Babies and children are the masters of ritual—
and tend to benefit deeply from its rhythm and predictability. You
can benefit deeply from ritual, too: rituals offer us stability and the
opportunity to reflect on and sync up with the new reality of our lives
during times of radical transformation.

I like to think of ritual as a way to put a pin in the map of our lives
and say, "this matters"—a way of marking the important moments
in our days, seasons, and years.

We humans are and have always been ritual beings. Cultures and traditions around the world, historic and present, mark the meaningful moments of people's lives with ritual. Many cultural worldviews would argue, in fact, that major life transformations like matrescence cannot be considered complete until they are marked with ritual. But a lot of us in modern Western culture have lost connection with the rituals of our lineages. Mythologist and psychologist Sharon Blackie, PhD, has a name for this, calling those of us who experience this loss "cultural orphans."[12] As a result, many of us find ourselves outsourcing the rituals of birthday parties, retirements, and weddings to Pinterest—or worse, appropriating the rituals of lineages that are not our own. And so, despite the almost magnetic pull we have to make meaning of our lives through ritual, our earnest attempts fail, ultimately, to do the important work of allowing us to pause and take stock of our experiences, transition from one phase of life to another, and to mourn, honor, and celebrate it all along the way.

In the following paragraphs, I'm going to share more about how ritual works as well as some examples of how I've woven meaningful ritual into my mothering life, and in the "Your Turn" section, I will offer you a process to help you create your own.

There are two types of ritual, both of which I've already alluded to in this section: regular, everyday rituals like the particular way you brew your coffee in the morning and one-off transformative rituals like weddings, baby showers, and funerals.

Creating ritual can seem a little daunting, but as one of my teachers, death doula Sarah Kerr, PhD, puts it, ritual doesn't have to be all *bells and smells*.[13] It can be incredibly simple.

One of my very favorite rituals that I engage in every single day is one I began when I was home with a baby and a toddler and feeling stretched thin with the physical and emotional demands of the day. There was little to no time for what we typically think of as self-care—no hour to spend in the bathtub, and walks in the forest often only happened with a baby strapped to my chest, nursing the entire time. At that time, although a pedicure would have been lovely, I was deeply in need of the most basic self-tending, like drinking enough water throughout the day.

And so I created a ritual for drinking water. Instead of chugging back my eight-ish glasses per day without thinking, I would pause before I took a sip and just say to myself, *This is self-care*, and *This is nourishment*.

In effect, I *made meaning out of the moment* that I drank water each day. This took it from being simply a *routine* to being a *ritual*.

And true to Pavlovian form, I began to believe it. I began to *feel* really nourished—like I had the capability of looking after myself, *too*, even in all the chaos of being at home with two kids all day. In fact, the association that grew, for me, between drinking water and feeling nourished became so strong that I began to seek out a simple glass of water whenever I was feeling stressed out or sad.

Another favorite ritual of mine began when I started to get a little more autonomy as my mothering years progressed and I would go on a walk every morning before my husband left for work and my full-time mothering role commenced. Let me be clear that it was nothing short of monumental for me to orchestrate and plan this walk to make sure I was able to do it every day! But moving my body in a way that felt nourishing each morning was what I needed—and continue to need—the most. The last stretch of my walk takes me along the beach near my house, and so I began choosing a shell or a rock each time I completed my morning walk as a way of recognizing that I showed up for myself that day. Over time, I amassed proof—in the form of a growing pile of beautiful beach finds—that I actually *could* care for myself and tend to my own needs.

These two rituals are everyday ones—the kind that weave a familiar pattern of meaning and reflection into the fabric of our lives. Everyday rituals can be used to honor and be more intentional in our intimate partnerships, in our creative practices, or in the times that we connect with the communities and people that we love, for example. Especially when motherhood feels overwhelming or when one day seems to blur into the next, it is so nourishing to have the anchor of ritual in our lives to help us to pause, take notice, and reconnect with ourselves and what's most important to us.

Larger, transformative rituals have an important place in our matrescence as well. I'm guessing it's unlikely that the "pin the excrement on the diaper" game you played at your baby shower had any impact on your smooth transition to motherhood, but, done right, rituals can help you honor the life that you are leaving behind and welcome who you are becoming. Not only that, but these kinds of rituals carried out in the presence of loved ones help a mother feel deeply *witnessed* and held in her transformation, with people present to remind her of how well she is supported.

My friend Becca Piastrelli, author of the book *Root and Ritual,* told me the story of her mother blessing. Organized by a few friends and a community elder, Becca was asked to share the fears she had of motherhood before the ceremony began. Once everyone had gathered in a circle, each guest affirmed the validity of these fears and spoke blessings over them: *We hold you in your fears, and may they not come to pass.* Then, Becca's mother, holding a picture of her grandmother in a representation of her matrilineage, shared the story of Becca's birth. In a symbolic gesture, Becca then turned away from her mother and walked through a tunnel of roses created by her friends as they held the flowers high above her head. She exited the tunnel into the waiting arms of two friends who were mothers, who wrapped her in the warm embrace of a shawl, representing motherhood.[14]

Becca's ritual put a pin in the map of this tender moment before she became a mother, ritually and symbolically preparing her and her community for her birth and matrescence. Though many of the rituals I've shared in this section have had their roots in the pragmatics of self-tending or cultivating greater intentionality, what I have come to know about ritual is this: it is filled with mystery and magic, and sometimes, when all the "logical," material responses to our transforming lives come up short, ritual is just the medicine we need to support us.

I hope, upon reading this, you are beginning to see how ritual can be an incredibly powerful and meaningful way to support yourself through matrescence—and that you feel empowered to reintroduce and reclaim ritual as a tool for reflection and transformation in the wider world of your family and community.

## YOUR TURN

When I'm guiding people in the process of ritual design, we focus on two primary steps followed by four key considerations that enrich and enliven your ritual.

The first step is to decide what in your life is calling out to you for a ritual and what your ritual is *about*. See if you can sum up the intention or purpose for your ritual in one word.

For example, perhaps you want a way to mark your transition into motherhood, and so you want to create a mother blessing ritual that is about "beginning." My morning ritual is about "self-connection." Other ritual intentions might be release, celebration, honoring, completion, or healing, for example. A strong and clear intention is the root structure of your ritual, so it's worth taking the time to contemplate, really considering what your ritual *means* to you and why it matters.

The second step in designing your ritual is to brainstorm what processes or symbolic actions come to your mind when you think of the intention you've just set.

For example, when I think of beginnings, I think of planting seeds or stepping over thresholds. For me, a ritual of celebration *must* include cake and community. This part of your ritual design process is wildly creative and benefits from mind maps and friends to brainstorm with. It's also the *most important* step to creating a ritual that is authentic to you and that actually functions in the way a ritual should: to be so meaningful and resonant that its intention lives on in your body, mind, and spirit, even after the candles are blown out. In other words, if full moons and bonfires don't spring to mind when thinking about creating a releasing ritual or seeing how fast you can put a diaper on a doll at your baby shower doesn't float your boat, then this is your chance to make this process your very own.

From this second step, you should have a pretty good idea of what you will do to enact your ritual. Now, here are some questions for you to consider that will help you build on this to create a meaningful, memorable moment.

1. *Is your ritual a regular one that you repeat on a daily, monthly, or seasonal basis? Or is it a single event? Either way, the timing of your ritual—whether it's in the morning before the baby wakes up, on an anniversary of some kind, or on the full moon— can be just as meaning-laden as your ritual itself.*

2. *How does your ritual begin and end? Traditionally, the time and space inside of a ritual process was thought of as "nonordinary," where the preoccupations of day-to-day life fall away and the intention of your ritual is the solitary focus. And so, it helps to demarcate this space with an action—as simple as lighting a candle as you begin and blowing it out afterward or reciting a prayer or poem to begin and end your ritual.*

3. *How can you incorporate as many of your five senses into your ritual process as possible? Without overcomplicating your ritual or crowding out your original intention with "bells and smells," how might you weave a few sensory elements into your ritual process so that you may feel its intention in a deeply somatic way?*

4. *What support do you need to enact your ritual? Perhaps you need your partner to take the baby for a few hours, your friend to photograph it, or even*

*just someone to hold space for you afterward, sup-
porting you to integrate the power of the process.
Ritual is often also an act of community building—so
go ahead and ask for the support of your loved ones.*

And presto! You have a ritual! I kid, a little: though your
ritual may come together quickly and with ease, it's also
okay to take your time to consider all of these steps as you
dream up your ritual process. In a way, the energy and intention behind your ritual build in the time you take to prepare
for it. Think of a wedding: even though it's a fairly simple
ritual of rings and vows, the weeks, months, and sometimes
years of planning leading up to it imbue that simple moment
with so much potency that it might just be one of the most
important and meaningful rituals of your life.

......................................................................

## COMMUNITY

Even if you have had the most wonderful mother in the world,
you may eventually have more than one. And among them all
you will find most of what you need. Your relationships with
todas las madres, the many mothers, will most likely be ongoing
ones, for the need for guidance and advice is never outgrown,
nor should it be . . . there are no two ways about it: a mother must
be mothered in mothering her own offspring. She does not just
suddenly become a fully formed temporal mother all by herself
. . . for eons this role was served by the older women of the tribe
or village. These human "goddess mothers" constituted an
essential female-to-female nutritional system that nourished
the young mothers in particular, teaching them how to
nourish the psyches and souls of their young in return.
—Clarissa Pinkola Estes, *Women Who Run With the Wolves*

A new mother's most valuable resource is the community she sur-
rounds herself with.

Hands down.

We were never meant to mother in isolation. In her book *Mothers and Others*, anthropologist and primatologist Sarah Blaffer Hrdy, PhD, makes this abundantly clear. As I shared earlier, human babies, born relatively helpless, require more calories to stay alive than a sole foraging mother could provide.[15] Humans are also "reproductively hyperburdened," with the ability to have closely spaced offspring.[16] Both of these facts mean that we evolved to be social creatures so we could garner the assistance of alloparents in the community. Evidence of this evolution is obvious even in the instincts and physiology of modern humans: our babies are cute and loud, and, in so being, have ways of getting the attention of not just their mothers but others around them who can help assure their survival. The regions of our brains activated by helping others are the same regions of the brain that are activated when we experience other pleasures. We are literally wired for the empathy and altruism characteristic of what anthropologists call "pro-social engagement."[17] Interestingly, Hrdy also posits that the primacy—and sometimes tumultuousness—of friendships among girls and young women may even be ancestral. The creation and maintenance of friendships as well as the forging of a sense of belonging to the community during these years may mean the difference between life and death for a young hunter-gatherer woman's future offspring.[18]

What would our ancestors say about the villageless intensive mothering that many of us find ourselves engaged in now? Hrdy writes that "continuous care and contact mothering is a *last resort* for primate mothers who lack safe and available alternatives."[19]

Oof.

It wasn't always like this—nor is it currently like this for some mothers. Before industrialization and the privatization of the home, we mothered in community, much like our ancestors did. Rich writes about this phenomenon extensively in her book *Of Woman Born*, citing that this shifted by the mid-twentieth century when the mass movement out into the suburbs that income increases allowed meant that mothers became more isolated within their homes.[20] As Margaret Mead said, "Nobody has ever before asked the nuclear family to live all by itself in a box the way we do. With no relatives, no support, we've been put in an impossible situation."[21]

This phenomenon was (and is) one occurring most markedly among white families. In contrast, many Black families hold values around interdependence and what Black maternal theory scholars call "other-mothering." Social scientist Stanlie James, PhD, defines other-mothering as "acceptance of responsibility for a child not one's own, in an arrangement that may or may not be formal."[22] As I've shared earlier, in many ways, Black values around other-mothering came out of necessity, because the majority of Black mothers have always worked and have always needed support with childcare.

If you are a mother who lacks a sense of community in her life, reclaiming "the village" isn't as easy as just calling up a few friends. Well, maybe—I mean, I hope it is for you. But there are a few things that can get in the way of the kind of pro-social engagement we long for.

Isolated within the tiny worlds of our nuclear families, our single-family homes, and the increasingly private experience of getting up, going to work, coming home, and watching TV until we fall asleep, many of us have come to live in an incredibly hyperindividualistic culture. Those of us who can afford it have become accustomed to paying for the services that community would have otherwise provided: rather than other-mothers, for example, we pay babysitters and childcare workers. The exquisite sense of generosity and reciprocity inherent in community care has been replaced by the transactional trappings of capitalism. I'll never forget when, upon dropping some food off for a friend in need many years ago, she looked at me quizzically and said, "What do I owe you?" Relatedly, we've lost the art of the drop-in and forgotten how to track who among our friends and kin might need a casserole or their lawn mowed or their children cared for for a few hours. Now, we must wield our calendars and find a tiny slice of time when we're not busy—*you know, three weeks hence.* In our culture, we've also lost the art of truly holding space and deeply listening when we *do* connect with others. So often, we interrupt and try to one-up each other or formulate our clever responses without truly paying attention to the human in front of us.

Another factor at play in our ability to locate and benefit from community has to do with our attachment styles. A study on women's thriving during the transition to motherhood found that mothers with a secure attachment pattern perceive more available support and are more likely to seek support than mothers with insecure attachment patterns.[23]

Finally, as I shared earlier in the book, we are particularly vulnerable to identifying with and locating ourselves in communities based around mothering ideologies like "natural parenting," "gentle parenting," or "attachment parenting," among others, when we are in the early days of matrescence. While there is absolutely nothing wrong with these practices—I am a self-professed advocate for all of them, in the right dosages!—we can begin to mistake them for our *identities*, especially when we feel as though we've lost our pre-motherhood identity. These ideologies and communities fail us when we have trouble living up to their standards, which, inevitably, we do.

Mothering ideologies come part and parcel with the rise of intensive parenting in our culture and the myth of the "perfect mother," both of which have a lot to answer for when it comes to our modern villagelessness. The American Time Use Survey reports that in 1965, before women were as active in the workforce as they are now, mothers spent *fewer* hours per week on childcare than they did in 2012.[24] As Jennifer Senior writes in her book *All Joy and No Fun*, "Today, parents pour more capital, both emotional and literal, into their children than ever before, and they're spending longer, more concentrated hours with their children than they did when the work day ended at five o'clock and the majority of women still stayed home."[25]

There's a somewhat horrible irony here: culturally, the demands of motherhood have gone way, way up while the presence of alloparents and other helpers to share the load with has gone way, way down. What's more is that our culture of perfection surrounding motherhood makes it awfully hard to get help. With all compassion to those of us who feel this way—like I did for many, many years, and sometimes still do—it can seem terrifying to let go of the reins of perfect parenting and hand them over to someone else. We've been told, over and over again, that there's a "right" way to parent, and that doing it the "wrong" way will result in certain disaster for our little ones (see note for more).[26] What if the babysitter lets the baby cry too long? What if Grandma gives Junior a chocolate bar? And there's also this: the "perfect mother" is a mask that we wear that covers up our vulnerability and our humanity. Quite frankly, it's impossible to make genuine friends when you're not being authentic. Even if we are surrounded by community, striving for perfection will always keep us separate from each other and parenting in isolation.

Our modern antidote to our post-village culture is the "mommy group." In her book *The Mamas: What I Learned about Kids, Class, and Race from Moms Not Like Me*, Helena Andrews-Dyer shares her experience of navigating belonging in a local mommy group. She writes: "Sprouting up mostly in urban centers, since those spaces are the most devoid of family support, mommy groups can be the surest path to a parenting community. But you can't always find your kind in those spaces. It's tough. They have totally earned the reputation of being performative, competitive and judgmental. . . . Other mothers—Black, younger, working class—often don't find them to be safe or nurturing spaces, so they 'opt out.'"[27]

And yet . . .

There is something that an actually supportive group of mothers who are all going through or have gone through a similar experience offers you that is different from any parenting book or prenatal class or well-intentioned mother-in-law in the world. Not only are they able to listen to you when you need to vent, but they are also able to provide (ideally) nonjudgmental support. As a mother, you're likely doing enough self-judging and criticizing: the last thing you need is the unsolicited two cents of your supposed support people. This is the work of holding space for you as you transition into motherhood: just being there for you, allowing you to be in this process and holding a reassuring presence as you speak words to the magnificent highs and chest-heaving lows of motherhood. In this way, those who support you are able to *witness* you deeply in this transformative time in your life. In many traditional cultures, a rite of passage wasn't considered to be complete until the initiate had been *witnessed*. Though I'll share more about this in the final section of the book, in short, a witness is able to see us—truly *see* us—and all the ways we've changed and are becoming more and more ourselves in our new role.

The other thing a community of other mothers can offer you is a massive dose of normalization, which is something everyone needs as they navigate the journey of matrescence. With the loss of the village, we've lost our ability to socially reference our mothering experience in a healthy, nuanced way—like, through conversations, not through Instagram.

It looks like:

*"Oh my goodness, no. My baby didn't sleep through the night until she was almost four years old. I found this great locally roasted coffee though! Can I bring you a bag?"*

AKA: This is totally normal. You and your baby are normal.

*"I totally lose my shit on my kids every so often, too. Sometimes I yell. It makes me feel terrible, also. But I find that an apology and a good cuddle afterwards do wonders. And sometimes, it's because I need a bit of time away, or need to think about why I'm feeling so frustrated or angry."*

AKA: This is totally normal. You are normal. Bonus: You are not a bad mother.

*"I sometimes dream of the days before I was a mother too. I miss them a lot. I just wish I could pee alone or not have a baby attached to me all the time! But, it does pass, and I've been able to do some of the things I used to love doing again."*

AKA: This is totally normal. You are normal. You are not a bad mother.

Normalization is not just a form of emotional support: it's no less than the offering of a sense of belonging to all the other mothers in the world who have also done this and who have also wondered if they're okay.

When I was pregnant with my first baby, I knew all of this, and I knew that it was imperative for me to "find my village," as it were. I was living thousands of miles away from family, and most of my friends were fellow scuba instructors and master's students. In other words, they didn't really *get it*. I felt really lost as to who I could turn to for help. And that's one of the paradoxes of the work of building your village: you've never needed your support people so much, and yet the people who supported you in the weeks, months, and years leading up to your transition to motherhood aren't always the same people who will be your supportive community afterward. Indeed, during any kind of radical transformation in your life, when you find yourself asking, *Who am I now?* you will also, inevitably, find yourself asking, *Where do I belong now?*

Though becoming a mother usually represents a significant shift in your community of support, which can invoke feelings of loss and sadness as you bid some formerly supportive relationships "bye for now," it can also be the opportunity of a lifetime, unveiling an entirely new network of connections with other women who totally get you and who are deeply supportive of you as you traverse matrescence.

You see, I can't help but view this dire state of our support networks as a blank slate from which we get to build community that feels most meaningful and relevant and supportive to us now, as modern mothers seeking the village—the ancient idea of which is inscribed in our bones.

That's why I see community as a MotherPower: you have never had a stronger imperative than you do *right now* to begin to create the social structures you need to mother well—and *be* well.

Over the next few pages, I will share with you some of the ways that you can create stronger support networks, including by contributing to your community and by learning how to effectively ask for help.

Although I certainly haven't gotten this locked down, there is one rule of thumb I've followed as I've endeavored to create community in my own life and guided other women to do the same for themselves. It is: *create what you crave.*

Or, as Gandhi put it: *Be the change that you want to see in the world.*

Before I go on, I just want to say: I know. You're already doing a tremendous amount of emotional labor to support yourself and your family in these wonderful and challenging early years. I know. And although you may be lucky enough to happen upon or already be a part of a community who loves and supports you, if you're like me, you may indeed be faced with creating it yourself.

As I contemplated the question of community in my own life, I noticed I was craving what I've come to call *unconditional support.* It's not the highly orchestrated playdates where calendars and pencils are wielded and days and times and places thrown around and soccer practices rescheduled. Unconditional support is the kind of support that you can call on at three o'clock in the morning, when you have to take your croup-y baby to the emergency room and someone needs to stay home with the toddler. Unconditional support shows up when it's needed—and even when it's not. And there's usually a far higher threshold of acceptable snot and tears in a relationship that includes unconditional support.

Most of us expect only to receive unconditional support from our closest family members. But with more of us living farther and farther away from that kind of community, it behooves us to expand our networks.

I began thinking about the concept of unconditional support when my daughter was two years old, I was pregnant with my son, and my husband was deployed for six months overseas. It was probably one of the darkest times in my mothering experience so far, when I was too tired and emotional to parent my daughter, who was going through the typical—and often deeply frustrating—process of, well, being a toddler.

I was sitting on the couch at the time of my revelation in unconditional support, my rear firmly implanted in the deep indentation created there during my first maternity leave; a year of nursing a baby to sleep, it seemed. I had a pilling, well-loved crocheted blanket over my legs, and it covered the tiny, endlessly bouncing legs of my daughter as well. We were one sentence into her favorite book, and I was crying, ceaselessly, bitterly, and pathetically, as I tried to pretend that I was fine and that I could eke out the words of the story I was reading without choking on them.

I distinctly remembered the words of my friends and colleagues echoing through my mind during this time:

*"Call if you need anything."*

*"Let me know if there's anything I can do."*

If you're like most others, you've uttered these words many times before, directed with varying levels of sincerity toward family, friends, and acquaintances. Those you've offered to support will never call, and you will assume that they do not need your help.

What I've learned is that probably the opposite is true. When I was feeling most desperate, I struggled with finding a safe way to expose my vulnerability, possibly dissolving into gasping tears on the phone as I asked a friend to walk my dog that day. Many days I was so low, so despairing, that I couldn't even begin to articulate what kind of help I needed. But I knew, deeply, that I couldn't go on without some kind of support.

What I needed was for someone to just *show up at my door* with a container full of soup. Maybe they would come in, play with my daughter for a while as I napped, or maybe just make a cup of tea and sit with me, keeping me company for a while.

I needed someone not to proffer a general offer of support, not to wait for me to swallow my own vulnerability and tears and ask, and certainly not to scold me for not calling when I needed help. *I needed someone to assume that I needed help, and simply offer it, without asking, without judging.*

Perhaps it feels chivalrous, offering help where maybe none is needed. But I assure you, chivalrous support does not feel like a judgment on a person's abilities or situation. It feels *unconditional.*

It opens up the door for a person to ask for help again. It preserves a person's dignity, not having to risk tears when they finally pick up the phone and ask you to walk their dog—when they finally pick up the phone and admit they can't do it all, not even part of it, and they're not doing okay.

And so it is that after this challenging season of my life drew to a close, I started a practice of dropping by friends' and clients' houses with jars of homemade granola, or soup, or a cup of takeout coffee from the local café. I like to think that in "creating what I crave," I am contributing to a sort of microculture within my community that has a shared language of generosity and reciprocity.

This story begs the question that so many new mothers ask me: How do you create and care for community—how do you create what you crave—when you can barely care for yourself? When *you* are the one needing care? This is something I've thought deeply about and have talked to many experts on community building about, and as far as I can tell, there's no hack for it. I also believe that the times we're living in are not getting any easier, and the old adage of never pouring from an empty cup is not going to continue serving us much longer. If we all wait until we are fully resourced and have capacity to help others, we will continue to live lives of isolation. What I have also found, though, is that even when I am at my most underresourced, I am able to offer *some kind* of support to my community. For example, I have a little reminder in my phone that pings every week to nudge me to text a few friends to see how they're doing. It takes me just a few minutes. When I'm able to offer more support than that, I do, but I try to make my weekly text-fest my bare minimum. Interestingly, I also find that though I have a narrative that supporting others is an energy *expenditure* on my part—and subsequently convince myself I don't have the energy for that kind of thing—the truth is I usually find it life-giving. One of my dear teachers, somatics coach and trauma repatterning practitioner Carmen Spagnola, reminded me once that people actually love to be "spiritually employed."[28] People love to be a listening ear, to send flowers, drop off the lasagna, or show up to the ritual. Like our pro-social ancestors, we feel good when we help. So it may be, too, for you.

So far I've focused on what you can offer your networks of support as you work to create community. But asking for help builds community too: it offers our people the opportunity to be spiritually employed and to positively impact our lives. Even though I've posited that truly unconditional support might offer us what we need *without* us having to ask for it, I also deeply believe that we have a responsibility, as people who want and desperately need community, to do our best to figure out what we need and how to ask for it. Being able to *articulate* your needs is an act of respect for those who might wish to help us. We can be transparent and in deep integrity with our request, asking for exactly what we need—no more and no less—and, in so doing, letting our potential support person know what they are committing to. I *love* being told, in response to my offer of support, *Why yes, Jessie, I really need someone to walk my dog on Wednesday. It takes about an hour.* What a gift being clear about your needs is to the potential giver! What a gift to know not only what is expected of you but that you're helping with *the exact thing* someone needs (not, say, dropping off a lasagna to the dairy-intolerant, for example). Articulating your needs when you're feeling underresourced is a skill, and it's not always easy—as I demonstrated wholeheartedly in my story about my second pregnancy. Thankfully, you might be getting some practice at this after having read the self-tending section of this book.

It's also important here to mention the idea of what I call *nonlinear reciprocity* when it comes to offering and receiving community support. Nonlinear reciprocity moves away from the transactional support that we tend toward in our culture—I help you, you help me; I help you, you owe me one. Instead, nonlinear reciprocity imagines that I might receive a lot of support when I am in need and offer little in return, but that receiving that support might position me to help someone else in my community. I "pass it on."

*All* of this work of revillaging and engaging in community care is *deeply* countercultural. You've probably noticed a pattern, by now: the MotherPowers, by definition, are not only helpful to your individual experience of matrescence, but they subvert and disrupt the culture that makes it so impossible to mother—and heck, be a human—in our modern times.

The editors of *Revolutionary Mothering* propose that "there will be no liberation without us knowing how to depend on each other, how to be encumbered with and responsible for each other."[29] Being *encumbered with* each other is the polar opposite of the hyperindividualistic paradigm most of us have been steeping in. In fact, it is being encumbered with the needs of your baby that may be the most challenging aspect of new motherhood, for you and for so many other mothers like you. But in the challenge of this encumbrance is also one of the gifts of matrescence. Mothering asks us to decenter ourselves and our individualistic propensities and put someone else's needs above our own. This doesn't necessarily mean we're trapped under the expectations of self-sacrifice inherent in patriarchal motherhood. It may simply mean that we're being asked to give up a hearty few teaspoons (cups?) of our autonomy in favor of relationality and interdependence.

Throughout this book so far, I've shared with you many ways in which matrescence *grows us up*, offering us experiences that demand we make a developmental leap into more mature adulthood, into potential leadership and eldership in our communities. This shift into interdependence is one of them. Being able to see from the perspective of others—especially when their perspective might oppose your own personal desires or goals—is a hallmark of mature adult development. Contrary to what we may believe, moving from a hyperfocus on the self to an expanded perspective of the interrelatedness of us all, from hoarding our autonomy to becoming *encumbered,* ultimately, and perhaps paradoxically, means that we might experience the *freedom* of being a part of something—of caring for and being cared for by a larger whole.

I don't know about you, but *that* is the world that I want to live in.

## YOUR TURN

..................................................................

Building community is the work of a lifetime. It's a practice, not a to-do list. It's one thing to drop off a batch of your favorite homemade granola to your neighbors—but building a culture of mutual care among the people that surround you takes *time*. It can be hard to know where to begin, so here are a few prompts to get you off to the right start.

> *It can be challenging to find and build community when you don't feel like you know who you are anymore. And so: think back to the questions from the Momifesto Workbook that you answered a couple chapters back. There, you explored some of the things that are most important to you as a woman, and as a woman who happens to be a mother. Do you have a fierce passion for social justice? A built-in need for travel and adventure? Note, here, some of the key things—no matter how big or how small— that are important to you. These may be bread- crumbs along the trail toward a like-hearted village of your own.*

> *Who are your soul sisters on this journey of mother- hood you're on? Who are the people you admire? Who are the people you can count on?*

> *How can you be a support to other mothers in your life? What strengths or capacities do you have that you can share as a member of your community of mothers?*

> *What are five ways that you can begin to build your community of mothers right now? Maybe*

*you can email a friend who has just had a baby to offer your support. Maybe you can go to the mom and baby yoga class at the studio in your neighborhood. Maybe you can drop off a lasagna on a mama friend's doorstop. Maybe you can ask someone for help and give them the gift of being "spiritually employed."*

·············································································

## INNER KNOWING

Inner knowing refers to your intuition—that mysterious way of perceiving things that exists beyond all the logic and reasoning our culture typically values. It is the part of us that *just knows.* Inner knowing often comes in the form of a physical sensation—a sense of discomfort, butterflies in the stomach, a constriction in the chest—but intuition can also come in other forms as well—as an idea, or a thought that nudges you, or a sudden image that flashes in your mind. Sometimes our intuition can be called upon to offer us even more detailed information, as accessed through visualization, meditation, or dreams. Others find intuitive hits happen throughout their day, especially when they're engaged in an activity that allows for the physical and mental space they need to hear their inner voice speaking to them.

Mothers' experience of inner knowing is often what we refer to when we say "mother knows best." But the related concept of "maternal instinct" has come under some controversy in recent years because of the way it has been weaponized against mothers. The idea of maternal instinct has been used to justify a lack of support for mothers as a result of the idea that mothering should come naturally to women. It has also justified burdening mothers with the emotional labor of childrearing: if mother knows best, then the implication is that *no one else does,* so we should leave it to her. Ruddick, in her theory of *maternal thinking,* advocates that we recognize mothering not as instinctual and "natural," but as a series of skills and cognitive capacities that are carefully honed over hours and years of nurturing.[30] More recently, we've tried to unpack the concept of maternal instinct with science, and I've shared earlier in the book that although there is maternal physiology that *primes* us for caregiving, there is also a great portion of this work that is indeed learned behavior.

This all might be true, but it's an incomplete way of regarding the complex work of mothering. After fifteen years of on-the-ground birth, breastfeeding, and mothering support, this is what I know to be true: mothers *absolutely* have an exquisite intuition about what is best for themselves and their babies. I *just know*. Is their intuition shaped by the things mothers learn, cognitively, about their babies through repeated caregiving experiences? Probably. Is it *only* mothers who have intuition about their babies? Of course not. Is intuition "natural"? Definitely.

Do you want to know how I know? Because even though mothers usually see me as the "expert," I make a practice of asking them what *they* know to be true first.

And then?

I believe them.

And you know what happens next?

They start trusting themselves. They start listening for their own inner knowing. They hear it more often. And then they start advocating for it.

After witnessing the births of more babies and mothers than I can count, I have to admit that I have a favorite birth story, and it's the perfect way to highlight what mothers' inner knowing looks like.

My client was in labor, at home, with her second baby. Things were moving quickly, and it became clear that I would be the only birth attendant in the room. It would be my first birth where I had no other person in a professional capacity there to work with and lean on as I supported this mama. Dear reader, between you and me? I was terrified. I mean, I trust birth and I trust women's bodies, but also . . . I was terrified. Deep breaths calmed my racing thoughts, and I brought cold washcloths into the humid September bedroom, my voice low and soft and my eyes steady. My client was in the birth pool, on her knees, pushing, when she looked up at me and said:

"There's the head."

And then a look of panic washed over her and she panted, "Jessie! What do I do next?"

Anyone who has attended a birth will know that this moment, when a baby's head has been born but his body is still inside his mother, is one of the most tenuous of a birth. In milliseconds, my mind worked through a dozen responses to her question: take a deep breath; try a new position; PUSH! But in those milliseconds, I also remembered the ultimate paradox of birth: I realized I knew enough to know that I didn't know what she should do at all. Any of my responses would merely have reflected my own fear, my own desire to *do something*, my brain's deep compulsion to try to *control* the situation. But there was absolutely nothing to indicate that anything had gone wrong or that my panic was warranted at all; my fear had no place here. And so, in deep consciousness of what my words would call her into, I said: "I don't know."

The words were still fresh on my lips as another contraction soared through my client's body and she lunged, as fast as I've ever seen a pregnant person move, back onto one knee and birthed her son.

She knew.

She knew.

She knew.

I've seen a thousand versions of this story—enough to know that you probably know, too.

But it helps to have the space to ask yourself what you know. It helps to have someone who cares for you ask you, too, and then believe what you say.

But this is the thing: we often find ourselves disconnected from our inner knowing. It's something I have noticed changing dramatically in the past ten years, and something I've become increasingly worried about in my practice. In this world where we have so much information at our fingertips, so many new mothers, in all their vulnerability and uncertainty, outsource their knowing to Google. Arguably, in fact, women's sense of intuition about their bodies and their babies is interrupted the minute they first seek external knowledge to validate their internal experience of pregnancy. A great many women know they're pregnant before they pee on a stick, let alone before a doctor insists they have a blood test to confirm their knowledge. We continue to be encouraged to outsource our inner wisdom throughout our pregnancy, birth, and mothering years. This experience is amplified by our culture's assertion of the perfect mother myth, which insists that there is a "right" way to parent—the implication being, of course, that it's not something you *already know*, that it's something you're probably going to have to look up.

In *Ordinary Insanity*, Menkedick argues that the outsourcing of our wisdom has insidious roots: "The male solution to female reproductive power was experts. If the child was to depend on the mother, then the mother was to depend on male experts. The latter offered stern and often contradictory advice on feeding, on bathing, on sleeping and thumbsucking."[31]

While it's okay and sometimes very helpful to ask for advice and support and information to inform our decisions, it doesn't always work in our favor to seek this out as a proxy for, rather than a complement to, our *own* wisdom. What happens is marathon scrolling sessions (usually in the middle of the night) when the baby isn't latching properly or when their poop looks different than usual, which typically lead to exhaustion and confusion before they lead to helpful answers. More concerningly, though, is that this outsourcing has led to perhaps the first generation of mothers who actually *don't* believe they know what's best.

And there's also this: we live in a world that rotates upon the axis of scientific evidence and proof. There is little space in our culture—and often within our mothering decisions—for "just knowing," for intuition, and especially not for magic or mystery. In addition, our intuition needs space and safety to thrive—the kind of space and safety we experience when we're able to tend to our needs and listen to the language of our bodies—to that entire realm of experience we're having below our necks. But so much in our busy lives works against our inner knowing: we are constantly barraged with information and activity, and we must work actively if we want to hear ourselves. Not just within the context of pregnancy, birth, and mothering, but widely throughout our information-driven society, so many of us have *literally lost the skills* required to hone and use a powerful sense of inner knowing.

Fortunately, when you're a mama experiencing the Big Slowdown and the liminal space, you have access to this necessary sense of spaciousness, at least in some ways (during long nights rocking your baby to sleep or during drive-naps, anyone?!). I believe that this is one of the reasons why motherhood has the potential to enhance our intuition and why I consider inner knowing to be a MotherPower.

There's more to this than just "knowing what's best." When we *insource* our way of knowing—and when we can cultivate the self-trust and self-confidence to *believe in it* and then even perhaps *act on it*—we unlock a new level of self-authority and sovereignty as mothers and as women. We can use this inner wisdom not only to discern how best to mother our children but also to navigate *all* of our decisions and to do so in such a way that aligns with our values and our deepest sense of authenticity. And like so many of the other capacities we cultivate in matrescence, insourcing rather than outsourcing your knowing and your decisions is another characteristic of mature adult development. As I've mentioned earlier, this is what developmental psychologists refer to as "self-authoring," or the ability to hear outside information but, ultimately, know for yourself what is right and what is needed.

And so it is that, as with so many of the MotherPowers we're cultivating here together, reconnecting with your inner knowing is a radical act, poised not only to change your own world, but to impact the world we live in.

## YOUR TURN

· · · · · · · · · · · · · · · · · · · · · · · · · · · · · · · · · · · · · · · · · · · · ·

Intuition is, simply put, a choice to pay attention to and make meaning of the possible signs, symbols, and messages around you. You get to decide what has meaning and what meaning you want to apply. Intuition is a choice to look for magic in your everyday life and to trust that you have an inner compass that will point you in the direction you need to go. Intuition is also like a muscle: it needs to be flexed on a regular basis in order to develop strength. Below, find a few ways you can begin.

*Do you feel connected to your inner knowing? Has that connection changed since you became a mother? Remember, intuition doesn't have to be "precious," magical, or earth-shattering. It may just be that you're craving oatmeal instead of your usual scrambled egg breakfast, only to remember that you've just menstruated and perhaps your body was letting you know it needed a boost of iron.*

*If you do feel connected to your intuition, how do you experience it? Is it visual, auditory, embodied, or just a "knowing"?*

*Make note of a time when you got feedback that your intuition was right. Remember that your relationship with your intuition thrives on feedback and "proof." One of my favorite ways to support women to cultivate their intuition is through the use of an Intuition Journal. In it, just jot down the random urges or thoughts that come into your mind that might be intuitions. Then, if you receive feedback that they were right—even if it's weeks or months down the line—make a note of it!*

· · · · · · · · · · · · · · · · · · · · · · · · · · · · · · · · · · · · · · · · · · · · ·

## EARTH CONNECTION

Matrescence has been the most ecological,
biological experience of my life.

—Lucy Jones, *Matrescence: On the Metamorphosis
of Pregnancy, Childbirth, and Motherhood*

There is nothing as primal, as mammalian, as birthing and mothering a child.

For those of us who carried our babies in our bodies, we are confronted with that reality from the minute we become pregnant: we are the vessel for new life, with the sore breasts, nausea, and existential exhaustion to show for it. When it comes time to birth, our animal nature takes over; in fact, the thinking-planning-Pinterest part of our brain (known to most as the frontal cortex) is not usually very useful anymore—if it weren't for the need many of us have to navigate a sometimes-confusing medical system, we wouldn't have any requirement for that part of our consciousness at all. Mothering is just as wild: from the minute her baby is born, a mother and child enter an exquisite dance of subtle, embodied communication, with glances, sounds, and movements attuned to each other's signals and cues. And though we thrive with the support of others, we also very often have what our mothering demands *already encoded within us*—in our gut feelings and the heightened physiological capacity for learning we experience in the early days of motherhood.

The primal nature of mothering continues to thread its way throughout our caregiving lives: any mother who's looked knowingly up at the full moon when her baby just won't settle for the night has had a taste of that primacy. Any mother who has *perhaps quite literally* growled at a judgmental friend, a schoolyard bully, or even her own child when they step out of line has encountered that instinctual nature. Any mother who has tried to tame her child into sleeping when she wants them to sleep or sitting still when she wants them to sit still has witnessed that wildness.

In her book *Grounded*, UK geotherapist Ruth Allen, PhD, defines *wildness* in terms well beyond the physical and mammalian.

She writes of a wildness that includes behaving in ways we don't expect of ourselves, declarations of independence, intentions to be subversive, resolutions to be different, and resistance to boundaries, restrictions, and the word *should*. She defines wildness in terms of our changeability, our boldness and tenacity, and our desire to live more authentically and in rhythm with the seasons.[32]

If that isn't a definition of matrescence—or at least the potential that matrescence holds for mothers—then I don't know what is.

I often say that I became an ecofeminist when I became a doula, and then even more so when I became a mother. I could not help but see the wildness of it all. I also could not help but notice the entire medical and cultural paradigm within which there was ever-so-much *taming* going on. The wildness and complexity of birth and mothering have become yet another flowchart of symptoms and solutions that can be controlled and made more predictable, "safer," or more *palatable* in some way. With Google an arm's reach away, with the increasing alienation we feel from our bodies and intuition, with the myriad corporations and "experts" selling us the idea that somehow they know best, and often with the fear of being judged for "doing it wrong," we fail to live fully into the innate wildness within us that mothering engenders.

So why does all this matter? It demonstrates that matrescence is a time when we experience a heightened potential in our connection with the earth and to ourselves as a part of nature, too. Earth connection can support both your own matrescence and the wider world, and that's why it is a MotherPower.

Let's start with how earth connection can support you, individually, as you traverse the transition into motherhood. Indeed, in so many ways, the living world can midwife us through matrescence and *all* the radical transformations we might find ourselves navigating in our lives. This is an ancestral truth: people have embarked on wilderness quests and otherwise turned to the support of the earth and her seasons to honor the major transformations in their lives since time immemorial.

In our modern consciousness, it's become well-known that connecting with the earth holds myriad benefits for our physical, emotional, and spiritual health. The following are some of the ways I witness these benefits supporting mothers, specifically.

First of all, in times of transition, when we are disoriented and our nervous systems tend to be dysregulated, the earth offers us a coregulating balm. In addition, the spaciousness we can experience when out in the woods or swimming in the ocean offers us the ability to metabolize the changes in our lives and hear the tiny quiet voice of our inner knowing when everything feels uncertain. What's more? When we witness the changing of the seasons, we can lean into and trust in the natural cycles of birth, death, and rebirth, considering them as metaphors for the cycle of transformation we're in. The discomfort of the Big Slowdown can be assuaged even just a little when we are able to pay closer attention to the way the earth's timing seems slow, often, but always exquisitely perfect. As Jones writes in her book *Matrescence,* "I . . . found relief in the woods: witnessing ecological processes, cycles of growth and decay. Here were the hazards, mortality, symbiosis, relationality, possibilities and new ways of seeing that matrescence rocketed me into."[33] Finally, I often think that what draws people to the earth in the midst of a life transition is that, in a time when you're not sure where or what or who you belong to anymore, you always belong, as Mary Oliver writes, "in the family of things."[34]

Earth connection is not *only* something we can cultivate for our own benefit—for the revelation of tracking the lunar cycle or of the sense of belonging we might find among the trees. In fact, that, too, harmless as it may seem on a physical level, is still exploitative on an energetic level—as in using Mama Earth for our mental, emotional, and spiritual well-being; *consuming* her like we might otherwise consume medication to make us feel better.

There is indeed a wider benefit to our enhanced connection with the living world during the transition to motherhood. Many mothers experience an *ecological awakening* in matrescence.[35] In part, this may be a result of an acute awareness of the future our children will live in. The wildness of mothering certainly also plays a role in this heightened awareness of our mammalian nature. And as I shared in the section on community, motherhood attunes us to the larger whole and toward interdependence: we become more aware of the ecosystem of humans around us, and it is only a small leap to begin to more deeply consider the nonhumans around us.

Maternal ecopsychology researcher Allison Davis, PhD, has studied this experience of ecological awakening in motherhood, positing that it is an important but thus far largely unrecognized aspect of matrescence. She suggests that eco-distress, manifesting as eco-anxiety and eco-grief, is often a part of the disorientation and difficulty that so many mothers experience as they traverse the transition to motherhood.[36] Davis has also researched the ways mothers can turn to the ideology of "green motherhood" as a way to resolve this distress.[37]

Earlier in this book, I described how mothers who are in the most vulnerable phases of matrescence can turn to mothering ideologies, looking for certainty and community. Green motherhood is a form of intensive motherhood that, as Davis writes, "emphasizes an individualized, consumption-based maternal identity and gendered, human-centered advocacy as a solution."[38] For example, many of the practices of green motherhood are predicated on the capitalism-driven purchase of the "right" products. Within the four walls of your home, this might translate into a fierce dedication to cloth diapering or only ever purchasing organic food or wooden toys, for example. While there's nothing wrong with these practices, Davis says, "This activism depletes mothers and removes responsibility from the corporations and governments driving climate change [and] privatizes the work of planetary wellness onto mothers."[39] This saddles mothers with an "environmental third shift" of doing the housework of cleaning up environmental change—as well as the guilt of not being able to make a significant impact as an individual.[40] Furthermore, the ideologies of green motherhood are in close relationship with the ideology of "natural motherhood." While I am an avid supporter of many of the same things natural motherhood might advocate for, I also try to remember that any ideology held too dearly becomes a prison. In the case of natural motherhood, this prison can begin to look deeply frightening, obsessed as it can become with the notions of nostalgia and purity also characteristic of far-right ideology.

And so it is that while I posit that earth connection may be a MotherPower that enables mothers to be uniquely poised as powerful advocates for the earth, it's not because I think cloth diapers are going to save the world. It's because in matrescence we have the potential to begin to realize ourselves as ecological beings, helping us to remember that "nature" isn't only what exists outside our windows: *we* are nature. Ecopsychologists often posit that we cannot protect what we do not love, and we cannot love that with which we have no relationship. Motherhood is an invitation into relationship with our wildness, and, in so being, with the earth. Motherhood is our invitation to *love* the earth in a new way.

## YOUR TURN

A note before you begin: it is important, when considering reconnecting with the earth, to be aware of your relationship with the land you live on. If you live on Indigenous land, start by learning about its original people and the history of colonization there.* Learn and acknowledge the original name given to the land you occupy. It is important, also, to be aware of appropriating the practices and beliefs of cultures that are not your own. If you are of settler ancestry, you may not have a lineage and practices of earth connection to lean on. You might feel awkward trying to forge a relationship with place, having had no one to teach you how. Try to stay in this discomfort and imagine ways you could be a culture creator rather than a culture appropriator.

One of the simplest and most powerful practices to support you to reconnect with the earth is to find a place in nature near your home where you can visit a few times

* Head to https://native-land.ca to find out.

a week. Sit there for at least fifteen minutes at a stretch, which is when the creatures around you will stop noticing you as "other" and are more likely to continue their daily comings and goings in your midst. Just sit there, and notice your surroundings. Over time, you will begin to *know* the landscape, to notice its subtle shifts over the seasons, and to feel that sense of reconnection and kinship.

Remember that anytime you benefit from the abundance of the earth—even if it's just the opportunity to sit and feel calm for a few minutes—you should offer a token of reciprocity. This might be just a simple whispered thank-you or perhaps an offering of some kind. In the winter months, I will often bring a little bit of birdseed to scatter on the ground as an offering, but in a pinch, even a hair plucked from your head—a part of you offered in reverence—is the perfect form of reciprocity with the earth.

We can also enjoy a sense of earth connection without having access to the outdoors or to wilderness. Here are some journal prompts to help you deepen your connection to the earth even further:

*Right now, how are you like . . .*

> . . . *water?*
> . . . *fire?*
> . . . *air?*
> . . . *earth?*
> . . . *spring?*
> . . . *summer?*
> . . . *fall?*
> . . . *winter?*

*What is your connection with the earth like right now?*

*How would you like to be more connected to the earth?*

*How can you tend to Mother Earth just as you are learning to tend yourself and your baby?*

..........................................................................

Welcome to your MotherPowers, mama.

May they awaken in you a new source of nourishment, a new connection with yourself and who you are now that you're a mother.

May you also see that when you cultivate these capacities in yourself you are nurturing the change our world needs the most right now. You are nurturing a *revolution*.

# 8

# Becoming Mother

*How to Complete Your Rite of Passage,*
*Embody Motherhood, and Share the*
*Wisdom You've Received along the Way*

> Becoming a mother is like discovering
> the existence of a strange new room
> in the house where you already live.
> —Unknown

Many, many (many!) women ask me how they will know they've *completed* the transition to motherhood.

It's true that many say that a woman is *postpartum* forever. We will forever be changed by our motherhood. The author of the book *Transformed by Birth*, Britta Bushnell, PhD, phrases it beautifully: "Though our motherhood journeys will always be evolving as our children go to school, fall out of the treehouse, dye their hair blue and leave home, most of these shifts and transitions require us to edit and update our *skills and capacities* as mothers, but the initial transition into motherhood is what shifts our *identity* the most." (See note for more.)[1]

My answer to the women who ask, "How will I know I've Become a Mother?" is always rather unsatisfying, in a Yoda-counsels-Jedi kind of way: You'll know when you know, you know?

One of the most *tangible* ways I've found to describe feeling *embodied* in your motherhood is that when someone yells out "mommy!" at the playground, you can conceive that they might be hollering for *you*, not someone else who more appropriately bears that title.

I remember feeling a distinct shift in the way I bore my Mother role when my daughter was about two and a half years old. I had slowly come to accept the presence of Goldfish cracker crumbs in every corner of my purse and the theme song to *Dora the Explorer* on repeat in my head, yes, but there was something more, too. In a way, there was an absence. An absence of the way that I had, in the early days, railed against the fact of my own motherhood. There was an absence of the ghost of the parallel life I *wasn't* living while I nursed my toddler to sleep at night.

My *whole life* has changed shape because I am a mother. It has re-formed and grown and evolved because of my motherhood, with my motherhood integrated within it. To be sure, there are times even now, over twelve years from the day I first held that beautiful little one in my arms, that I long to check into a hotel for a weekend, eat Thai takeout, watch Netflix, and sleep undisturbed, preferably in full starfish position, until I wake up. There are times when I need breaks, when I long for more autonomy, and even times when I miss my old life. But there's also a part of me that knows that my old life doesn't exist anymore, nor does the woman who lived it.

This experience is corroborated in research by Laney and colleagues. Among their study participants, they found that "becoming a mother involved fracturing or compressing a woman's identities so they were able to incorporate a motherhood identity and their children into their sense of self."[2] Incidentally, in this study, the mothers who struggled the most with a sense of self-loss reported ultimately being more satisfied and confident with themselves and their mothering abilities as they "came back" from the rite of passage into motherhood than the mothers who didn't struggle as much with a loss of self.[3]

As you traverse these early years of mothering, perhaps one day while in the shower or picking up Lego blocks you might also have a moment of clarity where you see *all* the pieces of your life that have shifted—or are beginning to shift—as you become who you are now that you're a mother. You might see the parts of you that you've left behind as you've traversed your way into motherhood but feel more compassion and love than sadness and grief. You might see the ways in which your holy anger at the conditions of modern motherhood catalyzed a shift in your family dynamics, work, or community. You may have experienced your transition to motherhood as an initiatory firewalk of depression or anxiety but be finding fledgling new life emerging from the ashes of everything matrescence has burned away. You might see the parts of you that have been created, explored, or fortified because of your motherhood and feel a sense of curiosity and wonder. You might have realized the impossibility of the perfect mother myth—maybe because you failed to live up to it—and have found a way to mother that doesn't require you to negate your own humanity in the process. You may have come to peace with the both/and-ness of it all and attained a certain comfort in the messy middle.

In other words, you'll know in your own way when you've crossed that threshold into an embodied motherhood, into motherhood as a part of your identity. You'll know when you know, you know?

But remember, all this takes time, mama. And remember, embodying your motherhood in a world that devalues mothers is challenging. Embodying your motherhood when you're unsupported by our culture to have motherhood *completely rearrange you* is challenging.

It's important to have compassion for yourself and for this process—and also to have confidence and trust. You are here: you've nearly made it to the end of this book, and you've explored a great many concepts, tools, and resources to support you along the way. You *are*, by definition, well on your way.

Your motherhood is unfolding, and so are you along with it. You are transforming—in your own unique, perfectly imperfect way.

✳  BIRTH OF A MOTHER  ✳

Oh, sweet mama,

I know.

You're wondering: So when does it end?

When do I feel like myself again?

When do I feel just a little less like there's a thread tied to the ventricles of my heart and fastened so securely to this tiny being . . .

a red thread that tugs and pulls and opens and sometimes tangles

a dance of joy and sorrow and skinned knees and sleepless nights

tender

—*tenderizing*, too—

I know. They said forty days. They said two years, maybe.

That other mother, around the corner from your house,

the one with the *Instagram color theme*

(I know)

she's in Costa Rica or hiking the Camino with a baby strapped bravely to her chest, or snug at home with an idyllic grandmother figure

and you're scraping crusted oatmeal off your shoulder and serving snacks *on a bed of Goldfish crackers.*

Mama, can I say?

It was only a handful of years ago that I dropped my children off for the first day they would both attend "big kid" school. Tuna sandwiches, crusts cut off; brand-new lunch boxes. A tiny plaid shirt on my boy; my girl, with her hair brushed, much to her chagrin.

Sliding the door of the minivan shut behind me, I walked up my front steps and pulled the cool early fall air into the deep part of my lungs, . . .

and had no idea how to begin.

I chuckled to myself:

"Eight years postpartum."

I chuckled, but the truth was there.

Five hours of time alone, in a silent house, lay ahead of me. Five hours of going to the bathroom by myself and drinking my coffee hot.

Eight years of longing for this day, if I'm being honest.

Of course, there have been milk-drunk smiles and astounding Lego towers and sweet, soft little heads against the skin of my breast

and also

longing.

As I traipsed from room to room, picking up the occasional stray stuffy and listening to the laundry chug in the basement, I felt an urge to *metabolize* everything that had changed since that day eight years prior, when I brought a spindly-legged preterm baby home . . .

and had no idea how to begin.

Here I was:

- Always walking the thin, gray, wavering line between being a mother and being a woman. A woman who happens to be a mother, but also loves great swaths of time alone, reading a book in a sushi restaurant, and writing by candlelight in the morning. Many days, I felt the tension between wanting to be with them all the time and desperately wanting to escape. Many days, it felt like a perpetual grass-is-always-greener: flashing memories of eyelashes on freckled cheeks as I completed monthly expense reports, dreams of completing monthly expense reports (or just peeing by myself) while they fought over who-said-what or who's-first.

- Still navigating the sometimes choppy waters of being in a marriage whose requirements of devotion and connection and occasionally sleeping in the same bed without a child between us were often antithetical to the needs of the very humans our love created. Eight years in, some counseling, and a good many fresh starts later, we were finally figuring a few things out. We tried, as often as we could, to draw a circle around just the two of us for half an hour and tell the children *not right now*, so that we remember who we are together.

- More fiercely dedicated to the care of my own heart, to the thriving of my relationships, to the tending of my own longings because: they're watching; because: they need a well mother; because: the need to plant my feet in the ground of my own selfhood had never been so necessary or so encroached upon; because: as they say, the days are long but the years are short; the time is now.

I've caught myself more than once, from the vantage point of *five hours of a silent house and hot coffee*, saying to the new mamas I work with, "This too shall pass."

But I know how trite and unsatisfying that feels sometimes. This is the truth I've learned:

- Time is a medicine, yes, and also motherhood will continue to change and change you. You will have many a time when you feel like you've released—or have had wrenched from you—a part of your mothering identity as you evolve and grow alongside your children. Breastfeeding will transform into bullying and into boyfriends as the source of your midnight worries.

- It's normal. The complexity of your feelings, your joy and ambivalence interwoven, the feeling of being lost, the renegotiation of relationships and values—it's *all* a part of this, and there's nothing wrong with you.

- It's not easy. Trust me. No one else *actually* has this figured out—despite what you see on Instagram.

- Everything else is going to change, too. You might move to the suburbs or start volunteering or find a new job. Your values will be tested, and you will learn to draw a circle around what's most important, be it *organic* Goldfish crackers, taking yourself on sushi dates, or always being there for bedtime.

• This is an opportunity to become more *yourself*, more whole, to start saying yes to your life because: they're watching; because: they need a well mother; because: the need to plant your feet in the ground of your own selfhood has never been so necessary or so encroached upon; because: as they say, the days are long but the years are short; the time is now.

## THE RETURN

The experience of beginning to integrate the fact of your motherhood into your identity and your life aligns with the final stage in the classic model of rites of passage, known as the Return.

One way of thinking about the Return is in the traditional sense. In rites of passage theory, the Return happens when you have completed your time of transformation and you must reintegrate your new self into your home community—*or find a new community.*

The concept of the Return is one of the many ways in which our ideas of how rites of passage happen and how people traverse big changes in their lives fall short of describing the specific and nuanced experience of *women*—and especially mothers. When anthropologists and mythologists began using this turn of phrase, it was in response to studying the rites of passage undertaken by boys and men, which often involved a literal separation from and then return to their home communities.

Mothers are usually relationally—and biologically—embedded in our families and communities; we don't usually *get* to separate, nor do we really "return." Then again, women have always had their rites of passage encoded right into their bodies through menarche, childbirth, and menopause: no need to leave home on the quest for transformation. But I digress.

What *does* ring true about the idea of the Return is that any rite of passage asks us not only *who we are now*, but where we *belong* now. When we navigate the Return, we must take our newly minted selves and ideas about who we are and what matters most now that motherhood has rocked us to the core and integrate into the fold of the wider community, the wider world.

Of course, you have been *living in the world* from the day you knew you were going to have a baby, but as I've shared earlier in the book, you may find your sense of belonging shifting and find yourself wanting to explore support networks that more deeply nourish you and your fledgling *motherself*.

I should tell you, dear mama, that in the world of rites of passage theory, the Return is otherwise known as the Hard Part.

I know. You thought you were past the hard parts already.

As anyone who has taken a gap year overseas or even just gone on a really fabulous vacation can attest, the Return can indeed be challenging. In short, you are fundamentally a different person now, and the way you see and participate in the world around you will be different, too. Bringing your fledgling sense of self into the world and saying: "Here I Am: New and Different" can be really gnarly. It's because belonging is *actually* what we're hardwired for as humans. We evolved knowing that we survive best in community, and so when we don't feel like we belong to our community anymore because we've changed, it's *really* hard. Have lots of compassion for yourself as you traverse the Return and explore where you belong now that you're a mother. It takes time, and the best thing you can do in the process is to keep "returning" to *yourself*—to become all the more deeply assured of who you are and what matters most to you. That knowing will act as a compass that will guide you home, quite literally, to where you belong.

## EMBODYING MOTHERHOOD

Another word commonly used in place of or alongside the Return in rites of passage theory is *reincorporation*. To me, this speaks life into the idea of *embodying* your motherhood: the root of the word *incorporate* is the Latin *corpus*, or "body." So incorporation means "to bring into whole of the body"—to bring your motherhood into the whole of who you are. And it can also mean to bring the body into the whole: to bring your new *motherself* into the whole of your life.

There are four ways that you can support yourself—or ask to be supported by others—so that you can begin to embody motherhood in your own, unique way.

The first of these is to tend to the shifts that have already occurred or are occurring in your life as a result of your matrescence.

Earlier in this book you began to explore, engaging in Tiny Experiments as you got curious—and maybe even playful!—about who you are becoming. In the process, you may have learned that there are other areas of your life that are calling out to you to shift and grow and evolve as you shift and grow and evolve into motherhood. You may have found yourself taking a new course or dreaming of starting a cupcake stand at your local farmers market. Maybe you started writing again. Maybe you found yourself scrolling through real estate listings closer to your extended family or other community of support. Maybe your sense of reincorporation was quite literal, and you're feeling ready to accept your *motherbody*, ditch the clothes that don't fit anymore, and have a giant bonfire for all your underwire bras.

The next step in the Tiny Experiments process is to expand on and grow what feels good and authentic and exciting—or the good kind of scary—so that you are no longer quietly trying your new self on for size, but beginning to truly shift the ecosystem of your life. You have allowed motherhood to shape you, to become a part of you, and now it is time to shape your life around the fact of you as Mother.

The second way you can become more deeply embodied in your motherhood is to find ways to be *witnessed* in your process of Return and reincorporation. In traditional ways of knowing, a rite of passage wasn't complete until the members of your community acknowledged your transformation. A witness is simply someone who says, either metaphorically or literally: "I see you. You have changed. I honor the journey you've traversed. Good job!" This is the time when the work you've done to create community for yourself and to rediscover where you belong now that you are a mother earns its weight in gold.

The third way to support yourself during the Return or reincorporation is to mark your transformation with ritual. You may have experimented with this in the section on ritual, but now is the time that symbolically crossing the threshold into motherhood can have a dramatic impact on your ability to move into a more embodied experience of your new role. Witnesses are important here too: a ritual that is seen and honored and celebrated by those that love you is even more potent.

The final way to support yourself through the Return is one that often gets overlooked, but is absolutely crucial to the process of *becoming*. Traditionally, the initiate traversing a rite of passage returns to their home community with "a gift and a task."

As you feel more deeply embodied in your motherhood, it's time to reflect on the abundance of gifts you've harvested as you've traversed this journey: the lessons learned, the wisdoms collected, the stories unmasked and brought to light.

Now is the time to consider offering these gifts to other mothers, to your children, to those still living in the darkness of challenging times, or to those who may feel they are walking this journey alone.

This is your task.

Our world needs empowered and powerful mothers more than ever.

In emphasizing mothers' role as *change agents*, matrescence researcher Athan says it's time to "talk back to the culture when it devalues you. Speak truth to power. We know, better than anyone else, what is distorted in the way we raise mothers in our culture, what is broken, and what is making so many of us sick."[4]

Beyond "just" speaking for change to the way we raise mothers, which is, of course, incredibly important in and of itself, the journey of matrescence is now, more than ever, *also* a call to step into *leadership in the wider world.*

What you've learned as a mother, as you've traversed this rite of passage, is how change gets made; it's how to *change everything.* We, in becoming mothers, have learned how to lead our lives and our communities with compassion and empathy. We've nurtured our creativity and explored how to make decisions from a place of deep knowing, rather than in response to external expectations. We've cultivated a sense of self-trust and navigated a new way of belonging, both within our own skin and within the world. We've walked the line between fierceness and kindness more times than we can count, and we have at least one tiny, dimple-knuckled reason to want the world to be a better place.

> Our task, therefore, is to consider, take up, and then wield unapologetically
> *our power*
> *(in a world that has, for so long, relegated mothers to the realm of powerlessness).*

Menkedick writes that when we begin to see the many ways in which we hold tremendous power not *in spite of* our motherhood but *because of it,* "it becomes possible to imagine a different kind of motherhood, fierce and frightening, free and bold, of female camaraderie and knowledge that could reshape cultural, social and political paradigms."[5]

And so.

Though you may emerge from this rite of passage with a great many gifts to bring to your child, your family, yourself, and your community, may you not forget the gift—and the task—that you bring to the *world.*

> You, as mother,
> as a well-nourished, embodied, creative human
> are what your child needs most

what *you* need most
and what the *world* needs most.

Do not take your wellness lightly. Do not underestimate the value of your motherhood, and the process of embodying—and claiming— your role as Mother. Do not dismiss the power of the work you're doing, right now, becoming and becoming and becoming, forging this new self, stepping into this new way of being, seeing the world through new eyes.

And do not forget: you are not alone.

Mama, I see you.

I see your courage and your willingness as you traverse this path—as you explore and choose for yourself a journey into mother- hood that can be, at times, so deeply disorienting, and yet, in the same breath, utterly transformative.

Sweet mama,
You are doing brave work.
May you journey well.

# GRATITUDE

An entire village supported me to birth this book, over many years of writing and over fifteen years of mother support. Naming all the people who lifted me and this work up feels like an impossible task that I am going to tackle anyway—not unlike the work of birth and mothering, not unlike the work of writing a book, too.

Dylan: This book would not have been possible without you. I know there's the part where you made me a mother, but there's also the part where you have steadfastly supported my dreams for the last almost two decades. And, lest anyone mistake the latter statement for some kind of trite placation, let it be known: you have held the flashlight while I swam through shipwrecks, been the arm I bit while birthing both(!) of our children, built every cool thing I found on Pinterest, and solo parented while I spent a month on a mountain looking for god, to name just a few. You make it *all* possible. I love you, I love who you're becoming, and I love doing life with you.

Ada and Max: Thank you for accepting me into your rigorous apprenticeship program. Under your tutelage, I have learned more about gratitude and grief, patience and no-patience-at-all, suffering and joy, how to tie a friendship bracelet and the name of a great many more dinosaurs than I would have otherwise. I love your eyelashes and your knuckles and your humor and your bigheartedness for the human and nonhuman alike. Humanumah.

Mom and Dad: What a life you have given me! Thank you for shuttling me to creative writing classes and mailing off poetry submissions, mostly staying quiet about my dubious career choices and for always supporting me to live a life worth writing about. Thank you for breaking all the stereotypes about what mothering and fathering could look like, and always having the patience to watch me run as far as I could in the opposite direction before realizing that you might have been right all along anyway.

Kate: You're the best. We have become *very* cool adults, and I love the friendship we've grown. Ever the whole enchilada and more, you are also the coolest aunt my kids could ask for.

Katharina: I am ever-in-awe of the myriad ways the universe has brought us together, over and over again, in this lifetime. You took my hand on that winter night so many years ago and showed me what was possible in motherhood and in life. Thank you for holding me as I birthed my babies and myself.

Maggie, Renée, Vanessa, Elizabeth, Shelley: Our time together has been the biggest car ride of YES in my writing life. Thank you for the soft place for my words to land. Thank you for the magic.

Erica and Cynthia: So many of my ideas about birth and mothering have been formed in our precious coven, over brunch and in the woods and during post-birth debriefs. I love you.

Lois Jackson and Helen Hayward: Your unabashed use of the red pen in my early writing days showed me that you believed in my best work before I did. I always write with your keen eyes in mind, and it hasn't led me astray.

Lianne: Thank you for helping me to hear my own wisdom and for your warm guidance through all the ups and downs of this book journey.

This book has been many, many years in the making, and so there have been countless folks who have spelled each other off as midwives in this long labor. I stand on the shoulders of a great many wayshowers, scholars, feminists, birth workers, mothers, and grandmothers whose work to more deeply understand and improve the lives of mothers has informed and shaped my own work in a million different ways. They are named and their contributions uplifted throughout this book, and I owe a debt of gratitude to all of them.

To Joelle Hahn: Thank you for the early developmental edits of this manuscript—when it was just an embryo and a lot of Clarissa Pinkola Estes quotes. To Richelle Fredson: Thank you for your enthusiasm, keen eye, and generosity with my proposal and everything it took to get to the book deal part of this journey. To Mara Glatzel and Becca Piastrelli: Thank you for your belief in this work, for helping me get this book into the right hands, for the check-ins and podcast dates and sweet emails. It's been so good to have you in my corner. To Kate Inglis (and Tara Jaskowiak, for introducing us): You took me, a total stranger, under your wing and guided this book on the final leg of its journey toward the warm and welcoming arms at Shambhala Publications. May every author be so lucky; may I pay it forward, again and again.

To Beth Frankl: Your loving, attuned, and patient presence has been such a gift during the adventure of writing this book. To Samantha Ripley and the rest of the team at Shambhala: It has been a delight and an honor to have your support for and belief in this work.

A deep bow to the nonhuman supporters of this book: To Mystery, for placing this work and these words in my care. Thanks for all those moments of flow. To the Great Mother, the biggest arms to fall into, the lap I curl up in, all tree roots and mossy pillows and generous creeks: you are my home, you are always there, you are the reason I am still here. To Mi'kmaq'i, for all the medicine you offer. To all the places that have held me as I've written these words, including but not limited to: the Goldfish-encrusted back seat of my minivan parked at the beach (many, many hours), the libraries full of books and encouragement, the woodstove-stoked cabins, the Airbnb kitchen tables, and just about every café with a decent caramel latte, London Fog, or muffin within a fifty-kilometer radius of my usually-too-chaotic-to-write home.

Finally, the most important people to thank have been the mothers and birth and postpartum support workers I have had the deep honor of supporting over the last fifteen years. This book is for you.

# NOTES

## INTRODUCTION

1. Policy Center for Maternal Mental Health, "Maternal Mental Health Disorders," accessed February 1, 2024, https://www.2020mom.org/mmh-disorders.

2. Aurélie Athan, "Postpartum Flourishing: Motherhood as Opportunity for Positive Growth and Self-Development" (PhD diss., Columbia University, 2011).

3. Alexis Pauline Gumbs, China Martens, and Mai'a Williams, *Revolutionary Mothering: Love on the Front Lines* (New York: PM Press, 2016), xv.

4. You might rightfully be wondering: If mothering can be done by anyone, then why not call it by a more gender-neutral term, like parenting? Andrea O'Reilly, PhD, expert in the sociology of motherhood and founder of the term *matricentric feminism*, shares that positioning mothering as a gender-neutral term "allows for an appreciation of how mother-work is deeply gendered *and* how this may be challenged and changed through empowered mothering." She goes on: "While the actions of mothering could be performed by anyone, they are overwhelmingly performed by women. Using the term 'parents' . . . .deflects, disguises and denies the very real and prevalent gendered oppressions of motherwork."

5. Adrienne Rich, *Of Woman Born: Motherhood as Experience and Institution* (New York: W. W. Norton, 2021).

6. Because this differentiation between *mother, mothering,* and *motherhood* is unfamiliar to most folks, I will continue to use the "lowercase m" motherhood to refer to the experience of being a mother, not necessarily the institution of Motherhood.

7. Olivia Fischer, "Forging Crossroads: The Possibilities and Complexities of Parenting outside the Gender Binary," in *Maternal Theory: Essential Reading*, ed. Andrea O'Reilly (Bradford, ON: Demeter Press, 2021), 795–816.

## CHAPTER ONE: BEYOND PELVIC FLOORS
## AND EMOTIONAL ROLLER COASTERS

1. Heng Ou, Amely Greeven, and Marisa Belger, *The First Forty Days: The Essential Art of Nourishing the New Mother* (New York: Stewart, Tabori & Chang, 2016).
2. Kimberly Ann Johnson, *The Fourth Trimester: A Postpartum Guide to Healing Your Body, Balancing Your Emotions, and Restoring Your Vitality* (Boulder, CO: Shambhala Publications, 2017).
3. Dana Raphael, "Matrescence, Becoming a Mother, a 'New/Old Rite de Passage,'" in *Being Female: Reproduction, Power, and Change*, ed. Dana Raphael (Berlin, NY: De Gruyter Mouton, 1975), 65–72.
4. Aurélie Athan, Zoom interview, August 28, 2020.
5. Amy Taylor-Kabbaz, *Mama Rising: Discovering the New You through Motherhood* (Alexandria, NSW: Hay House Australia, 2020), 111.
6. "Statistics on Postpartum Depression," PostpartumDepression.org, accessed July 27, 2023, https://www.postpartumdepression.org/resources/statistics.
7. "Supporting Black Women's Maternal Mental Health Journey," AHA Institute for Diversity and Health Equity, accessed July 27, 2023, https://ifdhe.aha.org/news/news/2022-07-19-supporting-black-womens-maternal-mental-health-journey.
8. Clayton J. Shuman, Alex F. Peahl, Neha Pareddy, Mikayla E. Morgan, Jolyna Changing, Philip T. Veliz, Vanessa K. Dalton, "Postpartum Depression and Associated Risk Factors during the Covid-19 Pandemic," *BMC Research Notes* 15, no. 102 (2022).
9. Chelsea Conaboy, *Mother Brain: How Neuroscience Is Rewriting the Story of Parenthood* (New York: Henry Holt, 2022).
10. Sarah Menkedick, *Ordinary Insanity: Fear and the Silent Crisis of Motherhood in America* (New York: Pantheon, 2020).
11. "WHO Statement of Caesarean Section Rates," World Health Organization (2015), accessed October 15, 2020, https://www.who.int/publications/i/item/WHO-RHR-15.02.
12. Sarah J. Buckley, "Hormonal Physiology of Childbearing: Evidence and Implications for Women, Babies, and Maternity Care," Washington,

DC: Childbirth Connection Programs, National Partnership for Women & Families, January 2015.

13. Cheryl Tatno Beck, Sue Watson, and Robert K. Gable, "Traumatic Childbirth and Its Aftermath: Is There Anything Positive?" *Journal of Perinatal Education,* 27 no. 3 (2018), 175–84.

14. If you are a woman who has experienced medical intervention of any kind during your birth, please be assured that my words here are, in no way whatsoever, a judgment on your personal choices. First of all, some medical interventions are necessary and lifesaving—*and* it is often nearly impossible to discern which of these interventions have indeed been necessary and lifesaving and which may have been avoided. But it is of the utmost importance to name that what I do see, as a doula, is the extent to which our birth culture has limited women's choices before they even walk through the doors of a hospital. Many doctors and medical students I work with have *never seen* an unmedicated vaginal birth, and so to ask them to be proficient in supporting that process is, unfortunately and devastatingly, unrealistic. To choose against medical intervention in the context of modern birth is to swim against the tide during the most vulnerable time in our lives—in other words, not easy to do. The medicalization of birth is a cultural, institutional problem, not a reflection of individual women's choices. And, in fact, I believe that we keep ourselves small and distracted when we spend our time pointing fingers at ourselves and each other when, truly, if we all pointed our fingers at the institution of medicalized birth, we might effectively change it.

15. Donna L. Hoyert, "Maternal Mortality Rates in the United States, 2021," Centers for Disease Control and Prevention (2021), accessed July 27, 2023, https://www.cdc.gov/nchs/data/hestat/maternal-mortality/2021/maternal-mortality-rates-2021.pdf; Maternal Mental Health Leadership Alliance, "Black Women, Birthing People, and Maternal Mental Health Fact Sheet," accessed July 27, 2023, https://22542548.fs1.hubspotusercontent-na1.net/hubfs/22542548/Black%20Women%2c%20Birthing%20People%2c%20and%20Maternal%20Mental%20Health%20-%20Fact%20Sheet%20-%20July%202023.pdf.

16. Menkedick, *Ordinary Insanity.*

17. Sarah Blaffer Hrdy, *Mothers and Others: The Evolutionary Origins of Mutual Understanding* (Cambridge: Harvard University Press, 2009), 100.

18. Hrdy, *Mothers and Others.*

19. Andrea O'Reilly, "Normative Motherhood," in *Maternal Theory: Essential Reading*, ed. Andrea O'Reilly (Bradford, ON: Demeter Press, 2021), 477–82.

20. Helena Andrews-Dyer, *The Mamas: What I Learned about Kids, Class, and Race from Moms Not Like Me* (New York: Crown, 2022), 11.

21. Rich, *Of Woman Born*; Menkedick, *Ordinary Insanity*.

22. Sharon Hays, "Why Can't a Mother be More Like a Businessman?" in O'reilly, ed., *Maternal Theory*.

23. Shari Thurer, "The Myths of Motherhood," in O'reilly, ed., *Maternal Theory*, 190.

24. Kathryn Lazarus and Pieter Rossouw, "Mother's Expectations of Parenthood: The Impact of Prenatal Expectations on Self-Esteem, Depression, Anxiety, and Stress Post Birth," *International Journal of Neuropsychotherapy* 3, no. 2 (2015): 102–23.

25. Aurélie Athan and Heather L. Reel, "Maternal Psychology: Reflecting on the 20th Anniversary of Deconstructing Developmental Psychology," *Feminism and Psychology* 25, no. 3 (2015): 1–15.

26. Alexandra Sacks and Catherine Birndorf, *What No One Tells You: A Guide to Your Emotions from Pregnancy to Motherhood* (New York: Simon & Schuster, 2019); Molly Millwood, *To Have and to Hold: Motherhood, Marriage, and the Modern Dilemma* (New York: Harper Wave, 2019).

27. Alexandra Sacks, "Matrescence: The Developmental Transition to Motherhood," *Psychology Today*, accessed October 20, 2020, https://www.psychologytoday.com/ca/blog/motherhood-unfiltered/201904/matrescence-the-developmental-transition-to-motherhood.

28. Aurélie Athan, "Matrescence: The Emerging Mother," *Medium*, accessed July 27, 2023, https://medium.com/@ama81/matrescence-the-emerging-mother-69d1699ff0cc.

29. Athan and Reel, "Maternal Psychology," 8.

30. Allison Davis, "Matrescence Theory: What Is It? How to Start Using It." *Matrescence Monday Newsletter*, February 13, 2023.

31. Allison Davis and Aurélie Athan, "Ecopsychological Development and Maternal Ecodistress during Matrescence," *Ecopsychology* 15, no. 2 (May 2023), http://doi.org/10.1089/eco.2022.0084, 7.

32. Menkedick, *Ordinary Insanity*; Millwood, *To Have and to Hold*.

33. Aurélie Athan, "Reproductive Identity: An Emerging Concept," *American Psychologist* 75, no. 4 (2020): 445–56.

34. Orit Taubman Ben-Ari, Shirley Ben Shlomo, Eyal Sivan, and Morde-Ochay Dolizki, "The Transition to Motherhood—A Time for Growth," *Journal of Social and Clinical Psychology* 28, no. 8 (2009): 945.

35. Aurélie Athan and Lisa Miller, "Motherhood as Opportunity to Learn Spiritual Values: Experiences and Insights of New Mothers," *Journal of Prenatal and Perinatal Psychology and Health* 27, no. 4 (2013): 240.

36. Alyssa Cheadle and Christine Dunkel Schetter, "Mastery, Self-Esteem, and Optimism Mediate the Link between Religiousness and Spirituality and Postpartum Depression," *Journal of Behavioural Medicine* 41, no. 5 (2018): 711–21.

37. Athan and Miller, "Motherhood as Opportunity," 220–53.

38. Christina Prinds, Niels Christian Hvidt, Ole Mogensen, and Niels Buus, "Making Existential Meaning in Transition to Motherhood—a Scoping Review," *Midwifery* 30, no. 6 (2014): 733–41.

39. Athan and Miller, "Motherhood as Opportunity," 247.

40. Arnold van Gennep, *The Rites of Passage* (Chicago: University of Chicago Press, 1961); Joseph Campbell, *The Hero with a Thousand Faces* (Novato: New World Library, 2008); Maureen Murdock, *The Heroine's Journey* (Boulder, Colo.: Shambhala Publications, 1990).

41. Van Gennep, *The Rites*.

42. It wouldn't be the first time white folks have observed the belief systems of traditional peoples, turned them into sweeping theories, and actually been kind of wrong. Maslow's Hierarchy of Needs has been similarly critiqued.

43. Elizabeth K. Laney, M. Elizabeth Lewis Hall, Tamara L. Anderson, and Michele M. Willingham, "The Influence of Motherhood on Women's Identity Development," *Identity: An International Journal of Theory and Research* 15, no. 2 (2015): 126–45.

44. Some matrescence thought leaders posit that matrescence lasts a lifetime. The same has been said about postpartum. I differentiate from this perspective. Although our motherhood journey certainly continues to unfold for a lifetime, there are certain aspects of this journey, not least of which are the disorientation, sense of loss, and certain shifts in gender roles that I will describe later, that are quite specific to the first two to three years of matrescence and become less adaptive if they last longer.

45. bell hooks, "Theory as Liberatory Practice," Yale Journal of Law and Feminism 4, no. 1 (1991).

CHAPTER TWO: EARTH

1. Lazarus and Rossouw, "Mother's expectations of parenthood," 102–23.
2. Amanda Montei, "How American Moms Got 'Touched Out,'" *Slate*, July 14, 2022.
3. R. Chris Fraley, Omri Gillath, and Pascal R. Doboeck, "Do Life Events Lead to Enduring Changes in Adult Attachment Styles? A Naturalistic Longitudinal Investigation," *Journal of Personality and Social Psychology* 120, no. 6 (2021): 1567–1606.
4. Ellie Lisitsa, "Bringing Baby Home: The Research," *The Gottman Institute*, accessed August 1, 2023, https://www.gottman.com/blog/bringing-baby-home-the-research/.
5. Johnson, *The Fourth Trimester*, 44.
6. Elly Taylor, *Becoming Us: The Couple's Guide to Parenthood* (Chatham: Bowker Press, 2021).
7. Conaboy, *Mother Brain*.
8. Darcy Lockman, *All The Rage: Mothers, Fathers, and the Myth of Equal Partnership* (New York: Harper, 2019), 30.
9. Jodi Pawluski, "Rethinking 'Mummy Brain,'" January 18, 2021, on *The Good Enough Mother Podcast*, produced by Dr. Sophie Brock, https://drsophiebrock.com/podcast49.
10. Hrdy, *Mothers and Others*.
11. Menkedick, *Ordinary Insanity*, 14.
12. Conaboy, *Mother Brain*.
13. Hrdy, *Mothers and Others*.
14. J. F. Leckman, R. Feldman, J. E. Swain, V. Eicher, N. Thompson, and L. C. Mayes, "Primary Parental Occupation: Circuits, Genes, and the Crucial Role of the Environment," *Journal of Neural Transmission* 111, (2004): 753–71.
15. Hrdy, *Mothers and Others*.
16. Eyal Abraham, Talma Hendler, Irit Shapira-Lichter, Yaniv Kanat-Maymon, Orna Zagoory-Sharon, and Ruth Feldman, "Father's Brain Is Sensitive to Childcare Experiences," *Proceedings of the National Academy of Sciences* 111, no. 27 (2014): 9792–97.
17. Conaboy, *Mother Brain*. 147.
18. Lucy Jones, *Matrescence: On the Metamorphosis of Pregnancy, Childbirth, and Motherhood* (London: Penguin Books, 2023), 202.
19. Hrdy, *Mothers and Others*.
20. Deeply passionate feminists—me included—have found the gendered division of labor in motherhood *particularly challenging*. Matricentric feminism scholar O'Reilly writes: "Feminist theory . . . positions gender

difference as central to, if not the cause of, women's oppression. This apprehension over gender difference is the elephant in the room of academic feminism; it has shut down necessary and needed conversations about important—and yes gendered—dimensions of women's lives." My experience is that when mothers are caught in the tide of both biologically shaped and socially constructed gender roles, they feel either that feminism has failed them or that they are "bad feminists," when the truth is that feminism has often failed to take physiological difference into account.

21. Dear reader, it is no secret that I am an unabashed *fan* of breastfeeding. But we can also point the finger toward breastfeeding as a big influence on the heavy burden of caregiving that often falls to mothers. With the option of formula, pumping, or donor milk, there is more flexibility in feeding choices available to modern mothers. Your choice depends on your personal values, capacity, and resources. Perhaps you will find that breastfeeding is a burden and choose to share the feeding responsibility among your baby's other caregivers; perhaps you will find it empowering and uncover other ways to achieve more balance in your caregiving load.

22. Ou, *First Forty Days.*

23. It is imperative to note that there needs to be *another* concentric circle of support around your partner. They—and consequently you—need to be held and cared for by others, whether that's relatives or friends or community members. This can present a challenge particularly for male partners who may have been socialized to be "providers" or not to show vulnerability with others.

24. Gus Wezerek and Kristen R. Ghodsee, "Women's Unpaid Labor is Worth $10,900,000,000,000," *New York Times,* March 5, 2020.

25. Wezerek and Ghodsee, "Women's Unpaid Labor."

26. Eve Rodsky, *Fair Play: A Game-Changing Solution for When You Have Too Much to Do (and More Life to Live)* (New York: G.P. Putnam's Sons, 2019).

27. bell hooks, *Feminism Is for Everybody* (New York: Routledge, 2015), 82.

28. Lockman, *All the Rage,* 154.

29. Lockman, *All the Rage,* 271–72.

30. Samantha Tornello, "Division of Labour Among Transgender and Gender Non-Binary Parents: Association with Individual, Couple, and Children's Behavioural Outcomes," in Frontiers in Psychology 11 (2020): 15.

31. Margaret Gibson, ed., *Queering Motherhood: Narrative and Theoretical Perspectives* (Bradford, ON: Demeter Press, 2014).

32. Rodsky, *Fair Play.*

33. Britta Bushnell, *Transformed by Birth: Cultivating Openness, Resilience, and Strength for the Life-Changing Journey from Pregnancy to Parenthood* (Louisville, CO: Sounds True, 2020).

34. Sophie Brock (@drsophiebrock), "Here is one reason why there can be tension and judgement between different generations of mothers," Instagram post, April 17, 2023, https://www.instagram.com/p/CrI CeyLpv1L/?img_index=1.

35. Rich, *Of Woman Born*, xix.

36. Dani McClain, *We Live for the We: The Political Power of Black Motherhood* (New York: Hachette Audio, 2019), chapter 3, 00:13:10.

37. Tami Kent, *Mothering from Your Center: Tapping Your Body's Natural Energy for Pregnancy, Birth, and Parenting* (New York: Atria Books, 2013), 3.

38. Jennifer Senior, *All Joy and No Fun: The Paradox of Modern Parenthood* (New York: Ecco Books, 2014).

39. Leslie Davis, "Motherhood Gave Me an Identity Crisis. Solving It Was Simple, but It Wasn't Easy,," *Washington Post,* October 4, 2018, https://www.washingtonpost.com/news/parenting/wp/2018/10/04/motherhood-gave-me-an-identity-crisis-solving-it-was-simple-but-it-wasnt-easy/.

40. Danya Ruttenberg, *Nurture the Wow: Finding Spirituality in the Frustration, Boredom, Tears, Poop, Desperation, Wonder, and Radical Amazement of Parenting* (New York: Flatiron Books, 2017), 237.

41. Aurélie Athan and Lisa Miller, "Spiritual Awakening through the Motherhood Journey," *Journal of the Association for Research on Mothering* 7, no. 1 (2005): 19.

42. Robert Kegan and Lisa Laskow Lahey, *Immunity to Change: How to Overcome It and Unlock the Potential in Yourself and Your Organization* (Brighton, MA: Harvard Business Review Press, 2009).

43. Trudelle Thomas, *Spirituality in the Mother Zone: Staying Centered, Finding God* (New York: Paulist Press, 2005), 90.

44. Tricia Hersey, "The Nap Ministry," accessed July 1, 2023, https://thenapministry.com.

45. McClain, *We Live for the We,* chapter 2, 00:05:04.

46. Leah Carroll, "Michelle Obama Tells Us How She Really Feels about the Lean In Movement," *Refinery29*, December 4, 2018, https://www.refinery29.com/en-ca/2018/12/218580/michelle-obama-lean-in.

47. Rich, *Of Woman Born*, 31.

48. Rich, *Of Woman Born*; Dawn Marie Dow, "Integrated Motherhood: Beyond Hegemonic Ideologies of Motherhood," *Journal of Marriage and Family* 78 no. 1 (2015): 180–96.

49. Patricia Hill-Collins, "The Meaning of Motherhood," in *Maternal Theory: Essential Readings,* ed. Andrea O'Reilly (Bradford, ON: Demeter Press, 2021), 152.

50. bell hooks, "Revolutionary Parenting," in O'Reilley, ed., *Maternal Theory*, 87.

51. Rich, *Of Woman Born*, xxxiii.

52. Jessica Grose, *Screaming on the Inside: The Unsustainability of American Motherhood* (Boston: Mariner Books, 2022), 145.

53. Anne-Marie Slaughter, "Why Women Still Can't Have It All," *Atlantic*, July/August 2012, https://www.theatlantic.com/magazine/archive/2012/07/why-women-still-cant-have-it-all/309020.

54. Sophie Brock (@drsophiebrock), "The Care-Career Conundrum," Instagram post, April 26, 2022, https://www.instagram.com/p/CcOF7gBpR5J/.

55. Tucker, *Mom Genes*.

56. Katrina Leupp, "Depression, Work and Family Roles, and the Gendered Life Course," *Journal of Health and Social Behaviour* 58 no. 4 (2017): 422–41.

57. Hill-Collins, "The Meaning of Motherhood," 152.

58. Hill-Collins, "The Meaning of Motherhood," 155.

59. Chris Luedecke, *The Early Days* (Waterdown, ON: True North Records, 2015).

## CHAPTER THREE: WATER

1. Pam England, *Labyrinth of Birth: Creating a Map, Meditations and Rituals for Your Childbearing Year* (Santa Barbara, CA: Birthing From Within Books, 2010).

2. Denise Lawler and Marlene Sinclair, "Grieving for My Former Self: A Phenomenological Hermeneutical Study of Women's Lived Experience of Postnatal Depression," *Evidence Based Midwifery* 1, no.2 (2003): 36.

3. Sarah Kerr, Ritual Skills for Living and Dying (Online course, 2021).

4. Andrews-Dyer, *The Mamas*, 47.

5. Sarah Kerr, Ritual Skills for Living and Dying.

6. Martin Prechtel, *The Smell of Rain on Dust* (Berkeley: North Atlantic Books, 2015).

7. Paula Nicholson, "Loss, Happiness, and Postpartum Depression: The Ultimate Paradox," *Canadian Psychology* 40 (May 1999): 162–78.

8. Barbara Almond, *The Monster Within: The Hidden Side of Motherhood* (Berkeley: University of California Press, 2011), 11.

9. Christine H.K. Ou, Wendy A. Hall, and Robyn Stremler, "Seeing Red: A Grounded Theory Study of Women's Anger after Childbirth," *Qualitative Health Research* 32, no. 12 (2018): 336–46.

10. Almond, *The Monster Within*, 11.

11. Ou, Hall, and Stremler, "Seeing Red."

12. Sophie Brock, "The Anger-Guilt Trap and How to Start Breaking the Cycle," accessed August 1, 2023, https://motherhoodstudies.newzenler.com/courses/angerguilttrap.

13. Rich, *Of Woman Born*, 30.

14. Montei goes on to assert the point that the "hot mess mom" is a likely a hot mess because of the injustices of our political and economic context on mothers, but that the hot mess narrative instead focuses on mothers' individual (and laughable, and relatable) "failings" to thrive in a culture that is not set up for their success. See Amanda Montei, "The 'Hot Mess Mom' Is an Economic Problem, Not a Mom Problem," *Mutha Magazine*, January 28, 2021.

15. Susan Maushart, "Faking Motherhood," in *Maternal Theory: Essential Readings,* ed. Andrea O'Reilly (Bradford: Demeter Press, 2021), 276–77.

16. Susan Maushart, *The Mask of Motherhood: How Becoming a Mother Changes Our Lives and Why We Never Talk About It* (New York: Penguin Books, 2000), 460–61.

17. Petersen, *Momfluenced.*

18. Menkedick, *Ordinary Insanity.* 247–48.

19. *Weeeelll*, mostly. Arguably, the spoken and unspoken pressures toward motherhood in our society still do a lot to make it feel like less than a choice.

20. Kate Figes, *Life After Birth* (London: Little, Brown UK, 2008). Chapter 3, Kobo.

21. Maushart, *The Mask of Motherhood*, 244.

22. Athan and Miller, "Spiritual Awakening," *Journal of the Association for Research on Mothering* 7, no. 1 (2005): 18.

23. Sarah Menkedick, *Homing Instincts: Early Motherhood on a Midwestern Farm* (Ashland, OR: Blackstone Audio, 2017), chapter 2, 00:21:26.

24. Sophie Brock (@drsophiebrock), "We've been sold a lie in motherhood that we prove our love for our children through our 'selflessness,'"

Instagram post, June 29, 2021, https://www.instagram.com/p/CQuS
_jNg-0Q/.

25. Athan and Miller, "Motherhood as Opportunity," 220–53.

26. Lisa Marchiano, *Motherhood: Facing and Finding Yourself* (Louisville, CO: Sounds True, 2021), 20.

27. Pauline Boss, "Ambiguous Loss: A Complicated Type of Grief When Loved Ones Disappear," *Bereavement Care* 33, no. 2 (2014): 63–69.

28. Shauna Janz, Coming Back to Ourselves (Online course, 2022).

## CHAPTER FOUR: AIR

1. Timothy Carson, "A Liminality Primer," accessed July 31, 2023, https://www.theliminalityproject.org/the-liminality-primer.

2. Carson, "A Liminality Primer."

3. Mary Douglas, *Purity and Danger* (London: Routledge and Kegan Paul, 1966).

## CHAPTER FIVE: FIRE

1. Laney, Lewis Hall, Anderson and Willingham, "The Influence of Motherhood," 126–45.

2. Taylor-Kabbaz, *Mama Rising*, 12.

3. Sophie Brock (@drsophiebrock), "Mothering can be experienced as both a limitation to becoming our 'full selves,' and as a path through which we become our 'full selves,'" Instagram post, November 21, 2022, https://www.instagram.com/p/ClP0-2EJ43J.

4. Rich, *Of Woman Born*, 17–18.

5. David Snowden, Training Retreat on Complex Adaptive Systems Theory, Safe-to-Fail Experiments, Cynefin and the Sensemaker Program (Nova Scotia Department of Health and Wellness, Halifax, 2014).

6. Snowden, Training Retreat on Complex Adaptive Systems Theory, Safe-to-Fail Experiments, Cynefin and the Sensemaker Program.

7. Danielle LaPorte, "Procrastination Can Be a Form of Intuition," accessed August 1, 2023, https://daniellelaporte.com/procrastination-can-be-a-form-of-intuition/.

## CHAPTER SIX: MOTHERHOOD AS REVOLUTION

1. Menkedick, *Ordinary Insanity*, 262–63.

2. hooks, "Revolutionary Parenting," in O'Reilly, ed., *Maternal Theory*, 134–35.

3. bell hooks, "Homeplace," in O'Reilly, ed., *Maternal Theory*, 100.

4. Hill-Collins, "The Meaning of Motherhood."

5. Jennifer Brant, "Indigenous Mothering: Birthing the Nation from Resistance to Revolution," in *Routledge Companion to Motherhood,* ed. Lynn Hallstein O'Brien, Andrea O'Reilly, and Melinda Vandenbeld Giles (Oxfordshire: Routledge, 2019), 112.

6. Andrea O'Reilly, "Matricentric Feminism: A Feminism for Mothers," in O'Reilly, ed., *Maternal Theory*, 461.

7. Rich, *Of Woman Born*.

8. Gumbs, Martens, and Williams, eds., *Revolutionary Mothering*, xv.

9. Angela Garbes, *Essential Labor: Mothering as Social Change* (New York: Harper Wave, 2022), 14.

10. McClain, *We Live For The We*, chapter 3, 00:24:24.

## CHAPTER SEVEN: YOUR MOTHERPOWERS

1. Sarah Ruddick, *Maternal Thinking: Toward a Politics of Peace* (Boston: Beacon Press, 1995), 24.

2. Ruddick, *Maternal Thinking*.

3. Carolyn Coughlin, The Art of Developmental Coaching (Online course, 2022).

4. Shauna Janz, Coming Back To Ourselves (Online course, 2022).

5. Dan Michels, "The Sensitivity Cycle and Nourishment Barriers," accessed July 14, 2023, https://danmichels.com/the-sensitivity -cycle-and-nourishment-barriers/.

6. Edward Z. Tronick and Andrew Gianino, "Interactive Mismatch and Repair: Challenges to the Coping Infant," *Zero to Three* 6, no. 3 (1986): 1–6.

7. D.W. Winnicott, *The Child, the Family, and the Outside World* (New York: Penguin, 1973).

8. Erika Hayasaki, "How Motherhood Affects Creativity," *Atlantic* September 13, 2017.

9. Lucy Pearce, *The Moods of Motherhood* (Shanagarry, Ireland: Woman-craft Publishing, 2012).

10. If this is the case for you, please go gently here. Though the suggestions I make in this section will likely be healing for you, at least at some point in your journey, it's of the utmost importance that you get the support you need to do this work in a safe and slow enough way.

11. Shauna Janz, Coming Back To Ourselves.

12. Sharon Blackie, *If Women Rose Rooted: The Journey to Authenticity and Belonging* (Tewkesbury, UK: September Publishing, 2019).

13. Sarah Kerr, Ritual Skills for Living and Dying (Online course, 2021).

14. Becca Piastrelli, personal communication to author, July 20, 2023.

15. Hrdy, *Mothers and Others*.

16. Hrdy, *Mothers and Others*.

17. Hrdy, *Mothers and Others*.

18. Hrdy, *Mothers and Others*.

19. Hrdy, *Mothers and Others*, 85.

20. Rich, *Of Woman Born*.

21. Margaret Mead, *Culture and Commitment: A Study of the Generation Gap* (London: Vintage/Ebury, 1975).

22. Stanlie James, "Mothering: A Possible Black Feminist Link to Social Transformation," in *Theorizing Black Feminism: The Visionary Pragmatism of Black Women*, ed. Stanlie James and A. P. Busia (Oxfordshire: Routledge, 1999), 45.

23. Taubman, Ben Shlomo, Sivan and Dolizki, "The transition to motherhood."

24. Guilia M. Dotti Sani and Judith Treas, "Educational Gradients in Parents' Child-Care Time across Countries 1965–2012," *Journal of Marriage and Family* 78 no. 4 (2016): 1083–96.

25. Senior, *All Joy and No Fun*. 10.

26. Also, full props to you, mama, because perfect mother myth or not, you've likely spent hundreds of hours of practice in addition to using your cognitive and intuitive skills to figure out what your kiddo needs, and this isn't something that's easily passed on to another caregiver. This,
    of course, also speaks to the need for our caregivers to be woven into our families rather than parachuted in for the occasional date night.

27. Andrews-Dyer, *The Mamas*, 150–51.

28. Carmen Spagnola, The Numinous Quest Course (Online course, 2020).

29. Cynthia Dewi Oka, "Mothering as Revolutionary Praxis," in Gumbs, Martens, and Williams, eds., *Revolutionary Mothering*, 53.

30. Ruddick, *Maternal Thinking*.

31. Menkedick, *Ordinary Insanity*, 199.

32. Ruth Allen, *Grounded: How Connection with Nature Can Improve Our Mental and Physical Well Being* (Herefordshire, UK: Mortimer Press, 2021).

33. Jones, *Matrescence*, 227.

34. Mary Oliver, "Wild Geese," in *Devotions: The Selected Poems of Mary Oliver* (New York: Penguin, 2019), 347.

35. Davis and Athan, "Ecopsychological Development," 1.

36. Davis and Athan, "Ecopsychological Development," 7.

37. Allison Davis, "The Double Bind of Carework in Green Motherhood: An Ecofeminist Developmental Path Forward," *Women's Studies International Forum* 98 (2023), https://doi.org/10.1016/j.wsif.2023.102730.

38. Davis, "The double bind of carework," 1.

39. Davis and Athan, "Ecopsychological Development," 1.

40. Davis and Athan, "Ecopsychological Development," 6.

## CHAPTER EIGHT: BECOMING MOTHER

1. See Bushnell, *Transformed by Birth*. In my work with mothers, I have noticed another identity shift that may happen to mothers whose children become ill or receive a diagnosis of special needs. In these instances, mothers often have to renegotiate the idea of and expectations for their motherhood based on how the life of their child is unfolding. Often, for these mamas, there is another identity shift into "becoming the mother my child needs," which may not be the motherhood they had envisioned for themselves when they first navigated matrescence.

2. Laney, Lewis Hall, Anderson, and Willingham, "The Influence of Motherhood," 131.

3. Laney, Lewis Hall, Anderson, and Willingham, "The influence of motherhood," 126–45.

4. Aurélie Athan, "Matrescence—the Developmental Experience and Spiritual Awakening of Motherhood," September 28, 2019 on *The Seasons of Matrescence Podcast*, produced by Nikki McCahon. https://podcasts.apple.com/ca/podcast/matrescence-the-developmental -experience-and/id1476334846?i=1000451599862.

5. Menkedick, *Ordinary Insanity*, 178.

# BIBLIOGRAPHY

Abraham, Eyal, Talma Hendler, Irit Shapira-Lichter, Yaniv Kanat-Maymon, Orna Zagoory-Sharon, and Ruth Feldman. "Father's Brain Is Sensitive to Childcare Experiences." *Proceedings of the National Academy of Sciences* 111, no. 27 (2014): 9792–97.

AHA Institute for Diversity and Health Equity. "Supporting Black Women's Maternal Mental Health Journey." Accessed July 27, 2023. https://ifdhe .aha.org/news/news/2022-07-19-supporting-black-womens-maternal -mental-health-journey.

Allen, Ruth. *Grounded: How Connection with Nature Can Improve Our Mental and Physical Well Being.* Herefordshire, UK: Mortimer Press, 2021.

Almond, Barbara. *The Monster Within: The Hidden Side of Motherhood.* Berkeley: University of California Press, 2011.

Andrews-Dyer, Helena. *The Mamas: What I Learned about Kids, Class, and Race from Moms Not Like Me.* New York: Crown, 2022.

Athan, Aurélie. "Matrescence—the Developmental Experience and Spiritual Awakening of Motherhood." September 28, 2019, on *The Seasons of Matrescence Podcast.* Produced by Nikki McCahon. https://podcasts .apple.com/ca/podcast/matrescence-the-developmental-experience -and/id1476334846?i=1000451599862.

———. "Matrescence: The Emerging Mother." *Medium.* Accessed July 27, 2023. https://medium.com/@ama81/matrescence-the-emerging -mother-69d1699ff0cc.

———. "Postpartum Flourishing: Motherhood as Opportunity for Positive Growth and Self-Development." PhD diss., Columbia University, 2011.

———. "Reproductive Identity: An Emerging Concept." *American Psychologist* 75, no. 4, (2020): 445–56.

Athan, Aurélie, and Lisa Miller. "Motherhood as Opportunity to Learn Spiritual Values: Experiences and Insights of New Mothers." *Journal of Prenatal and Perinatal Psychology and Health* 27, no. 4 (2013): 240.

———. "Spiritual Awakening through the Motherhood Journey." *Journal of the Association for Research on Mothering* 7, no. 1 (2005): 18.

Athan, Aurélie, and Heather Reel. "Maternal Psychology: Reflecting on the 20th Anniversary of Deconstructing Developmental Psychology." *Feminism and Psychology* 25, no. 3 (2015): 1–15.

Beck, Cheryl Tatno, Sue Watson, and Robert K. Gable. "Traumatic Childbirth and Its Aftermath: Is There Anything Positive?" *Journal of Perinatal Education* 27, no. 3 (2018): 175–84.

Blackie, Sharon. *If Women Rose Rooted: The Journey to Authenticity and Belonging.* Tewkesbury, UK: September Publishing, 2019.

Boss, Pauline. "Ambiguous Loss: A Complicated Type of Grief When Loved Ones Disappear." *Bereavement Care* 33, no. 2 (2014): 63–69.

Brant, Jennifer. "Indigenous Mothering: Birthing the Nation from Resistance to Revolution." In *Routledge Companion to Motherhood,* edited by Lynn Hallstein O'Brien, Andrea O'Reilly, and Melinda Vandenbeld Giles. Oxfordshire, UK: Routledge, 2019.

Brock, Sophie. "Here is one reason why there can be tension and judgement between different generations of mothers." Instagram, April 17, 2023. https://www.instagram.com/p/CrICeyLpv1L/?img_index=1.

———. "Mothering can be experienced as both a limitation to becoming our 'full selves,' and as a path through which we become our 'full selves.'" Instagram, November 21, 2022. https://www.instagram.com/p/ClP0 -2EJ43J.

———. "The Anger-Guilt Trap and How to Start Breaking the Cycle." Accessed August 1, 2023. https://motherhoodstudies.newzenler.com /courses/angerguilttrap.

———. "The Care-Career Conundrum." Instagram, April 26, 2022. https://www.instagram.com/p/CcOF7gBpR5J/.

———. "We've been sold a lie in motherhood that we prove our love for our children through our 'selflessness.'" Instagram, June 29, 2021. https://www.instagram.com/p/CQuS_jNg-0Q.

Buckley, Sarah J. "Hormonal Physiology of Childbearing: Evidence and Implications for Women, Babies and Maternity Care." Washington, DC: Childbirth Connection Programs, National Partnership for Women & Families, January 2015.

Bushnell, Britta. *Transformed by Birth: Cultivating Openness, Resilience, and Strength for the Life-Changing Journey from Pregnancy to Parenthood.* Louisville, CO: Sounds True, 2020.

Campbell, Joseph. *The Hero with a Thousand Faces.* Novato, CA: New World Library, 2008.

Carroll, Leah. "Michelle Obama Tells Us How She Really Feels about the Lean in Movement. *Refinery*, December 4, 2018. https://www.refinery29.com/en-ca/2018/12/218580/michelle-obama-lean-in.

Carson, Timothy. "A Liminality Primer." Accessed July 31, 2023. https://www.theliminalityproject.org/the-liminality-primer.

Cheadle, Alyssa, and Christine Dunkel Schetter. "Mastery, Self-Esteem, and Optimism Mediate the Link between Religiousness and Spirituality and Postpartum Depression." *Journal of Behavioural Medicine* 41, no. 5 (2018): 711–21.

Conaboy, Chelsea. *Mother Brain: How Neuroscience Is Rewriting the Story of Parenthood.* New York: Henry Holt, 2022.

Davis, Allison. "The Double Bind of Carework in Green Motherhood: An Ecofeminist Developmental Path Forward." *Women's Studies International Forum* 98 (2023). https://doi.org/10.1016/j.wsif.2023.102730.

———. "Matrescence Theory: What Is It. How to Start Using It." *Matrescence Monday Newsletter*, February 13, 2023.

Davis, Allison, and Aurélie Athan. "Ecopsychological Development and Maternal Ecodistress during Matrescence." *Ecopsychology* 15, no. 2 (May 2023). Accessed July 3, 2023. http://doi.org/10.1089/eco.2022.0084.

Davis, Leslie. "Motherhood Gave Me an Identity Crisis. Solving It Was Simple, but It Wasn't Easy." *Washington Post*, October 4, 2018. https://www.washingtonpost.com/news/parenting/wp/2018/10/04/motherhood-gave-me-an-identity-crisis-solving-it-was-simple-but-it-wasnt-easy.

Dewi Oka, Cynthia. "Mothering as Revolutionary Praxis." In *Revolutionary Mothering: Love on the Front Lines*, edited by Alexis Pauline Gumbs, China Martens, and Mai'a Williams, 53. New York: PM Press, 2016.

Dotti Sani, Guilia M., and Judith Treas. "Educational Gradients in Parents' Child-Care Time across Countries 1965–2012." *Journal of Marriage and Family* 78, no. 4 (2016): 1083–96.

Dow, Dawn Marie. "Integrated Motherhood: Beyond Hegemonic Ideologies of Motherhood." *Journal of Marriage and Family* 78, no. 1 (2015): 180–96.

England, Pamela. *Labyrinth of Birth: Creating a Map, Meditations and Rituals for Your Childbearing Year.* Birthing From Within Books, 2010.

Figes, Kate. *Life after Birth.* London: Little, Brown, 2008.

Fischer, Olivia. "Forging Crossroads: The Possibilities and Complexities of Parenting outside the Gender Binary." In *Maternal Theory: Essential Reading,* edited by Andrea O'Reilly, 795–816. Bradford, ON: Demeter Press, 2021.

Fraley, R. Chris, Omri Gillath, and Pascal R. Doboeck. "Do Life Events Lead to Enduring Changes in Adult Attachment Styles? A Naturalistic Longitudinal Investigation." *Journal of Personality and Social Psychology* 120, no. 6 (2021): 1567–1606.

Garbes, Angela. *Essential Labor: Mothering as Social Change.* New York: Harper Wave, 2022.

Gibson, Margaret, ed. *Queering Motherhood: Narrative and Theoretical Perspectives.* Bradford, ON: Demeter Press, 2014.

Grose, Jessica. *Screaming on the Inside: The Unsustainability of American Motherhood.* Boston: Mariner Books, 2022.

Gumbs, Alexis Pauline, China Martens, and Ma'ia Williams. *Revolutionary Mothering: Love on the Front Lines.* New York: PM Press, 2016.

Hayasaki, Erica. "How Motherhood Affects Creativity." *Atlantic,* September 13, 2017.

Hays, Sharon. "Why Can't a Mother Be More like a Businessman?" In *Maternal Theory: Essential Reading,* edited by Andrea O'Reilly, 225. Bradford, ON: Demeter Press, 2021.

Hersey, Tricia. "The Nap Ministry." Accessed July 1, 2023, https://thenap ministry.com.

Hill-Collins, Patricia. "The Meaning of Motherhood." In *Maternal Theory: Essential Readings,* edited by Andrea O'Reilly, 152. Bradford, ON: Demeter Press, 2021.

hooks, bell. *Feminism Is for Everybody.* New York: Routledge, 2015.

———. "Homeplace." In *Maternal Theory: Essential Readings,* edited Andrea O'Reilly, 100. Bradford, Demeter Press, 2021.

———. "Revolutionary Parenting." In *Maternal Theory: Essential Readings,* edited by Andrea O'Reilly, 134–35. Bradford, ON: Demeter Press, 2021.

———. "Theory as Liberatory Practice." *Yale Journal of Law and Feminism* 4, no. 1 (1991).

Hoyert, D. L. "Maternal Mortality Rates in the United States, 2021." Centers for Disease Control and Prevention (2021). Accessed July 27, 2023.

https://www.cdc.gov/nchs/data/hestat/maternal-mortality/2021
/maternal-mortality-rates-2021.pdf.

Hrdy, Sarah Blaffer. *Mothers and Others: The Evolutionary Origins of Mutual Understanding*. Cambridge, MA: Harvard University Press, 2009.

James, Stanlie. "Mothering: A Possible Black Feminist Link to Social Transformation." In *Theorizing Black Feminism: The Visionary Pragmatism of Black Women*, edited by Stanlie James and A. P. Busia, 45. Oxfordshire, UK: Routledge, 1999.

Johnson, Kimberly Ann. *The Fourth Trimester: A Postpartum Guide to Healing Your Body, Balancing Your Emotions, and Restoring Your Vitality*. Boulder, CO: Shambhala Publications, 2017.

Jones, Lucy. *Matrescence: On the Metamorphosis of Pregnancy, Childbirth, and Motherhood*. London: Penguin Books, 2023.

Kegan, Robert, and Lisa Laskow Lahey. *Immunity to Change: How to Overcome It and Unlock the Potential in Yourself and Your Organization*. Brighton, MA: Harvard Business Review Press, 2009.

Kent, Tami. *Mothering from Your Center: Tapping Your Body's Natural Energy for Pregnancy, Birth, and Parenting*. New York: Atria Books, 2013.

Laney, Elizabeth K., Elizabeth Lewis Hall, Tamara L. Anderson, and Michele M. Willingham. "The Influence of Motherhood on Women's Identity Development." *Identity: An International Journal of Theory and Research* 15, no. 2 (2015): 126–45.

LaPorte, Danielle. "Procrastination Can Be a Form of Intuition." Accessed August 1, 2023, https://daniellelaporte.com/procrastination-can-be
-a-form-of-intuition.

Lawler, Denise, and Marlene Sinclair. "Grieving for My Former Self: A Phenomenological Hermeneutical Study of Women's Lived Experience of Postnatal Depression." *Evidence Based Midwifery* 1, no. 2 (2003): 36.

Lazarus, Kathryn, and Pieter Rossouw. "Mother's Expectations of Parenthood: The Impact of Prenatal Expectations on Self-Esteem, Depression, Anxiety, and Stress Post Birth." *International Journal of Neuropsychotherapy* 3, no. 2 (2015): 102–23.

Leckman, J. F., R. Feldman, J. E. Swain, V. Eicher, N. Thompson, and L. C. Mayes. "Primary Parental Occupation: Circuits, Genes, and the Crucial Role of the Environment." *Journal of Neural Transmission* 111 (2004): 753–71.

Leupp, Katrina. "Depression, Work and Family Roles, and the Gendered Life Course." *Journal of Health and Social Behaviour* 58, no. 4 (2017): 422–41.

Lisitsa, Ellie. "Bringing Baby Home: The Research." *The Gottman Institute.* Accessed August 1, 2023. https://www.gottman.com/blog/bringing -baby-home-the-research.

Lockman, Darcy. *All the Rage: Mothers, Fathers, and the Myth of Equal Partnership.* New York: Harper, 2019.

Luedecke, Chris, *The Early Days.* Waterdown, ON: True North Records, 2015.

Marchiano, Lisa. *Motherhood: Facing and Finding Yourself.* Louisville, CO: Sounds True, 2021.

Maternal Mental Health Leadership Alliance. "Maternal Mortality Rates in the United States, 2021." Centers for Disease Control and Prevention (2021). Accessed July 27, 2023. https://www.cdc.gov/nchs/data/hestat /maternal-mortality/2021/maternal-mortality-rates-2021.pdf.

Maushart, Susan. "Faking Motherhood." In *Maternal Theory: Essential Readings*, edited by Andrea O'Reilly, 276–77. Bradford, ON: Demeter Press, 2021.

———. *The Mask of Motherhood: How Becoming a Mother Changes Our Lives and Why We Never Talk about It.* New York: Penguin Books, 2000.

McClain, Dani. *We Live for the We: The Political Power of Black Motherhood.* New York: Hachette Audio, 2019.

Mead, Margaret. *Culture and Commitment: A Study of the Generation Gap.* London: Vintage/Ebury, 1975.

Menkedick, Sarah. *Ordinary Insanity: Fear and the Silent Crisis of Motherhood in America.* New York: Pantheon, 2020.

———. Homing Instincts: Early Motherhood on a Midwestern Farm. Ashland, OR: Blackstone Audio, 2017.

Michels, Dan. "The Sensitivity Cycle and Nourishment Barriers." Accessed July 14, 2023, https://danmichels.com/the-sensitivity-cycle-and-nourishment-barriers.

Millwood, Molly. *To Have and to Hold: Motherhood, Marriage, and the Modern Dilemma.* New York: Harper Wave, 2021.

Montei, Amanda. "How American Moms Got 'Touched Out.'" *Slate*, July 14, 2022.

———. "The 'Hot Mess Mom' Is an Economic Problem, Not a Mom Problem." *Mutha Magazine*, January 28, 2021.

Murdock, Maureen. *The Heroine's Journey.* Boston: Shambhala Publications, 1990.

Nicholson, Paula. "Loss, Happiness, and Postpartum Depression: The Ultimate Paradox." *Canadian Psychology* 40 (May 1999): 162–78.

Oliver, Mary. "Wild Geese." In *Devotions: The Selected Poems of Mary Oliver.* New York: Penguin, 2019.

O'Reilly, Andrea. "Matricentric Feminism: A Feminism for Mothers." In *Maternal Theory: Essential Readings*, edited by Andrea O'Reilly, 461. Bradford, ON: Demeter Press, 2021.

———. "Normative Motherhood." In *Maternal Theory: Essential Reading*, edited by Andrea O'Reilly 477–82. Bradford, ON: Demeter Press, 2021.

Ou, Christine H.K., Wendy A. Hall, and Robyn Stremler. "Seeing Red: A Grounded Theory Study of Women's Anger after Childbirth." *Qualitative Health Research* 32, no. 12 (2018): 336–46.

Ou, Heng, Amely Greeven, and Marisa Belger. *The First Forty Days: The Essential Art of Nourishing the New Mother.* New York: Stewart, Tabori & Chang, 2016.

Pawluski, Jodi. "Rethinking 'Mummy Brain.'" January 18, 2021, on *The Good Enough Mother Podcast.* Produced by Dr. Sophie Brock. https://drsophiebrock.com/podcast49.

Pearce, Lucy. *The Moods of Motherhood.* Shanagarry, Ireland: Womancraft Publishing, 2012.

Petersen, Sara. *Momfluenced: Inside the Maddening, Picture-Perfect World of Mommy Influencer Culture.* Boston: Beacon Press, 2023.

Policy Center for Maternal Mental Health. "Maternal Mental Health Disorders." Accessed February 1, 2024. https://www.2020mom.org/mmh-disorders.

PostpartumDepression.org. "Statistics on Postpartum Depression." Accessed July 27, 2023. https://www.postpartumdepression.org/resources/statistics.

Postpartum Support International. "Perinatal Mood and Anxiety Disorders Fact Sheet." Accessed July 27, 2023. https://www.postpartum.net/wp-content/uploads/2014/11/PSI-PMD-FACT-SHEET-2015.pdf.

Prechtel, Martin. *The Smell of Rain on Dust: Grief and Praise.* Berkeley: North Atlantic Books, 2015.

Prinds, Christina, Niels Christian Hvidt, Ole Mogensen, and Niels Buus. "Making Existential Meaning in Transition to Motherhood—a Scoping Review." *Midwifery* 30, no. 6 (2014): 733–41.

Raphael, Dana. "Matrescence, Becoming a Mother, A 'New/Old Rite de Passage.'" In *Being Female: Reproduction, Power and Change,* edited by Dana Raphael, 65–72. Berlin, New York: De Gruyter Mouton, 1975.

Rich, Adrienne. *Of Woman Born: Motherhood as Experience and Institution.* New York: W. W. Norton, 2021.

Rodsky, Eve. *Fair Play: A Game-Changing Solution for When You Have Too Much to Do (and More Life to Live).* New York: G.P. Putnam's Sons, 2019.

Ruddick, Sarah. *Maternal Thinking: Toward a Politics of Peace.* Boston: Beacon Press, 1995.

Ruttenberg, Danya. *Nurture the Wow: Finding Spirituality in the Frustration, Boredom, Tears, Poop, Desperation, Wonder, and Radical Amazement of Parenting.* New York: Flatiron Books, 2017.

Sacks, Alexandra. "Matrescence: The Developmental Transition to Motherhood." *Psychology Today.* Accessed October 20, 2020. https://www.psychologytoday.com/ca/blog/motherhood-unfiltered/201904/matrescence-the-developmental-transition-to-motherhood.

Sacks, Alexandra, and Catherine Birndorf. *What No One Tells You: A Guide to Your Emotions from Pregnancy to Motherhood.* New York: Simon & Schuster, 2019.

Senior, Jennifer. *All Joy and No Fun: The Paradox of Modern Parenthood.* New York: Ecco Books, 2014.

Shuman, Clayton J., Alex F. Peahl, N. Pareddy, Mikayla E. Morgan, Jolyna Changing, Philip T. Veliz, and Vanessa K. Dalton. "Postpartum Depression and Associated Risk Factors during the Covid-19 Pandemic." *BMC Research Notes* 15, no. 102 (2022).

Slaughter, Anne-Marie. "Why Women Still Can't Have It All." *Atlantic,* July/August 2012. https://www.theatlantic.com/magazine/archive/2012/07/why-women-still-cant-have-it-all/309020.

Stern, Daniel, and Nadia Bruschweiler-Stern. *The Birth of a Mother: How the Motherhood Experience Changes You Forever.* New York: Basic Books, 1998.

Taubman Ben-Ari, Orit, Shirley Ben Shlomo, Eval Sivan, and Mordechay Dolizki. "The Transition to Motherhood—a Time for Growth." *Journal of Social and Clinical Psychology* 28, no. 8 (2009): 945.

Taylor, Elly. *Becoming Us: The Couple's Guide to Parenthood.* Chatham, NJ: Bowker Press, 2021.

Taylor-Kabbaz, Amy. *Mama Rising: Discovering the New You through Motherhood.* Alexandria, NSW: Hay House Australia, 2020.

Thomas, Trudelle. *Spirituality in the Mother Zone: Staying Centered, Finding God.* New York: Paulist Press, 2005.

Thurer, Shari. "The Myths of Motherhood." In *Maternal Theory: Essential Reading,* edited by Andrea O'Reilly, 190. Bradford, ON: Demeter Press, 2021.

Tronick, Edward Z., and Andrew Gianino. "Interactive Mismatch and Repair: Challenges to the Coping Infant." *Zero to Three* 6, no. 3 (1986): 1–6.

Tucker, Abigail. *Mom Genes: Inside the New Science of Our Ancient Maternal Instinct.* New York: Gallery, 2021.

van Gennep, Arnold. *The Rites of Passage.* Chicago: University of Chicago Press, 1961.

Webster, Bethany. "Mother Wound Glossary." Accessed June 30, 2023. https://www.bethanywebster.com/mother-wound-psychology-glossary.

Wezerek, Gus, and Kristen R. Ghodsee. "Women's Unpaid Labor Is Worth $10,900,000,000,000." *New York Times*, March 5, 2020.

Winnicott, D. W. *The Child, the Family, and the Outside World.* New York: Penguin, 1973.

Wolf, Naomi. *Misconceptions: Truth, Lies, and the Unexpected on the Journey to Motherhood.* New York: Anchor Publishing, 2003.

World Health Organization. "WHO Statement of Caesarean Section Rates." Accessed October 15, 2020. https://www.who.int/publications/i/item/WHO-RHR-15.02.

# ABOUT THE AUTHOR

Jessie is a coach and doula who has been supporting women to navigate rites of passage and other radical life transformations for over fifteen years. She is the founder of the internationally acclaimed matrescence support program *MotherSHIFT* as well as *The Village*, its sister program for postpartum support professionals. Jessie also works one-on-one with women and mothers in her practice and facilitates workshops, rituals, retreats, and nature-based experiences quests. She has a master's in health promotion and a B.Sc. in neuroscience, and her research on women's experiences navigating health and well-being has won multiple awards and been published in peer-reviewed journals internationally. Jessie's writing and work have also been featured in *International Doula Magazine*, *Spirituality & Health*, *Today's Parent*, *Green Parent*, Motherly, Expectful, She Explores, and more. She is the author of *Project Body Love: My Quest to Love My Body and the Surprising Truth I Found Instead* and the host of the Becoming Podcast. Jessie lives with her partner on the east coast of Canada where they raise their children and steward the land.

Find out more about Jessie's work at www.jessieharrold.com.